A Time &

| *BY JEAN*

'A Stewardship is entrusted to me'
1Corinthians 9:17

The Story of
St. Michael's House
Oxford

| *FOREWORD BY* | *THE ARCHBISHOP OF CANTERBURY* |

First Published 2000
by
The St Michael's House Fellowship
Coxboro' Cottage, Cookham, Berks SL6 9HR

ISBN: 0 9537902 0 7

Design and Print by
Wright's (Sandbach) Ltd
9 Old Middlewich Road
Sandbach, Cheshire.
CW11 1DP

"A Time and a Season"

THE STORY OF ST MICHAEL'S HOUSE OXFORD.

"There is a time for everything and a season for
every activity under heaven."

Ecclesiastes 3:1

Jean Cooke
11th October '01

Contents

Continued over

Foreword by
The Archbishop of Canterbury

"It has been said that behind every forward movement in the Church there is someone with a 'vision'".

The truth of those words, quoted in the opening pages of 'A Time and a Season', becomes ever clearer as the history of St Michael's House is unfolded. From its earliest beginnings in the 19th Century; to the various changes that brought it eventually to Oxford; to its golden days in the years following the Second World War; to its closure and the amalgamation with Dalton House, Bristol that, in turn, became one of the founding institutions of Trinity College, Bristol, the story is one of people with vision and spiritual and moral courage who were prepared to take God at His word.

Today, although its buildings have changed their use, or been demolished, the legacy of St Michael's lives on in the tens of thousands of people whose lives have been changed by those trained there, whether for ministry in the Church of England, or service in the Overseas Mission Field - in schools, hospitals or wherever. The spiritual disciplines which its students learnt have clearly served them well down the decades.

As someone who was engaged with the work of Theological Colleges for many years and who is convinced of the vital importance of the ministry of women, I know something of the difficulties that they have encountered in getting that ministry properly recognised. St Michael's was born from a vision and blazed a trail that many others would follow. Its tale deserves to be told for, without the foundational work of places like St Michael's, the recent developments in the roles of women within the Church of England simply would not have taken place, and we owe a debt to Joan Garwood and Jean Cooke for all they have done to bring this book together.

But, like many trailblazers, the story is also one in which the things that institution stood for became absorbed by the mainstream and its *raison d'etre* ceased to exist. As the title rightly says, it was there for a time and a season - but what a time and what a season. All of us, men and women, clergy and lay alike have benefited from the work of St Michael's and my hope is that many will gain fresh insights into its outstanding contribution as they read the pages of this book.

But let me leave the last words to Miss Dorothy Snow, that redoubtable Principal who piloted St Michael's through many choppy waters in the 1950's and 1960's. For these words, I believe, sum up the vision on which it was built, and sustained it for all its years, for the good of all.

'St Michael's House is, and always has been, a venture of faith, and we believe that in answer to prayer God will supply all our need so that we can go forward .... to work for the extension of His Kingdom to the glory of Our Lord Jesus Christ.'

ARCHBISHOP OF CANTERBURY

"I have a stewardship entrusted to me ."
(1 Corinthians 9:17. R.V)

Introduction

Late in 1996 it was realised that the remarkable history of St Michael's House, Oxford, had never been written. We have set out to write it, only in order that the work done in the College itself, and then in the years that followed by its former students, throughout the world, might be recorded to the **glory of God**. From them came the inspiration for the book and its title.

We acknowledge with gratitude the enormous help we have had from former students, in the contributions they have made, and in editing different chapters. We apologise to the very many who do not appear in the book by name, although they may recognise their work. We had hard choices to make, and we don't attempt to explain why some are included and others not. We admit too that it has not been possible to gain everyone's permission to quote something they have written - we trust that no one will be offended!

We wish to thank warmly the Most Reverend Dr George Carey, Archbishop of Canterbury, for his Foreword. We ventured to approach him firstly because he followed the Revd Alec Motyer as Principal of Trinity College, Bristol, and secondly because he has been a strong supporter of women's ministry.

We are indebted to the Lambeth Palace Library for access to the archives of Church Society - and to Trinity College, Bristol for making available to us documents relating to St Michael's House and Dalton House. Also to the Church's Ministry among Jewish People, the South American Mission Society, the Church Pastoral Aid Society, Tear Fund and W.B. Saunders Co Ltd for permission to quote from their publications. Further, to the Revd Dr Alister McGrath, Principal of Wycliffe Hall, Oxford for permission to quote from his book "To know and serve God" - the biography of the Revd Dr James Packer: and to the Very Revd David Gillett former Principal of Trinity College, now Bishop of Bolton, for permission to quote from his articles in Trinity News. We are particularly grateful to Dr Jennifer Bates, Miss Snow's niece, and Mrs Hilary Griffin, a friend, for information about the Snow family.

We were fortunate to obtain copies of all the newsletters, sent out from St Michael's between 1950 and 1968, and from St Michael's Fellowship from 1969 to 1998 - an invaluable source of information.

It remains for us to thank our two editors Grace Townshend (of Oxford) and Angela Butler (Grange-over-Sands) for the time taken to read the MSS and to make constructive criticisms. Above all we are indebted to John Stapylton-Boyce (Oxford) for his untiring labours in typing on to disk and producing innumerable copies for us.

It is our hope and prayer that those who read this book will be led to praise God for all He has done, and be inspired to pray for all who study now at Trinity College, Bristol, where the work of St Michael's continues.

Jean Cooke and Joan Garwood.

CHAPTER 1

Beginnings 1860 - 1940

Questions answered

As the party assembled on 7th November, 1996 for the 25th Anniversary of the founding of Trinity College, Bristol, the appearance of a number of older women as 'old' students raised questions. Who were they? Why were they there?

The answer is the subject of this book. These women were just a few of the many hundreds who had studied at St Michael's House, Oxford, either before or after the Second World War. Although St Michael's lost its full name and individual identity when it amalgamated with Dalton House, Bristol, in 1968, it remains today as one of the tributaries which flowed into Trinity College when, in 1971, Dalton St Michael's, Clifton Theological College and Tyndale Hall were united under that new name. Dalton House was the Women's College of the Bible Churchmen's Missionary Society (now Crosslinks).

Roots and names

The history of St Michael's actually spans over one hundred years. The story begins when a Training House for missionaries was opened in Barnet in 1860. How that came about we have not yet been able to trace. We do know that in 1864 it moved to London and became known as **Mildmay Deaconess House**. Later it received recognition by the Bishop of London for the training of deaconesses and lay workers, and the name changed to **St Catherine's Deaconess House**. By 1938 some seven hundred women had passed through the House and many had gone out to serve the Lord in England and overseas.

The House faced severe difficulties at times. For example, we read that in 1917 the Trustees 'discarded it'. The cause is not known but a new Warden, Dr. Weitbrecht Stanton, a former CMS missionary, was appointed. His untiring work saved the House from extinction and with the new Head Deaconess, Miss

Constance Hankin, the essentials of the evangelical Mildmay tradition were preserved. The training, licensing and status of women workers on the evangelical side of the Church was greatly developed during his Wardenship.

Another man with a vision
It has been said that behind every forward movement in the church there is someone with a 'vision'. It is certainly true of the founding of St Michael's. In Oxford, the Revd Christopher Chavasse was the Master of St Peter's Hall. He had previously been Principal of Wycliffe Hall and for a long time had cherished the conviction that Oxford was the place for an evangelical Training College for women workers in the Church. He knew of and admired the work being done at St Catherine's, and was also aware of their problems. Accordingly, in January 1937, he sent an invitation to that College suggesting its removal to Oxford. But, at that time, the authorities saw no special reason for moving.

A College in crisis
However, in July of the same year, news reached St Catherine's that the London County Council was intending to acquire the three large houses which they occupied. It was to be a compulsory purchase in connection with the Highbury Housing Scheme.

What was to be done to prevent the closure of the House? The invitation from the Master of St Peter's was looked at again, and after prayerful consideration was accepted. Mr. Chavasse, who later became Bishop of Rochester, had already ascertained that the new Bishop of Oxford would welcome the House in his Diocese. He was overjoyed by the decision and writing many years later to Miss Snow he revealed his deep feelings about it:

> I send you the letter I wrote to Mr. Foster-Carter setting out how St Michael's came to be established at Oxford. I had worked for this for years and I was glad that the way it happened meant that the Mildmay House with its long and good tradition was not snuffed out: but that the pioneer work for women's ministry in the Church has fallen like the mantle of Elijah upon the Elisha of St Michael's. Some day with all that you are doing you will be known as the real founder of St Michael's, in its new home after the war, and I shall become only the reason why it is in Oxford

at all. But I do thank God that my conviction that Oxford was the place for an Evangelical Training College for women has been proved to be more than right. I have a deep feeling for St Michael's, as if it were my baby: born indeed after great travail. No one knows what a lot of work and prayer it meant.

Moving words indeed. In the accompanying letter to Foster-Carter, Bishop Chavasse writes about the change of name:

> As the one who was the founder of St Michael's House, I write to you who was its first Warden, when it was opened at 1, Fyfield Road on September 26th, 1938. You will remember that when St Catherine's Deaconess House, Mildmay, went bankrupt and paid their debts by selling their property [to the L.C.C.] I (with £2,000 given me by Lady Hollenden, and other monies I had collected) re-opened it as a Training House for Deaconesses and others at 1, Fyfield Road. It was given the new name of St Michael's Deaconess House since St Catherine's was the name for the Non-Collegiate Delegacy of the University. For the next two years with the help of appeals, I kept the House going till the War brought the training of women workers to a close in 1940.

A day to remember
The removal of St Catherine's to Oxford during an intense heatwave in August 1938 was a never-to-be-forgotten experience. But with the help of many willing hands it was accomplished, and over the next few weeks everything made ready for the official opening and dedication on Monday, September 26th. This from the 1938 College Report:

> Order had to be created out of chaos, rooms had to be planned and re-furbished, carpets to be chosen, curtains to make, pictures to hang and so on. We were specially thankful for the hospitality given to our household on the day of arrival by the Master of St Peter's Hall and Mrs. Chavasse.

The opening of St Michael's was so significant for Oxford that a full report of the day's events appeared in the Oxford Times under the heading:

'Training Centre for Deaconesses Transferred to Oxford'

The many guests gathered in the marquee on the large lawn at 1, Fyfield Road for the first part of the ceremony. The Bishop of Oxford (Dr.K.E. Kirk) was supported by the Archdeacon of London (the Venerable E.N. Sharpe), the Master of St Peter's Hall and the retiring Warden of St Catherine's (the Revd C.E. de Vine). The Archdeacon had become the new Chairman of St Michael's, and in that capacity he welcomed Miss Elizabeth Crathorne as the new Head Deaconess, the Revd G. Foster-Carter as Warden and the Bishop of Oxford as College Visitor. Unfortunately, through the change they had been compelled to make, St Catherine's had lost the services of their Hon. Secretary, their Treasurer and their Warden. Archdeacon Sharpe paid tribute to them, saying that they would all be greatly missed.

Bishop Kirk made a kind speech in which he promised the House his full support and interest. The Master of St Peter's Hall said that to his mind not only was a great new chapter about to open in the honourable history of that Deaconess House, but also a new chapter in the work of the Church in Oxford. He appealed to those present to give their wholehearted support to St Michael's as it went forward in its work of training women for the ministry of the Church. Mr. Chavasse went on to pay tribute to the generosity of Lady Hollenden and said it had been hoped that the House would open free of debt; but unfortunately that could not be. The outstanding debt was nearly £300. He appealed to friends all over the country to play their part in wiping this out, and also in providing the £250 which was required annually. This appeal was evidently heeded. By the end of the first year, gifts amounting to £320 had been received.

The Dedication

Following the speeches, the Bishop and Archdeacon robed, and visited the chief rooms, saying prayers appropriate to each, coming last to the Chapel. In a short service the Chapel and its furnishings were dedicated

> to the honour and glory of the Eternal Trinity and in grateful memory of Herbert Uony Weitbrecht Stanton

the Warden who had carried on the House when the Mildmay work came to an end. Then the House was dedicated and re-named St Michael and All Angels.

Administration

This was put in place with great care, no doubt in view of earlier problems at St Catherine's. A St Michael and All Angels Trust was set up to undergird the College. The first five trustees named are the Bishops of Manchester, Southwell, Worcester, Leicester and Sodor and Man (see Appendix 1). Of the remaining thirty-six trustees, twelve men and women formed a Board of Directors. They believed wholeheartedly in God's guidance in the opening of St Michael's in Oxford, expressed in the foreword to the first Annual Report and to which we have already referred:

> The Church is becoming aware (as never before) of the need of a trained Ministry of Women: and that, in a variety of spheres such as parishes, colleges, schools, social settlements (set up in deprived areas), social welfare work and the like.

> Yet the few institutions that exist for the training of women workers are finding it difficult to maintain themselves, and in some instances are actually closing down.

> It is therefore a real venture in faith (in obedience to what is felt to be an unmistakable command of God to go forward) for St Catherine's Deaconess House to move to Oxford and, under the new name of St Michael's to seek to establish itself in a neighbourhood that seems ideal both from the educational advantages it offers and for its close proximity to the Women's Colleges.

Then they touch on the financial needs of the House:

> As the fees of the students are only £75 a year, the House cannot be self-supporting - at any rate at first. An annual revenue is therefore required from outside sources.

> The Directors believe they see their way towards obtaining nearly half this sum. They confidently appeal to all Church-people who realise the importance of the Ministry of Women, to support the Deaconess House, with its evangelical traditions as it opens a new chapter in its long and useful history.

And then in capitals,

THE MOVE TO OXFORD MUST MEAN A MOVE
FORWARD IN EVERY WAY IF IT IS TO JUSTIFY
ITSELF AND RISE TO ITS OPPORTUNITY.

Aims and Achievements

The inspiring start augured well for the future of the College. The
accommodation at 1, Fyfield Road, was good. There were single
rooms available for ten students and the two resident staff, the
Head Deaconess and Miss M.E. Harcourt, tutor.

Though the House had taken to itself a new name, it did not
change its primary purpose: to train evangelical women for the
Diaconate or as recognised lay workers in the Church of England
at home or overseas. The training was threefold: academic, practical and devotional. Oxford was to provide excellent facilities for
the academic aspect; Canon John Taylor, then Principal of
Wycliffe Hall, gave the doctrine lectures, the Vice-Principal lectured on the New Testament, Dr. Wheeler-Robinson on the Old at
Mansfield College, and the Revd G. Foster-Carter, Warden of St
Michael's, on Church History.

Head Deaconess Crathorne and Miss Harcourt taught
Pastoralia, Christian Worship and Christian Ethics. Tutorials were
held daily.

A short lecture course in Psychology was taken by Dr. Basil
Yeaxlee of the University's Department of Education. Lectures on
other specific subjects such as Moral Welfare were arranged from
time to time.

On the practical side through the kindness of clergy and others,
students were given opportunities for house and hospital visiting,
teaching in Sunday Schools and speaking at Women's Meetings
and Youth Fellowships.They also visited schools and acquired
some experience in Religious Instruction in Church Schools.

Training in the devotional life was of paramount importance.
Students attended Morning and Evening Prayer daily, interces-
sions at midday, a midweek celebration of Holy Communion in the
Chapel, occasional Quiet Days and the Annual Retreat.

In this way a pattern for the thorough preparation of women for
Christian Service was established and followed to great advantage
in the years ahead.

A secondary purpose of the House was to serve as a centre to
which past students could return for fellowship, refresher courses
or short periods of rest. During the first year they had a succession

of visitors and were especially glad to welcome three overseas deaconesses, Lilian Blake from Jamaica, Lily Stewart from China, and
Dorothy Genders from Western Australia.

The House also sought to foster fellowship with members of the
Reformed Churches on the Continent, and maintained a close link
with the Basel Missionary Society. That first year five girls from
Germany and Switzerland came for language study as part of their
preparation for missionary work in India, Africa and China.

A further intention expressed at that time was to extend the usefulness of the House in a new direction by co-operating with the
Oxford Pastorate in its work among women students of the
University. They planned to organise garden parties, tea and tennis
parties and other forms of recreation with a view to making social
contact with these students. Bible readings were shared and library
facilities were made available at St Hugh's and Mansfield Colleges
as well as the Bodleian. The first year in Oxford was promising and
much was achieved in a short time.

The storm clouds of war
But already war seemed imminent, and was declared on 3rd
September, 1939. The effect on St Michael's was grave. As a
wartime economy the College had to dispense with Miss Harcourt
as resident tutor. Mr Foster-Carter and staff of Wycliffe Hall, kindly gave additional help with lectures. Deaconess Grace Lewin came
to assist Deaconess Crathorne. In spite of the disorganisation of
some parochial activities, students continued to get good experience in the parishes of St Ebbe, Holy Trinity, St Giles and New
Marston. Some did intensive visiting among evacuated children.

The Revd Christopher Chavasse continued his support of the
College, but during that year he suffered a serious accident which
incapacitated him for some time; he was also elevated to the
Episcopate which meant, in due course, a move to Rochester.

War-time conditions meant the College faced a continuing deficit
and a decline in student numbers. It is not surprising that at a
shareholders' meeting held in March 1940 the following resolution
was passed:

> That the House be kept going until the end of the Summer
> term; and that, thereafter, if the War still continues and the
> prospect of new students is not considerably improved, the
> House be closed for the time being as a Deaconess Training

Centre and the building be let for the duration of the war with a view to paying off the overdraft.

This was qualified by another resolution to the effect that, if not less than six students were forthcoming at full fees, the House should carry on.

In the event, the College closed, and the building was let to Dr. Barnardo's Homes. This was a great help financially and St Michael's emerged from the war with all debts cleared and £1,000 in hand.

Several significant things happened during the time of closure. Proper articles of Association were drawn up for the Trust. The new Master of St Peter's Hall, the Revd J.P. Thornton-Duesbery, succeeded Bishop Chavasse as Chairman of St Michael's and, in 1945, control of St Michael's was handed over to the National Church League. More of that in the next chapter.

Eight years were to pass before it became possible to re-open and extend St Michael's. Nevertheless, what had been achieved in those two years formed a solid foundation for the future. And one former student of St Catherine's, Annette Tatton, was recorded as having given 'valiant help' in the move to Oxford, and was destined to become a valued Vice-Principal, in the new St Michael's, many years later.

CHAPTER 2

A Fresh Start 1948 - 1952

In October 1948, Miss Dorothy Barter Snow, a graduate in both Science and Theology, was invited to re-open St Michael's House, at the former Deaconess House, 1, Fyfield Road, Oxford, with just five students. It is interesting to trace the events which led up to this new beginning.

In January 1946, after a number of consultations, the St Michael and All Angels Trust had been wound up and its assets, together with the tenancy of the house in Oxford, transferred to the **National Church League**. This body had been formed earlier by the coming together of the Protestant Church Union and the Church of England (Ladies') League. It already owned a Church Sisters' Training College in London.

A new Council for St Michael's was set up and in their minutes of November 7th, 1946 there is a declared intention to re-open St Michael's as a residential College for women, as soon as possible. It would provide theological training for those desirous of deaconess work, or being trained for educational work at home or abroad. At the same time the National Church League was considering the future of their **Church Training College**. This had been opened in Chelsea, London, in 1900 under the auspices of the Ladies' League, and largely through the zeal and inspiration of one, Lady Wimborne, who became its first President. Later it removed to Hollenden House, in Putney, owing to the generosity of Lady Hollenden. It is reported that lady workers trained at Hollenden House, wore purple gowns and attracted the nick-name 'purple pussies'. For a number of reasons, the College had closed in 1930 and remained so throughout the war.

Nether Court, Hove
In 1946, the National Church League was offered a large and suitable house, Nether Court, in Hove, and accordingly, on October 1st that year, it re-opened with six students in residence, and with

19

Miss Eileen Ward as Principal and Miss Olga Forster as house-keeper. Local parochial experience was available especially at Bishop Hannington Church where the Revd Dick Rees was vicar. He also lectured at the College, together with other men and women of evangelical persuasion, who were willing to travel from London as visiting lecturers to meet the needs of the College. The President was now Lady Bates, and Nether Court had an excellent Council, chaired by the Revd T.G. Mohan (later to be chairman of St Michael's), with the Revd Llewellyn Roberts as secretary. All its members were well-known evangelicals.

The College was recognised by the **Council of Women's Ministry**, and offered the two-year course for the Inter-Diocesan Certificate as well as a shorter course of its own certificate. Miss Ward was a fine Principal, but very strict and although she was respected by all, some were a little afraid of her. She herself had trained at Mt. Hermon Missionary College, and had been detained in Egypt during the war. Students at Nether Court wore a distinctive green uniform, consisting of a hat, coat and tailored dress. It was smart and earned them the nick-name of 'the girls in green'.

Transfer of Nether Court to Oxford

In spite of being such a pleasant place, near to the sea and Downs, and offering such good courses, Nether Court did not attract many students, and even two years later there were only three in residence. It is not surprising that, with their new college in Oxford, the National Church League decided to close Nether Court and to transfer the students to St Michael's to complete their course. The decision, announced after Easter 1949, seemed cataclysmic, after such a short period in Hove. But, in the goodness of God, Miss Ward was led into Christian service in the parish of St Peter and St Paul, Dagenham and two of the students, Iris Tillett and Margaret Fish, went happily to Oxford in October of that year. Joan Marshall completed her course at Nether Court, and many years later was delighted to join the staff of St Michael's to oversee students in their practical training for parish work. Iris, who served in parish work right up to her retirement, died in 1997, but both Margaret and Joan in their retirement have been able to contribute to this book.

At St Michael's Iris became Senior Student, and wrote in the 1950 newsletter about the many opportunities in Oxford for the great variety of practical work, as well as the students going further afield to help, for example with a Parish Mission in Essex. Margaret writes of her long friendship with Iris, which began on Hove railway station, and became life-long. Her time in Oxford was very happy, and she found the atmosphere at St Michael's more relaxed than at Hove, where she had been rather scared! There were now about twenty students at the College, some of whom came from the continent.

In 1949, the College was still based in 1, Fyfield Road, and these earliest days are fondly remembered by former students. Pat Snow (now the Reverend) writes:

> I loved that house. One feature was a large airing cupboard used by a hard-up student as a study when her money for her gas fire ran out. Rations were still on, and we consumed quantities of kippers (they were not rationed). Unseemly hilarity upset lecturer Jim Packer during one of his lectures when he spoke about 'Yom Kippur'! There was a quince tree in the garden so we were treated to quince jelly. It was not popular. Even less popular was the concoction made from the pulp of quinces. It was the substitute for marmalade at breakfast. It remained untouched. Marmalade appeared again! These were tough days but Miss Carpenter, our cook-house-keeper, did her best to satisfy our appetites.

There continued to be a steady demand for women with a personal knowledge of the Lord Jesus Christ to undertake Christian work in schools, training Colleges, parishes and on the mission field. The aim of the College was to equip women who were called to Christian service with the necessary theological and pastoral knowledge, and to give them experience and training in practical Christian work. In addition, the College aimed to deepen the spiritual life of its students by prayer and the devotional as well as the academic study of the Bible as the inspired Word of God. How well it fulfilled these aims can be seen in the lives and work of its students, much of which can be found in later chapters.

In 1950, the control of the College passed to the **Church Society**, formed by the amalgamation of the National Church League with the Church Association. There continued to be a St Michael's House Council, which in time included representatives from Oxford, and which served the College well for many years.

'Thackley', Banbury Road

Soon the student body numbered twenty-four and not all could be housed in Fyfield Road, some had to be out in lodgings. It was in answer to the fervent prayers of many that, in 1951, the Church Society was able to buy Thackley, a large detached house, 119, Banbury Road, Oxford, for the expansion of St Michael's. The house had been built in 1904 for Professor Joseph Wright, on the one remaining plot of freehold land in the Banbury Road. It was the last acre of an estate bought by Miss Beale, of Cheltenham College fame, for St Hilda's College, but re-sold because she felt it was too far out of Oxford.

The Professor, a real Yorkshireman, wanted the house to be a 'big, old-fashioned, North Country house built of stone'. Everything in the house was to be of the best, with materials brought from Dorset and Derbyshire, and Joseph Wright, to crown it all, had the house roofed with stone slates from Yorkshire, each slate being almost as big as a grave stone. He named the house 'Thackley' after his birthplace in Yorkshire.

Since Joseph Wright was the leading Professor of German in the University, a most learned and serious scholar, it was not surpris-ing that the one dominating centre in Thackley was his study, real-ly a library but so much loved by the Wrights that they used it as their workshop, living-room and place of entertainment of hun-dreds of undergraduates, graduates and visiting professors. Professor Wright showed much interest in and kindness to his stu-dents, and many of them recalled the Sunday afternoon teas at Thackley to which they were frequently invited. One wrote to Mrs. Wright after her husband's death:

> What happy memories I have of his overflowing kindness and geniality. I don't know any more wonderfully welcoming house than yours. It is indeed a House Beautiful to all Oxford pilgrims!

How appropriate it was that a house with such a history should become the home of St Michael's.

When, in 1952, the house was officially opened, Miss Snow invited Mrs. Wright to be present. She wrote back graciously:

> It was kind of St Michael's to invite me to the official open-ing. I indeed appreciate the invitation and regret I am too

decrepit to attend. It is a great satisfaction to me that the house my husband built and where he worked for so many years should now be a centre for the very valuable work of the Church Society.

Courses for Teachers, Parish Workers and Missionaries

Academically, St Michael's had the recognition of the Ministry of Education for the one year Teachers' Supplementary Course in Divinity, and the Council of Women's Ministry for the Inter-Diocesan Course for the training of Parish Workers. Also a number of Missionary Societies had begun to recommend their women candidates for Bible training at the College. So the student body grew steadily in numbers, and judging from early newsletters, a happy family spirit remained. Students and staff were united in their love for the Lord and desire to serve Him.

Most students combined their professional studies for teaching or parish work with recognised examinations in Theology, including University degrees, diplomas or certificates. There was also the College's own Certificate in Bible Knowledge. The curriculum included, Christian Doctrine, Church History, Christian Worship, Pastoralia, Moral Theology, the Philosophy of Religion, the Book of Common Prayer, Christian Ethics, Non-Christian Religions, Missionary Methods, Teacher Training, Public Speaking, Elementary Psychology, Hebrew, New Testament Greek and Music.

In addition to the regular College courses, lectures were arranged on First Aid, Home Nursing, Hygiene, Moral Welfare and Social Service.

A far-seeing Principal

Throughout these years Dorothy Barter Snow was the inspiration and guiding-light of the College community, although she always had good supportive staff. Her commitment to the work at St Michael's and her conviction that it was for the extension of God's Kingdom is enshrined in 'Such a candle' the pamphlet she wrote in 1955.

There is in Oxford a more recent centre of reformed teaching than any of these just mentioned. Seven years ago an Evangelical theological college for women was opened. St Michael's House began its present work in 1948 with five stu-

23

dents. It has now sent nearly a hundred trained women to work for God in Evangelical parishes in England, to schools where old St Michael's students teach as Scripture specialists, and to the far places of the earth where old students are doing missionary work, evangelising, teaching, healing. St Michael's has old students in Israel, Arabia, Uganda, Nigeria, Ethiopia, India, Pakistan, Ceylon, and most European countries, as well as in England. Shortly the College will be represented in Malaya and the Far East.

The choice of Dorothy Barter Snow as the Warden - Principal of the new St Michael's was an inspired one. It will be shown in later chapters that she made a deep impression on all who came into contact with the College. That is the testimony of bishops, other clergy, former members of staff and ex-students.

CHAPTER 3

A Visionary Principal 1948 - 1965

For seventeen years Miss Dorothy Barter Snow was Principal of St Michael's. She was a woman of outstanding intellect and integrity, totally committed to Jesus Christ and devoted to Him in her personal life.

Her Christian Family

She came from a strongly Christian evangelical family, with an interesting history. Her mother was Laura Anna Barter, fifth and youngest child of Lieutenant General Richard Barter and Mrs. Barter of Cooldaniel, County Cork. Born in India, during her father's service there in difficult times, Laura was a delicate child, but she grew up to be a wife, mother, and well-known Christian writer, particularly of tracts and magazine articles for women and girls.

On July 25th, 1896, Laura became the wife of Frank Trevelyan Snow, Vicar of St Peter's, Islington. It was a most happy partnership of two people who wanted to put God first in every department of their lives. Laura, a few years younger than Frank, threw herself into the work of the parish, alongside her husband. Her Irish wit and keen sympathy were strong factors in making things run smoothly in the parish.

It was just a year after their marriage on July 30th, 1897 that Laura gave birth to Dorothy at St Peter's Vicarage, Islington. Both she and the baby almost died during the birth. But in God's mercy both were saved and the baby was named Dorothy Mary Barter. There were to be five more children born to the couple and since General Barter had left no sons to carry on his name (his only son died tragically in India) all were given the third name Barter, at Laura's wish. Dorothy was the one who delighted to use the name in memory of a much-loved grandfather.

Over the years the Snows ministered in several widely differing parishes. From St Peter's, Islington, they were called to Holy

Trinity, Bordesley, and from there, in 1910, to the living of Broadway, Worcs. This unexpectedly proved to be the most difficult for them, as some members of the congregation came to resent the evangelistic thrust of Frank's preaching. However, they worked faithfully in Broadway for some six years and during that time were asked, when attending the Keswick Convention in 1913, if they would go out to West Africa for a few months. They were to take meetings in different parts of Nigeria for the deepening of the spiritual life of both Europeans and Africans. After much prayer and consideration (for their six children had to be cared for in England - as well as their parishioners) they accepted. Their time in Nigeria was a tremendous encouragement to them for they saw a spiritual hunger and an outpouring of the Holy Spirit, which they had not found in England. It gave them a great burden to pray for more workers to go to the harvest fields of the world, and to do all they could to stimulate interest in overseas Mission.

Shortly before the end of World War 1 the family moved to Birling in Kent, a small parish and an ideal country living for Frank as he was beginning to feel his age. They were to stay there for eight and a half years. Laura's writing flourished and it was for the family a time of happiness and peace after the strenuous work in previous parishes.

Sadly, after several years in Birling, Dorothy's father became unwell, and to the great grief of the family was called Home on 3rd October, 1925. His death meant a swift and difficult move from Birling to Hadleigh in Suffolk, where, with Christian foresight, Frank had bought Topplesfield Hall, an old roomy house (not as its name might imply, a huge country manor) with a rambling garden and orchard.

Laura's ministry
Here Laura lived for fourteen years writing, speaking, working indefatigably in God's service, until her own health failed and she died in 1939. Laura Barter Snow's books and writings continued to be read widely. One book in particular, 'Just for me', went into several editions and sales reached many thousands. It is reported that a copy of this was even seen in an anti-God museum in Russia. Except for the short time in West Africa, Laura never left home to go abroad to those far places of earth where she would have loved to take the good news of the Gospel in person. Instead, God used

her pen to write messages which went in print to far more places than she could ever have visited as a missionary.

It was a privileged home in which the Snow children grew up. From childhood they were surrounded by human love and immersed in an atmosphere of God's love that attracted them to Him from the start. The greatest influence was their mother Laura, whom they loved intensely. After her death, her daughters compiled her biography, entitled **The Joyous Servant**, and in it they wrote of the special joy of Sunday evenings in the Vicarage:

> When the older members of the family departed for Church, the rest of us sat around the fire while our mother read to us all sorts of stories, historical and moral, but always stories with God and the spiritual life as their background. Old-fashioned stories, perhaps, but we were old enough to take hold of what was eternal in them, and young enough to disregard the ephemeral. After the reading there would follow prayers, real, personal, intimate for the people and causes we all had at heart. The experience was unforgettable and left one with a life-long impression of the reality of God, His nearness and dearness and His concern with our small lives.

Enthusiasm for overseas mission

In the home too, Dorothy's parents did so much to stimulate the children's interest in overseas missions. When they were still quite small they began to meet missionaries who enthralled them with stories of foreign lands and the work waiting to be done for the Lord. They grew familiar with the faces of Africans, Chinese and Indians in missionary magazines and it seemed to them that to be allowed to take the Gospel of Christ to these people was the highest possible vocation. Missionary enthusiasm in the family showed itself, not only by collecting boxes, and the getting up of missionary entertainments of an amateur kind, but also by the holding of family missionary meetings arranged by the younger members among them.

Small wonder that Dorothy's brothers and sisters, after their education in England, all went abroad into different kinds of Christian service. Dr. Eileen Snow became Principal of the Christian Medical College at Ludhiana, India, and her sister Olive, Administrative Secretary of the same Institution. Her brother Frank served with the Church Mission Society at the Stuart

Memorial College, Isfahan, where for some time he was Acting
Head. Her second brother, Dick, also a doctor, went first to India
and then ultimately to Bahrein where he was in charge of the
Government Hospital. Dorothy's third sister, Kathleen, found her
vocation in the Order of the Sacred Heart and ended her days
working in an Ashram in Poona.

School and College

Financially the Snows were never well off, but Dorothy's parents
made great sacrifices to see that their six children were well educated. Laura worked hard at her writing to earn something extra
towards the cost of home schooling with a governess when they
were young, and good schools and colleges when they were older.
Some were able to get grants or scholarships including those available for clergy children. At home, the children had all gained a
great love of books of all kinds and a respect for and love of nature,
which in the case of Eileen and Dorothy led on to the study of medicine and biology. Dorothy always claimed that an early tadpole-
catching expedition with her mother made her a zoologist! She
graduated with an Honours Degree in Zoology from King's
College, London.

Already very strong in the faith and committed to Christian witness and evangelism, she was one of the founder members of the
Inter-Varsity Fellowship at London University. She maintained a
strong prayer interest in this movement (now the U.C.C.F.) to the
end of her life. Like her mother before her, Dorothy's zeal for mission could have led her overseas but instead God's call was to mission at home. She became a biology teacher, and studied theology
in her spare time, working for the London BD. This equipped her
to teach scripture alongside her science, and this she did for some
twenty years in a number of schools, including Clarendon School,
Abergele. It was clearly of the Lord that Dorothy remained in
England, because at times of family crises, when her father died at
Birling and then her mother at Hadleigh, it was she, the eldest child
who was able to give greatest practical help. All her experience
helped to equip her for the Principalship of St Michael's.

A clear vision for training

Dorothy Barter Snow came to St. Michael's with a clear vision for
the content of that training. She herself chose the College motto : "I

have a stewardship entrusted to me" (1 Corinthians 9:17 RV). These words continued to inspire students long after they left St Michael's.

Of tall and dignified stature, Dorothy could appear stern - even forbidding - but she was possessed of an impish sense of humour (no doubt linked to her Irish ancestry) and a twinkle in the eyes which endeared her to many. As people got to know her they discovered a heart of compassion, a wisdom and spiritual depth which made her a much loved and respected Principal.

Dorothy's spiritual leadership was greatly appreciated, especially the way she led the daily prayers in Chapel. A teacher by nature, training and experience, she lectured in Old and New Testament, with a grasp of both Hebrew and Greek. Her own knowledge of Scripture was immense and she sought to impart this to students, believing it to be of prime importance in their future work. Thus she led the whole College in a life of devotion, prayer and Bible Study.

Writing in St Michael's newsletter after her own retirement as Secretary to the College, Miss Mary Long said:

> I have had the particularly great privilege of working closely with Miss Snow, and of seeing her walk humbly with God, through these years of building up this work of training, with its tests and disappointments as well as its joys and victories of faith. I have seen her deep love for every student, past and present, and have realised more deeply year by year, the faithfulness of her prayer life - here is one whose life is indeed hid with Christ in God.

House rules

Miss Snow aimed to help every student in the development of Christian self-discipline, which she believed would be essential in a life of Christian service. There were, therefore, rules at St Michael's. They included attendance at Chapel - morning and evening, lights out, and compulsory rotas for gardening and housework. Another custom, which some students found difficult, to say the least, was the changing of rooms and room mates every term. Miss Snow felt it was important for students in training for mission to learn to live with people whose habits were different from theirs. Anyone who has lived on the mission field, for any length of time, would probably agree with this.

But Miss Snow was far from inflexible and could bend the rules when necessary. For example, Effie Smith told Miss Snow that she could not possibly do a Diploma in Theology in one year if she had to put her lights out at 10.30 p.m. Miss Snow promptly abolished the rule for one year and resumed it after Effie had left. Another rule forbade male visitors to remain in College after 7 p.m. But on one occasion when someone was visiting his fiancée in St. Michael's and had not left by the appointed time, Miss Snow invited him to stay for dinner and the evening as her guest.

Even the time-table was not sacrosanct. One former student writes:

> Happiest of all were the days off when Miss Snow thought we were all looking tired. Going with her to buy a boat and then sail it on the river are memories of that time.

Former staff and students also recall with some amusement summer punting on the river when Miss Snow's large dog, Andy, brought the outing to a near disaster.

Studies and Hobbies
In spite of her exceedingly busy life, Miss Snow found time to pursue her own studies and hobbies. Her first degree was in Natural Sciences and she was teaching Biology at Clarendon School when invited to come to St Michael's. It was a great joy to her and to the student body when she went on to gain her BD in 1950 and then, in 1960, her B. Litt. (Oxon).

Of her hobbies there are many stories. Lorna Manners, formerly on the staff, writes:

> I remember the silkworms. On one Vacation Miss Snow asked me to look after them during her absence. Thankfully, they all survived, although some had changed to the spinning, then chrysalis stage, by the time she returned.

Miss Snow was a skilful weaver, but she liked to find, dye and spin the wool herself. On one occasion she took a little party (L. Manners, H. Sobek and D. Nelson) to the Scilly Isles. As well as walking, of which she was very fond, they spent much time collecting, from the rocks, the many lichens from which she made her dyes. That little holiday was remembered too for the sighting of unusual seabirds, including puffins, as well as grey seals on the islands.

When Dorothy was scarcely more than a child, her mother had given her her first beehive, bees and appliances, and Dorothy became a very experienced bee keeper. Peter Dawes tells two delightful stories from the time when he was a visiting lecturer:

> I'm not sure if it was I or my Rector who met her one day looking down the Banbury Road - " I am waiting for the Queen," she said. It turned out that you can get bees by post and that certain ones (? Italian) were valued for their docility. For myself, I was a 'townie' and told her that the country would drive me mad, which horrified her. She never forgot our conversation for she quoted me in a St Michael's letter after her retirement.

One day she took Peter to see the bees, which were buzzing about very actively. He said nonchalantly "Jolly little chaps" at which she exploded "Chaps! Chaps! They are girls, everyone of them!"

Miss Snow became a regular and loyal member of St Ebbe's Church as did many of her students, and a valued friend of Rectors and Curates; to the latter she always gave a book as a gift at Christmas. Attendance at St Ebbe's and other city churches was not easy because students were not expected to use public transport on Sundays. However, most had bicycles, and these were used also to get to and from meetings in Oxford and around. Since she herself enjoyed physical exercise, Miss Snow encouraged it in the students. If a student could avail herself of a lift in a car Miss Snow laid it down that she must always pay the equivalent of the bus fare to the driver, demonstrating in this way the principles of honesty and integrity in which she set a clear example.

The Bible - her inspiration and authority

For Dorothy Snow the scriptures were her inspiration and authority. She lived by them and encouraged students to do the same. She believed that total devotion to Christ's service really meant separation to Him, from the world, and that included abstention from doubtful practices such as theatre and cinema going. One former student recalls how seriously the Principal spoke one morning to the whole College because one member had been seen going to an

Oxford Theatre. "The play might have been innocuous," she said, "but how would anyone know whether that servant of Christ did not make a habit of going to anything in such a place." For her the principle of consideration for the weaker brother or sister was paramount.

But no one would have criticised Miss Snow for being narrow-minded. The breadth of her knowledge and interests was so great. Keith Weston was very aware of this whenever he visited the College. He writes:

> She would often invite me to her study - a veritable Aladdin's cave of books, papers, weaving equipment and other para-phernalia, so thick on furniture and floor that it might be dif-ficult to find a place to sit. And of course in the company of her large and faithful dog, Andy. She would sometimes share problems about the College, or about individuals, but always expressing her anxieties with wonderful kindness and love and always followed by prayer together.

Retirement - and a dream come true

Miss Snow retired from St Michael's in 1965, and surprised herself as much as anyone else by fulfilling her dream to work overseas for a short time. She was appointed to the staff of the C.M.J. School in Jerusalem (the Anglican International School) on a voluntary basis, to teach Religious Knowledge and Science. She stayed for a year before finally settling in Hampshire.

Appreciation

When Dorothy Barter Snow left in 1965 students and staff alike expressed appreciation for her years as the first Principal of the College. Annette Tatton, her Vice-Principal, wrote:

> We - members and friends of St Michael's - praise God for all He has done through His Servant, and cannot help feeling sad that a great chapter in our history is drawing to a close. Seventeen years of skilful teaching, careful planning, inspired foresight, Irish humour, and above all spiritual vitality, have been lived out by God's servant in blessing for St Michael's House. To those of us who have worked on the Staff has been afforded the special privilege of knowing Miss Snow as Principal, colleague and friend and of serving under one

Dorothy Barter Snow.

Laura Barter Snow and her family. (Dorothy is second from the left, back row.)

Staff in Ridley Garden.

Nether Court, Hove.

St. Michael's, 1 Fyfield Road, Oxford.

Ridley (119 Banbury Road)

Latimer (117 Banbury Road)

whom to know is to respect and love. We have seen, and learnt much of the Lord in His radiant Servant.

CHAPTER 4

Chaplains and Clergy -
Remembered and Remembering

Throughout its existence, St Michael's benefited enormously from the intellectual, spiritual and pastoral input of the clergy. Helped, no doubt, by her Vicarage background Miss Snow had a way of persuading such men that to come to St Michael's was just what God wanted them to do. They came as Chaplains, lecturers, friends of staff and students and as Chairmen of the St Michael's Council.

First Chaplain
In 1938, an Oxford clergyman, the Revd G. Foster-Carter, Vicar of St Andrew's Church, had been appointed Warden, Chaplain and lecturer at St Michael's Deaconess House. When the College reopened in 1948 he was the first clergyman to call on Miss Snow. He was invited to join the staff as a lecturer in Church History, and this he continued to be until only a few months before his death in 1966. The College expressed their appreciation of his faithful service with a gift in December 1965. He wrote:

> I did not open the envelope in which your amazing gift was enclosed until I got home tonight. And when I did it was difficult to believe my eyes. I can't imagine why you should have thought of giving me a present at all. It is quite true that I have been lecturing for some length of years. But I was paid for it and never felt the payment was inadequate. It comes at a most auspicious moment for me. We are putting space heating into the house, and this enables me to get an extra heater for the top landing. I shall think of it as St Michael's gift of heat and warmth and shall, by it, remember the happy work of so many years.

It was recorded in the 1966 newsletter that he died on Thursday 5th May.

Council Chairmen

Much could be written about the Chairmen of the St Michael's Council. These were all men of deep spirituality, already extremely busy in their different spheres. Yet they gladly gave their time and prayers to meetings of the Council and to visits to the College. When she was preparing to retire in 1965 Miss Snow wrote:

> I should also like to give thanks for our St Michael's Council. Their backing, their prayers and advice have meant very much to me - I could not have had a better Council with which to work. The Chairmen who have led our Council, the Revd Canon St John Thorpe, The Revd L.F.E. Wilkinson (Principal of Oak Hill Theological College), and the Revd Canon T.G. Mohan have been real personal friends to me and have given much of their time and interest to the work here.

Of 'Wilkie', who died rather suddenly in 1961, she wrote:

> St Michael's sustained a very great loss when the Chairman of our Council went Home to God quite suddenly only three weeks after a Council Meeting. We much miss his visits to us, his spiritual talks, his kindly humour, his wise advice and judgement. He was much beloved and his work amongst students most effective.

What Miss Snow felt about these men, Miss Cooke can also say about the Revd John Bournon, who succeeded Canon Mohan and saw St Michael's through the last few difficult years in Oxford, giving great support to her and the staff.

More Chaplains

Turning to those who served as Chaplains, first came the Revd Gordon Savage, Secretary of Church Society (and later the Bishop of Southwell) who, in addition to his chaplaincy duties gave lectures on the Prayer Book. A strong link was made with St Ebbe's Church and three of its Rectors became Chaplains. First was Revd Maurice Wood (later Bishop of Norwich) who gave lectures on his special subjects, Homiletics and Pastoralia, and all his work in the College was deeply appreciated. Many staff and students valued his friendship after he left Oxford for Islington. He himself remembers with a smile that the burning issue amongst the women students of his day was, 'Should parish workers wear hats when speaking at meetings?' He recalls:

> I took a Biblical and Pastoral line, suggesting that in princi-ple we should follow the advice of St Paul in I Corinthians 11:2-16 - our preaching and our hat should attract quietly rather than distract violently!

In a more serious vein he writes:

> We trained some fine Christian girls, who gave many years of devoted and pastoral service to needy parishes in the Church of England.

When Maurice left Oxford in 1952, the Revd Basil Gough fol-lowed him as Rector of St Ebbe's and Chaplain to St Michael's. He was to serve the College until he became Principal of Clifton Theological College in 1964. Basil's input into the spiritual life of St Michael's was incalculable. Former students write of the helpful-ness of his lectures, the Quiet Days he took, his sermons in the Chapel and his ministry at St Ebbe's. Of his and Stella's departure to Bristol Miss Snow wrote:

> The Revd Basil Gough and his wife Stella have given freely of time, encouragement, advice and hospitality, our loss is def-initely Clifton's gain.

Basil not only gave all this spiritual help but he was quick to meet other needs too, like cutting the enormous College lawns when the staff were clearly overpressed. Service indeed!

Canon Keith Weston

The relationship with St Ebbe's continued when the next Rector, the Revd K.A.A. Weston (later Canon) was appointed Chaplain, and elected to the St Michael's Council. He and his wife Margaret gave the same wonderful support as their predecessors. Keith (always modest) felt that Basil outshone him as a Pastoralia lectur-er. But students would not have said so. Often they told him how much his lectures helped them, and he records with surprise that years later one former student said she was still using his outlines in her parish. Many recall Keith's deeply spiritual, challenging sermons at Holy Communion Services or on Quiet Days. He in turn writes that he appreciated the Chapel Services - calling them 'precious' and 'moving'. On the St Michael's Council Keith gave wise and practical advice, and was a tremendous help in the difficult times in 1967/8 when preparations were being made to close St Michael's in Oxford. Like Basil and Stella Gough before them, Keith and Margaret were great friends of the College, offering practical help in times of need, and sharing their musical gifts in the social life of the College.

St. Peter's Hall

Another Oxford cleric to whom the College was indebted was the Revd J.P. Thornton-Duesbery, Master of St Peter's Hall (later, St Peter's College). He was a successor to the Revd Christopher Chavasse, who was instrumental in bringing St Michael's to Oxford in 1948, and who, as Bishop of Rochester, supported the work with very great interest. Mr. Thornton-Duesbery had also been on the St Michael's Council from the beginning in 1945 when plans to re-open in Oxford were in their infancy. He was a good friend to both Miss Snow and Miss Cooke, only leaving the Council when he retired in 1968. He was always ready to give advice on University Courses and to arrange introductions to University Tutors for the benefit of Theology students.

It is not possible to name all the Clergy who had a share from time to time in the work of St Michael's. They came to lead and preach at Holy Communion Services, to take Quiet Days, or to lecture. They include names of those who have become very well known in the evangelical world - Bishops and writers. A rough count brings us to a total of about fifty men who generously helped the College in this way.

The Stotts

Mention must be made however of the Revd Wilfrid Stott who lectured on the Bible between 1951 and 1961. He and his family had been missionaries in China, and with their young children had undergone the traumatic evacuation from that country, when the Communists took over. Wilfrid had become Vicar of Dowdeswell, near Cheltenham, and was able to come into Oxford for one morning of lectures each week, combining this with study for a B. Litt. His research made it necessary for him to stay in Oxford four nights in every week. This was difficult financially for him to do, so

Miss Snow allowed him to park his caravan at St Michael's for his 'sleep overs'. All was well until a bitterly cold spell in one November almost turned him into an icicle. Fortunately after this drama, friends offered him accommodation.

Wilfrid Stott was greatly appreciated as a lecturer, pastor and friend. He was a deeply spiritual man, with a sense of humour, and a wealth of experience of God's faithfulness during those years on the mission field. He was greatly missed when he responded to a call to go to the parish of St Philip, Cambridge. There he was able to lecture at Romsey House, and in due course became Chairman of its Council. Both he and his wife Jessie were totally committed to mission, and it was no surprise to hear that in 1964 they were off again to Kenya to serve God for a few years on the staff of the United Theological College at Limuru.

Quiet Days

Perhaps the most memorable times in which the clergy visited the College were the Quiet Days arranged at the beginning of each term. All the usual tasks and studies were set aside for the day. As one student puts it:

> To just sit still and listen, to learn of Him and to grow in the knowledge of Him, so that gradually the 'I' in our activities may diminish more and more, and the 'He' may grow in the same proportion.

Always helpful and appreciated, there were occasions when the subject for the day was particularly apt, both for the immediate circumstances as well as for future work at home or on the mission field. For instance, the Hilary Term 1952 Quiet Day was led by the Revd Frank Houghton with the general subject of 'Adaptability' which was a most appropriate and welcome preparation for students who had just moved from a comfortable house to one (119, Banbury Road) where 'planks, sand and mortar were all over the place.'

There were two talks on the urgent necessity for a Christian to be able to adapt and the following notes are quoted from the newsletter of that year:

> **(a) Adaptability to circumstances** (Phil. 4 v10ff) "Those", he said, " who intend to work in the mission field, will

experience a period of disillusionment when they start their work in a foreign country. They will find that things are different from the way they imagined them to be." Mr. Houghton warned such missionary candidates not to go out, who find it difficult to adapt themselves to difficulties in this country. Our attention was drawn to 2 Cor. 11 v.3 where a list of circumstances is given to which St. Paul had to adapt himself. He was able to do so because he was content with every situation, because he did not ask for more than he already had. 'I have learnt in whatsoever state I am, therewith to be content.'This spirit of complete contentment is needed if our service is to be effective.

The question was raised "Are we content with whatever God sends us?" Dwelling on this question Mr. Houghton eventually showed us that the problem of being able to be content is a spiritual one. 'I can do all things through Christ which strengtheneth me.'

(b) Adaptability to people (1 Cor. 9 vv 11 - 23) Adaptability to circumstances is only the background of the main task - adaptability to people. It is no good for a servant of Christ to sit at home; he has to go where the people are. In talking to them, however, the servant has to adapt him or herself to the people; their background and general outlook has to be understood if the conversation is to be fruitful.

If we want to be servants of Christ we have to become servants of our neighbours. Servants of the strong-minded and servants of the weak. Look at St. Paul. It must have been exceedingly difficult for him to suffer fools gladly, but he knew the necessity of not becoming a 'stumbling block' in the service of Christ. He knew of the necessity of adapting himself to all.

They also served
The contributions made to the College life by all these visitors were memorable. If 'variety is the spice of life' then a general 'Hallelujah' was expressed for the lectures of the Revd Peter Dawes, one of Basil Gough's curates (later to become Bishop of Derby). He tutored between 1957 and 1960. His stimulating lectures on

Doctrine and Worship, and his rich vein of humour enlivened every visit. He has memories too and writes of those days:

> My first impression was of a very mixed group of ladies with quite a varied experience in other fields, but for a number of them academic work seemed very heavy going. My memory is of students who, in the main, wished to learn, to be trained and eager to serve God, somewhere, in parishes at home or overseas - and everything was done in an atmosphere of prayer and enjoyment.

Former students will recall others who brought their own distinctive character to the subjects they lectured in, the Revds Jim Packer (see also next chapter), Jim Spence, David Pytches, Gilbert Gauntlett, and in the late sixties the Revd Bruce Smith - a particularly popular lecturer from Australia, who was 'shared' with Birmingham Bible Institute. Bruce has fond memories of Oxford and St Michael's, and has kept in touch over the years, through students who have found their way to Australia, and through his own return visits here. Rumour has it that Bruce has gained the reputation of being one of the best preachers in the Sydney Diocese.

Although, in general, the clergy came for the benefit of the training of the students, members of staff also have happy memories of their presence in the College. Coming regularly and punctually to fulfil their duties, they usually arrived in time for elevenses or lunch, and gave immense enjoyment and fellowship to the resident staff.

CHAPTER 5

A Tribute to the Staff 1948 - 1968

One of the great strengths of St. Michael's was the team of dedicated staff in every department, most of whom were appointed by Miss Snow. In her 1964 - 65 newsletter she wrote of the faithfulness of God:

> He has not only supplied our material needs but I owe Him much for the Staff that He has sent to us, both resident and visiting whom we have prayed into St. Michael's, and for none of whom we have advertised.

The first cook-housekeeper was **Miss Dorothy Carpenter**, the daughter of missionaries. Her brother, the Revd John Carpenter, had been the Rector of St. Ebbe's during the War and she introduced Miss Snow to that Church. Dorothy was remembered for her quiet efficiency and her care for students until her retirement in Oxford. Though virtually blind, she delighted to entertain ex-staff and students and continued to serve Christ faithfully to the end of her days.

At the end of Miss Snow's first year, she was most fortunate in acquiring as her secretary **Miss Mary Long**, who had worked for the Faith Mission Bible College in Edinburgh. For many years Mary proved a tower of strength until she had to leave to look after her ageing mother. In fact Mary returned for a short time after Miss Snow's retirement and gave the same untiring service to **Miss Jean Cooke**, the new Principal. Others who gave loyal and valuable secretarial help in the busy office were **Miss Ruth Underwood, Miss Mary Hawkins** and **Miss Joyce Gardner**.

No College can survive without a bursar and St Michael's was no exception. In 1958, **Miss Constance Bingham**, who had served in India with the Church of England Zenana Missionary Society, joined the Staff. She brought to the College not only perfect accounting and recording, but a nature that truly reflected Jesus Christ. After she retired in 1967 it was written of her:

Miss Bingham went in and out among us as a wise and loving counsellor, ever ready to listen, to encourage, to say a word in season.

In the early days **Dss Elsie Le Rougetel** was in charge of Pastoralia, a responsibility she fulfilled capably and with the love and respect of the students. The **Revd G. Foster-Carter** lectured in Church History and **Miss Vera Brandon** in Greek, Ethics, Philosophy and Christian Relationships (once described by Miss Snow as 'a strange mixture of psychology, education, moral theology and common sense'.) Already a qualified and experienced mathematics teacher, Vera Brandon had joined St. Michael's as a student in 1951. She stayed on as a tutor, and gave ten years faithful and loyal service to the College. She left in 1961 to join the staff of St. Peter's, Rushden, having been ordained a Deaconess on September 29th, 1960, St Michael's Day, at St. Andrew's, Oxford. Deaconess Brandon served God unwaveringly in the following years, first in parochial work, then on the staff of the Church Army Training College at Blackheath, and as a member of the Community of the Word of God. She has also been a wonderful prayer partner to all former members of St. Michael's. At Petertide 1998 she was ordained Priest at Rochester Cathedral, which was a fitting climax to a lifetime of dedication to Christ's service.

Miss Elizabeth Richards was also first a student at St. Michael's and then a greatly valued member of staff equipped with secretarial skills. Elizabeth studied theology at St. Michael's with a view to becoming a parish worker. Her 'slightly academic bent', however, fitted her for a different task. A message given by Miss Snow in a morning service at Chapel helped Elizabeth to realise where her gifts lay, and on being invited a little later to serve on the staff, she accepted joyfully. Students appreciated her both as teacher and tutor. She had spent two years in Africa (Nyasaland) working as her father's secretary and was very interested in missionary work. Subsequently her call to serve as a missionary in Paraguay with the South American Mission Society came through two St. Michael's students, Thea Wedgwood and Jocelyn Padbury. Elizabeth has worked in Paraguay for many years in Bible Teaching, Linguistics and Theological Education by Extension (SEAN = Seminary by Extension to all Nations). She was ordained Deaconess in South America in October 1964.

In 1950, a young man called **James Innell Packer** was research-ing for his Doctorate at Wycliffe Hall. He had just gained a First in Theology, after reading Classics for his first degree. Miss Snow engaged him to teach Biblical Theology and the Philosophy of Religion. Jim Packer was an excellent lecturer. His delivery was slow and deliberate, ideally suited to those taking notes. The experience at St. Michael's was valuable to him also, preparing him for his later work at Tyndale Hall and Trinity College in Bristol, and eventually at Regent College, Vancouver. Dr. Jim Packer has been deemed one of the great Christian writers and thinkers of the 20th century, and his books have become best-sellers. His biographer, Alister McGrath, wrote of him in 1997:

> he has exerted an enormous influence on the emergence and consolidation of evangelism in the last forty years.

Miss Margaret Morris, later to become Mrs. Habermann and known as 'Jock', was another outstanding member of the teaching staff. Miss Snow had persuaded her to come to St. Michael's both in order to help struggling students prepare themselves for taking theological examinations, and to be responsible for all aspects of Pastoralia. Miss Morris worked as tutor alongside Jim Packer and lectured in Christian Doctrine. After one student had failed her examinations (having a lot of knowledge but unable to produce it), Jock had an idea:

> I imagined her mind to be like one of those tape measures, concealed in a metal box with a little puller sticking out - pull it and the rest follows. Could I devise a 'puller'? I began writing doggerel for her:
>
> Bernard was a holy saint
> He said that man was evil
> That Christ had died to ransom him from bondage to the
> Deevil!

This worked splendidly; from then on she produced copious rhymes, which prompted and amused students as they tackled subjects such as Philosophy, Old Testament and Church History.

On becoming aware that students training as parish workers or missionaries needed help with voice production, Miss Morris introduced Christmas programmes of hymns and carols, interspersed with verses of Scripture, enjoyed by all who came to them; they greatly improved the speaking capacity of the students. When she left St Michael's Jock Morris was led to establish a theological College at Cambridge, known as Romsey House. An account of its birth and ministry is contained in her highly entertaining book 'Persistent Whisper'. Until 1995, Romsey House attracted many students, for varying courses and for different lengths of time. However, in that year it joined with Northumbria Bible College, Berwick-upon-Tweed in a similar merger to that undergone by St Michael's. A service of Thanksgiving was held in Cambridge, at which St Michael's was represented. The closing message was given by Professor Hugh Williamson, the Chairman of the Council, and the final hymn 'Great is Thy faithfulness' expressed everyone's feelings.

After Jock Morris left the College, **Mrs Nita Wright**, the wife of David Wright, member of St Michael's Council, joined the staff to teach speech production, part-time. Everyone enjoyed their sessions with Nita, who later became an actress with the Royal Shakespeare Company.

In the early 1960s, a number of well qualified women joined the teaching staff for varying periods of time. One such was **Dss Patricia Nelson**, a graduate in Theology from Moore College, Sydney, who came for a year. Pat has kept in touch with Lorna Manners, since returning to Australia and she was ordained to the priesthood in 1993.

In 1962 **Miss Peggy Knight**, an experienced and inspirational teacher, with a Degree in Classics and a Diploma in Theology, joined the staff. She had a very strong missionary interest and many practical gifts. Students especially appreciated her informal gatherings on Saturday evenings when they could drink coffee, listen to music and get their mending or knitting done.

Miss Theodora Parkinson, who had served for some years as a missionary in the Near East, came to fill a gap at very short notice in October 1961. Her work was greatly appreciated particularly in the Bible Knowledge Certificate course and in the organisation of school teaching practice. When she left to retire in 1963 she was greatly missed for her friendliness and generous, adventurous spirit.

Miss Joan Crewdson came to take Miss Parkinson's place on a part-time basis. Having graduated from Cambridge, she was studying for a further Degree in Theology at Oxford. After she left Joan continued to be a friend and visitor to St Michael's.

About the same time, **Miss Eva Parker** was appointed as a resident tutor. While a student at St Michael's, from 1955 - 56, Eva's intellectual and practical gifts had been evident. After gaining a Diploma in Theology, she was accepted by the China Inland Mission for service in Malaya, where she worked for four years until health problems brought her home. But the Lord had other work for her to do and for the next few years students benefited from her knowledge and experience. Her excellent teaching and ready wit held their interest. Thanks to her vigorous self-discipline she successfully gained her B.D., ran the library with great efficiency and in her free hours made time to work in the College garden.

Eva returned to Religious Education teaching in 1967, and continued until her retirement in 1980. For some fifteen years Eva put up a tremendous fight against cancer, accomplishing so much in that time, in addition to her teaching. She obtained another Degree through the Open University, and was at one point lay Chaplain to the Mayor of St Albans. Following her death in 1990, a former student (Kath Lefroy) wrote of Eva:

> I praise God for the life of Eva which, for me, had something of the quality of the grit in an oyster, for around that forms the pearl which is so valuable and of such inestimable worth.

Following Miss Dorothy Carpenter as housekeeper came **Miss Ivy Stiling, Mrs MacLean** - affectionately known as 'Mrs Mac', - **Miss Daisy Simmonds** and **Miss Lorna Manners**. Each contributed to the life of the community their experience, gifts and hard work.

Lorna Manners will be remembered not only for her first-class catering and cooking, but also for the garden she created and tended and for her flower arrangements. Since the budget was tight, when Lorna began working at St Michael's there was no refrigerator. For almost six years she had to use the basement cellar for storing food, making many trips up and down the steps each day. In addition to routine work, in the summer vacations Lorna gave time to making jam and bottling fruit which grew plentifully in the College gardens - no freezers in those days.

Lorna tells the story of how, eventually, a 'fridge' was acquired.

> Going up and downstairs was good for the figure, but oh, how I longed for a refrigerator - it certainly would have saved time and energy. I knew that there was not much money to spare for such things, so after one particularly hard day and much tiredness I decided I would pray one in! Day after day I spoke to the Lord about it. About six months later my prayers were answered. One day Miss Snow came to see me and said : "Could you make use of a large refrigerator?" She told me she had just received a 'phone call from a lady in North Oxford who was replacing her fridge with a more up to date one - and wondered if we could make use of it. Well, could we!! I thought I should then tell Miss Snow how long I had been praying for one and how much it was needed. It did not cost the College much - just £10. So that was how St Michael's got its first and only fridge.

When St Michael's closed in 1968, Lorna together with 'Auntie' Jackson played a huge part in sorting and packing everything that had to go to Bristol. At the same time they were seeking new homes and new jobs. It was not long before Lorna was appointed house-keeper to Ripon Theological College, Boars Hill, where she spent seven happy years in very lovely surroundings. Then, to her amaze-ment, she was involved in another merger and found herself pack-ing up Ripon to go to Cuddesdon Theological College, Wheatley. This time, however, she retained her job - becoming Domestic Bursar at Cuddesdon. For nine years she continued to be a valued member of staff, and was able to care for her widowed mother until they retired to Wiltshire in 1984.

Miss Joan Marshall, mentioned in Chapter 2, joined the Staff in 1967 as a part-time Pastoralia Tutor. St Michael's was required to set up the new three year Training for Parish Work, and Joan was appointed especially to oversee students' practical experience in parishes (she herself was ex-Hove Sisters' Training College - so in a way, a former student). Her warm friendliness and her practical help in sharing her own full experience of Christian work were much appreciated. In a time of need, she was also a great help to the Principal with her secretarial skills. When St Michael's left Oxford, Joan returned to parish work, for which she was so well-qualified.

She continued in the ministry until she retired to Sussex in 1988. She was active in retirement until her health began to fail. She died after a short illness in 1998.

From the beginning Miss Snow welcomed **girls from France, Switzerland, Germany** and **other countries** who came to give domestic help, improve their English and benefit from Christian teaching. They were given time to attend classes and encouraged to take an examination in the language. Their presence enriched the life of the College and lasting friendships were made with students and staff.

In 1950 **Miss Emily Jackson** came from Manchester as a student in training for parish work. She excelled in Pastoralia, but finding herself unable to reach the required academic standard, felt she should offer to help on the domestic side. She was taken on and for seventeen years served the College as a very efficient house-keeper. Affectionately known as 'Auntie', she was both loved and occasionally feared, for she could be stern with students who did not keep their rooms tidy or whose general housework did not come up to her northern standards. But she had a heart of gold, an infectious smile and quick wit. She was also the devoted owner of an irascible cat, Tim, quite as unique as his owner. He would brook no rivals.

As a trained tailoress Emily saved the College many pounds in the furnishings she herself made. But her greatest joy was to make wedding dresses for past students, and then to be invited to the weddings. Peter Dawes recalls another of her features : "I shall not forget dear 'Auntie' and her wonderful tricycle ('Trike') which appeared to be back to front." On this remarkable machine she cycled many miles in and around Oxford.

The following Farewell to Auntie was written by Frances Dallison (now the Revd Frances Edwards), a student in 1968. It sums up just what she meant to the College community:

"Ask Auntie!" Everyone at St Michael's House has heard that many times! "She will give you more polish, a clean duster, another blanket, a knitting pattern, advice about your contribution to the Christmas Gift Stall, a listening ear - in fact nearly everything you might need, including a slice of good North-Country sense"

No-one who was in College at the time will ever forget the day a wheel fell off 'Trike' as Auntie Jackson was turning into the drive, just a few days before the Garden Party and Dedication of the New Chapel. After the first thankful hours when we realised she was not seriously hurt, we thought of all the things she had been planning to do - as did Auntie herself; she proceeded to direct operations from her bed. There were the Guest-rooms to be prepared, books to be dusted, shelves, windows, floors to be cleaned and many things to check. These activities are just a fractional part of the tremendous work our Auntie had done for St Michael's over the years.

Her contribution to the smooth running of the College has been a great one, not only in practical matters. Many a student has been heartened by Auntie's "Well, how did it go? Yes, I was praying" on return from a women's meeting, a hospital service or teaching practice. She knew each of us better than we imagined, and has helped many of us by her understanding. She had an infectious sense of humour, and a study of students' and staff laundry books would reveal a fund of wit and talented drawing, including several portraits of Tim! Many of us carried on a regular correspondence with her through this medium - and she received a good number of 'Valentines' this way every February 14th.

So, dear Auntie, we will never forget you. We thank you for all the Lord has done for us through you, and we do pray that you will have many more years of joy in His service.

When St Michael's closed in 1968 Emily Jackson faced the trauma of becoming homeless and jobless with indomitable faith. God rewarded that faith in providing her with a modest home, and for some years a job, in North Oxford, where she continued to love and serve Him to the end of her days. For the last few years she suffered crippling arthritis and heart trouble (no doubt, in part, a legacy from the many stairs constantly negotiated at St Michael's), yet she kept in touch with former students and staff and delighted to be at every Reunion whether held in Oxford or London. When she died shortly before her 90th birthday in 1994 - for which she had already planned a celebration - the large congregation that attended her Thanksgiving service at St Andrew's Church was a tribute to Auntie's life of service and shining witness to Jesus Christ.

Deaconess Annette Tatton's association with St Michael's went back to the earliest days. She is mentioned in the 1938 report as one of the gallant band involved in the removal of St Catherine's Deaconess House from London to Oxford, and in its refurbishment as St Michael's. Annette applied for a post on the staff at a time when there was no suitable vacancy, but eventually took up an appointment in 1958. She came with a wealth of parochial experience, and in spite of serious illness remained teaching and caring for students until 1968. The 'Deac', as she was nick-named, was an outstanding Vice-Principal whose contribution to the College was invaluable. She made herself always available to staff and students to listen, counsel, advise and pray. Dss Joyce Hewitt's experience illustrates this.

Joyce had been sent to St Michael's by the Church's Ministry among Jewish people to receive biblical training in preparation for service in North Africa. As a qualified nurse and midwife she was asked by Miss Snow on arrival to act as College nurse. That term Joyce was kept busy caring for students in bed with 'flu or with limbs broken or sprained on the ice. Her limited time for study and the difficulty she had in coping with Theology and Church History meant that as the Easter term drew to a close she was sure she could not continue. On the very last evening of the term, she tried in vain to find someone with whom to share her doubts. In desperation, she knocked on the door of the Deac's small upper room in number 117. There, over a cup of tea, she found sympathy and understanding, and was able to unburden her problems. Joyce continues:

> Thanks to her practical ministry I was not only able to come back, but to complete the two year Inter Diocesan Certificate with success. And I found St Mike's very different from any previous experience. It was quite awe-inspiring, and stimulating with lovely Christian fellowship and memorable tutors and lecturers.

Joyce valued her friendship with Annette, as did many other students who had been helped by her in their struggles, and they remained friends until Annette's death in 1982. In the 1983 newsletter Miss Cooke wrote:

> When we think of our beloved 'Deac' who was gathered to the Lord on November 15th, 1982, this must be one of our

deepest impressions - a life lived through severe testing, but with unfailing serenity and faithfulness to the very end. When we say she was Christ-like, we really mean it and each of us had with her, as we do with Him, a unique relationship. She always pointed to Him and with genuine humility acknowledged that her gifts in teaching, evangelism and pastoral work were all due to His grace.

When the Bishop of Oxford ordained Annette Tatton as deaconess on September 29th, 1958, she was the first one to be ordained in the Oxfordshire diocese and the first of evangelical persuasion in the Church of England for many years. Bishop Peter Dawes notes how unusual it was, at that time, in evangelical circles. Only those who had served at least three years as parish worker could apply for Selection for the Diaconate. After her own ordination Dss Annette undertook to run a deaconess course at St Michael's House for evangelical women ordinands during the summer vacation. Attending the first one in 1959 were Sister Lorna Fry, Miss Vera Brandon and Miss Eileen Harding.

Many more men and women gave time and talents to the College for longer or shorter periods, and often on a voluntary basis. There was **Mrs Claire Spivey**, who lectured in Philosophy and Ethics and also gave invaluable help in the bursarial work. She and her pharmacist husband Paul went to Nepal with Interserve, and brought up their two sons there. Paul now works for the World Health Organisation in Geneva, and Claire, for the British Council in Berne.

Miss Hannah Wright succeeded Eva Parker as an academic lecturer and brought many talents with her. Soon she showed her prowess in art, sport, flower arranging and gardening. Many a meal time too was lightened by her anecdotes. Hannah went on to Dalton House in 1968 where she did post-graduate study, and some lecturing. In 1970 she married Peter Williams (staff and former St Michael's students recall the occasion with pleasure). After a spell in Scotland, they responded to a missionary call and went to Kenya, where they both served on the staff of St Paul's United Theological College, Limuru - and were blessed with two sons, Andrew and Reuben.

Dr Margot Roach from Canada was another whose excellent course on missionary medicine was much appreciated.

Although never a member of staff, **Mrs Stella Gough**, wife of the Revd Basil Gough - Chaplain and friend of St Michael's - is remembered by many with great affection and gratitude. As part of their practical work, students helped Stella with the Women's Fellowship at St Ebbe's, and joined in pastoral visiting in the parish. Some went baby-sitting for the Goughs on Sunday evenings, so that they could both get to a service. On one occasion Stella saw that Miss Snow was worried because a lot of the students had 'flu - even getting it twice! Stella says "As far as I can remember all I did was to call round morning and evening and tell them to stay in bed OR ELSE...." Miss Snow remembered this time, "I can never forget how Mrs Gough stepped into the breach as a daily nurse when most of us went down with Asian flu."

Ann Witchalls (Gilchrist) expresses what many past students felt about the staff at St Michael's:

> It was a real privilege to spend two years at St Mike's, to soak up teaching from so many godly staff and visiting tutors; to live in the lovely setting, the garden and the parks of Oxford, in all the changing seasons.

CHAPTER 6

The Students -
A Cross-Section of Society

One student's impression on arriving at St Michael's in October 1957 was the great variety of experience of those who had come there to study. There were teachers, from whose practical demonstrations in local schools students would benefit later. These had come to take the year's course in Religious Education, culminating in a Diploma or Certificate, even in one case a Degree in Theology. There were many who had come from very different jobs: a dental nurse, a medical social worker, an engineer from de Havillands, a cabaret artist (converted in a Billy Graham Crusade), a book-keeper from a London jeweller's and secretaries (one had worked for 15 years for The Law Society). Then there were nurses, some already accepted by a Missionary Society and sent to St Michael's for Bible/Missionary training. It was a wonderful cross-section of society. Firm friendships were formed as these women of differing temperaments lived and worked and played together as a family. Each set of students became aware of how much they learned from each other. Little wonder that one student remarked at the end-of-year prayer meeting: "I never imagined so many women could live together peaceably."

Enrichment from overseas
Every term too brought 'the world' to St Michael's, as folk from overseas joined 'the family'. Doreen Begernie (Senior Student) wrote in 1962:

> At College, this year, the world has been truly represented. From Australia we have enjoyed having Dss Nelson as a member of staff. Rachel Fuller from Tasmania has been a part-time student and also helped in the kitchen. Then, once more we have had the fellowship of visitors from India. This

year it has been Miss Nancy Basaviah, and Dr Aley Luke and we have learnt much from them and their devotion to the Lord. Some of us have even learnt how to put on a sari! From Germany has come Hannelore Sobek, who in no time became expert in the kitchen. From Tralee, in Ireland, came Daphne Giles, on the clergy-fiancee's course.

Many of those who came from overseas in the early days kept in touch for years through the prayer fellowship, some even until they were 'called Home'. Such were Dora Weymuller in Germany and Alice Masih in India. It is impossible to name all who became members of this international family at St Michael's, but many returned to their home countries, enriched for the time they spent there. Here is a typical testimony from Sarita Bolliger (1948-50) writing about England, before returning to Switzerland in 1953:

> All these differences of another language, other manners, another countryside, and another temperament did not disturb me very much. I even felt at home rather quickly. The main reason for this is that I had the privilege to meet here, at St Michael's House, and afterwards, elsewhere, real outliving Christians who love the same Lord as their Saviour and friend and with whom I enjoy always a deeper and more strengthening Fellowship in Christ. That is the most moving experience I had in England, and that makes me love the English people in their characteristics. I am therefore very thankful that I could come to St Michael's, Oxford, and hope to be able to return to my beloved country, to carry there a little flame of the fire which burnt in England for our Lord Jesus Christ.

One who came to St Michael's in 1950 was Aurelia Takacs. A Hungarian refugee, "Rika" came first as an 'au pair', but it was not long before her brilliance was discovered and she became a full-time student, easily passing her Diploma in Theology. She went on to become an undergraduate in the University of Oxford and studied at St Anne's for a Degree in Theology. Aurelia recorded her appreciation of St Michael's in the 1955 newsletter:

> Jesus said "When you pray, say 'Our Father'."

> For many years I have seen the wonder of these words, that God, Who revealed Himself in Christ, revealed Himself as

Father. But probably I am one of the many who have come to a deeper realisation of this truth while living in this household. For here the friendships take on likeness to family bonds - they continue in time, in spite of distance. And not only one - one special friend, but everyone with whom we lived, prayed, worked together here, in some way belongs to us.

Aurelia's academic success was outstanding, as was her consistent Christian witness. After gaining her Degree in Theology, she was awarded a scholarship at the Union Theological Seminary in New York, the first woman ever to achieve this. There she obtained her Doctorate in Theology, became an assistant tutor, and met and married Zoltan Fule, a fellow Hungarian. They were well-matched in every way. Rika obtained a teaching post in a Presbyterian College in Ohio and he a pastorate 800 miles away from her. That was a difficult time but the separation did not last too long. Soon they were together again and Zoltan became Chaplain to Bergen County, New Jersey, a position he held for 13 years. A son, Peter, and a daughter, Susan, were born to them. Sadly, Zoltan died suddenly in 1994, while on holiday in Australia, a great loss to the family and to the church. With staunch faith Rika moved to New Mexico to be nearer her children, by this time both married. She was greatly encouraged by the visit of the Habermanns and Effie Smith in 1996, and she wrote in a newsletter: 'It was like water in the desert'. She continues to work very hard, teaching Biblical Studies in adult education, writing and preaching, and to keep in touch with St Michael's.

Impressions of Oxford

Those who came to St Michael's from overseas were bound to be impressed by the city of Oxford. The following piece, written by a Dutch student Trix Johannes in 1951, won a prize in a College competition for the best essay on "Impressions of Oxford, the city with the 'dreaming spires'." The year after, she returned to the Netherlands to teach Classics.

Oxford! The very name leads one's thoughts to a centre of erudition and tradition, even when one has never visited the place before. The reality affirms this impression, received by hearsay, but adds other characteristics such as the architectural beauty of the city and the amiability of its surroundings.

The abundant amount of most beautiful and old buildings, colleges and churches amazes an inhabitant of the flat countries, where such riches are carefully and sparingly scattered. One can spend hours in visiting the imposing buildings, where the heart of the English academical youth beats, and notices with astonishment, that the students have their home and live their lives in surroundings in which almost no one else in the world lives - buildings dating from a time in which mankind knew how to build and how to construct their buildings so that they lasted, and how to combine an impressive appearance with beauty. Dining halls and chapels, which transpose us to an age and a mind quite different from ours; lecture rooms which remind us of the fact that light and fresh air were not taken into account in the time of the masters of these wonderful buildings.

It is no wonder that the sense of tradition and its high value is living in the hearts of those who dwell here. It is inspired by their surroundings quite naturally.

Walking along, one feels the atmosphere of ages of piled up learning descending from every façade, from every porch, and every 'quad' and tower. Added to this, the gowned personages, speeding to their various centres of wisdom, which picture every Dutchwoman invariably will associate with the highest mark of learning, since the privilege of wearing such a costume is only granted to scholars who have reached the highest possible rank of knowledge in her country.

And when one wants to enjoy nature, can one think of something more lovely than the beauty of the University Parks with their majestic trees of various sizes, shapes and shades of green and brown or a walk along one of the rivers and a view of the many towers and spires of Oxford?

More than one route
Many students have interesting stories about how they came to be at St Michael's, and clearly saw God's guidance in what happened. One such was Freda Yates, who became a student in September 1953. From her home in Dublin she had been returning to North Wales to her teaching post at the end of the Easter holidays. She

had only just been given notice by her school, and was wondering what the future held. She writes:

> While waiting for a train connection in mid-Wales I got into chat with a female in country dress with a somewhat anti-quated bicycle - I cannot remember the precise details, but her name rang a bell because my grandmother used to send me a magazine when I was in boarding school edited by Laura Barter Snow. So here was Miss Snow herself - she was on her way to or from Clarendon. And in the course of our conversation she told me about St Michael's, sent me litera-ture in a few days and I was in Oxford the following September! Coincidence? No! Guidance? Yes!

Freda has always sent in news to the Old Students' Fellowship Letter and was delighted to come back to the Special Reunion in 1994. Her teaching career in Ireland has been most fulfilling and in retirement she is as busy as ever, promoting Bible Reading for young people, in work for Scripture Union and for All-Ireland Interserve.

For some, life before St Michael's had been relatively easy - a good, often Christian home, a supportive evangelical church, a sat-isfying career, based on good qualifications. But for others the way had been quite hard, and to find themselves in an institution such as St Michael's was nothing short of a miracle. One such who is most happy for her story to be told is Margaret (Peggy) Hider, known and loved by hundreds during many years of service in dif-ferent parishes as 'Sister Peggy'.

Margaret was born in the mid-twenties, the sixth child in a family of twelve. Her father's work as a carpenter brought in little money and her mother had to work hard to supplement the family income. Margaret's schooling was frequently disrupted because she was required to care for younger members of the family. Then, in 1941, her mother died and Margaret had to leave school, barely able to read or write, and with an older sister had to concentrate on helping the family. She worked hard, at one time holding down eight different cleaning jobs to make ends meet. But at last, when her father married again, she was able to do a course in catering - not easy, but with hard work and her tenacious nature the necessary exams were passed. Even then Margaret had a strong personal faith in God's detailed guidance in her life. She began to feel that He was guiding her to full-time church work but, with no money and no qualifications, her hope of being trained as a church worker gave way to despair. She was now 23. Then, amazingly she was approached by a tutor from St Michael's offering her a domestic position together with private tuition. So with God's provision of a grant, and £1 a week spending money, she found herself back at 'school' and preparing to work in a church. Her determination and the support of other students and staff resulted, after four years, in her academic success and in 1957 she went to her first Parish - in Tooting, the first of many, mostly in London where she served the Lord as a much loved Deaconess.

Of the years at St Michael's Peggy has written:

> Four years at Bible college was a wonderful time for me. I found the study very hard but was so sure that God had called me to this work that I found it very worthwhile.

Some years later, when she spent two years working in Israel, Peggy was amazed to find she was able to learn quite a lot of Hebrew. During her last year at St Michael's, Peggy was Senior Student, together with Joan Ecclestone - a sure tribute to the way in which she had endeared herself to the community. Now, in retirement in Uphill near Weston-Super-Mare, Peggy has continued to serve the Lord, in spite of ill-health, as a non-stipendiary minister of St Barnabas Church.

In contrast, and showing again the variety of people who made up St Michael's family, Felicity Bentley-Taylor (Houghton) - another Senior Student - was born into a missionary family. Her parents were members of the China Inland Mission on the teaching staff of Chefoo School, Malaya. At nine years of age, when her whole family were in a Japanese internment camp in North China, Felicity first became interested in South America as a mission field, but it was not until she was actually at St Michael's that she felt sure that she should offer to the South American Mission Society. By this time she had gained a Degree, a Certificate in Education and some teaching experience. Of her two years at St Michael's Felicity writes:

> As I write, I have before me the photo of students and staff at St Michael's House in 1958 - 59. Happiness shines from the faces in it and the memories it evokes are also happy ones for me. We were forty students that year and thirteen members of

staff; teaching, administrative and domestic. It was a great privilege to me to be in that bunch of students whom I enjoyed and appreciated and in some cases grew to admire. The example of some of our set who were older than the rest and whose Christian experience was more mature than mine, was I think one of the most formative influences of my life then.

Felicity spent thirty-four years in Chile and Bolivia, mainly devoted to student work. After retiring she married David Bentley-Taylor, part of whose missionary career had also been given to student ministry.

Flexibility and choice
Perhaps it was the flexibility of courses which Miss Snow allowed that made this rich diversity of the student body possible. Women could come for longer or shorter periods from one term to several years, and choose the lectures to which they were most suited. Such a student was Dr Mary Eldridge. Already qualified as an Obstetrician, she was at St Michael's from January to July 1954 - and she has written about that time:

> My few months at St Mike's provided a wonderful interlude between busy hospital jobs in the UK and the Christian Medical College, Ludhiana, India, where I was to be in charge of the Obstetric Dept, and responsible not only for the patients but for teaching medical and nursing students, and where Miss Snow's sister, Eileen, was Principal. In two terms I wasn't expected to study for CRK, let alone a Diploma in Theology, so was free to choose the lectures I attended and was also free to go to any local group who wanted a speaker. I learned not to mind when the audience fell asleep when I addressed yet another women's meeting.

Mary mentions other things she learned, such as ice-skating on Port Meadow, playing just one hymn tune - apparently obligatory for parish workers - and discovering how many hymns could be sung to it! She continues:

> I appreciated the in depth Bible Study and still find use for my notes on the Creed. I made good friends and we helped one another and prayed together over practical work. My efforts at a church youth club were pretty disastrous as were

61

my flower arrangements. Forty years on we talk about discovering our gifts. At St Mike's we tried most things, even leading or speaking at Saturday morning chapel - an ordeal in front of 'Snowie' (Miss Snow's affectionately used nickname).

After serving eight years at Ludhiana, and interruptions of her career by illness, Mary went to Landour for four years and then to Nepal for fifteen wonderful years with the United Mission to Nepal (seconded by Interserve). In her retirement to Colchester, Mary still rejoices in the final message given to students leaving St Michael's in 1954 "Faithful is He who calls you who also will do it."

Some who went to St Michael's knew already what their future ministry would be. Others only experienced God's call to a particular field of service while at the College. Some were surprised by what happened. For example, there was Irene Kramer (1964) who, like Aurelia, had begun as a part-time student, helping in the kitchen. She expected to go on to train as a parish worker. Instead, God called her into the Church Army, where she met and married Captain Philip Hudson. In the Army they served the Lord together and brought up a family.

Rules and Room-mates
It is not surprising that for some the fairly rigid regime of those far off days was sometimes irksome. But for others it was a welcome change from the responsibilities of home, a job, church activities and sometimes of the care of parents. To have a programme laid out and time free for study in preparation for serving the Lord was bliss; even more so among such diverse companions and in the fascinating city of Oxford.

In the House, each student was allocated a house job for half an hour before breakfast. If it happened to be polishing the red tiles in the porch floor during the snowy or muddy season - tough! Rotas too were arranged for helping in the kitchen and dining room, and until more regular help was acquired, in the huge and beautiful gardens. Another Senior Student wrote in 1964:

> Most things which go to make up St Michael's training were tackled enthusiastically - even the gardening, in the first few weeks - until, alas, an over-enthusiastic student mistook the much treasured cat-mint for a weed! Fortunately it was discovered, still intact on the rubbish heap. (Pauline Dolby [Sturges]).

Students, however, were not entrusted with the care of Miss Snow's bees, until her Sabbatical - and then only under strict supervision. On her retirement, Judith Rose, an agricultural expert, was left in charge.

In the Hall of 119 stood a fine grandfather clock, irreverently named 'Miss Vick' after the lady to whom it had first been given. This, Pat Snow remembers 'ruled our lives and was quite hated by some'. But she herself found living by the clock, including times for getting up and lights out, a good discipline, since in parish life there has to be a measure of discipline coming from within.

Many women found themselves sharing a room with one or even two others for the first time since childhood. That was not easy, and even harder when they returned the following term to find that another room and another room-mate had been allocated. However, through this, deep and lasting friendships were made which neither time nor distance could diminish and which proved sustaining to many at home or abroad in difficult or isolated circumstances. Also there is no doubt that it helped the process of learning to live with others and knocked off a few awkward corners.

'A lively and happy place'
How did a member of staff feel about such a student body? Let 'Mrs Mac' conclude this chapter:

> The students were a very mixed bag which made life very interesting for all the staff. The older "professionals" - teachers, nurses - who were wanting some theological training to enrich their professional lives, teachers especially, to take examinations and to enable them to teach 'Scripture' in State Schools; parish workers - several girls engaged to curates!; a lovely Indian lady, with countless saris, who was Principal of a Women's College in India - and the missionaries in training. Several went to India, one to a lonely post in Nepal. Some of these subsequently married, and others remained single. It is a joy to me to read news each year of so many whom I remember with their likes and dislikes and idiosyncrasies, and I loved them all. St Michael's was a lively happy place.

CHAPTER 7

Beyond the Walls

Although St Michael's, both at 119 and later 117, Banbury Road, was separated from the road by attractive walls, as is the custom in North Oxford, students soon learned that the College was much concerned with a whole world of activity beyond those walls.

From inside - out

From their first weekend in College, students were expected to undertake practical work as part of their training. Bishop Chavasse had foreseen that Oxford, with its many churches, schools and hospitals would offer untold opportunities for this. Pastoralia tutors sought to 'match' students with these opportunities offering different experiences from term to term. Often a student was assigned to teaching or speaking to an unfamiliar age-group, or to boys as well as girls. This was not at all easy for some, at the time, but looking back they realised how valuable it had been and how God had enabled them to meet these new challenges.

Children and young people

Students helped with Sunday Schools, Bible Classes, Youth Clubs and Fellowships in many churches in Oxford itself, and many further afield. They were often greatly encouraged by the responsiveness of the youngsters. Churches were very grateful for the input of these enthusiastic, if inexperienced women. Getting to and from meetings, usually by bicycle, was not easy either. One student recalls a somewhat disastrous Sunday afternoon. Joan was asked to take on a primary Sunday School class in a village some miles from Oxford. Her only previous experience had been with teenagers. Nervously negotiating the busy main road on her new bike, she ran into the kerb, fell heavily, badly spraining her ankle. She ended up in casualty at the Radcliffe Infirmary and returned to College with her leg plastered to the knee. Entering the sittingroom where the Sunday Fellowship tea was still in progress, she was greeted with a great shout of laughter. It seemed unfeeling but it was later explained that Joan had been especially prayed for that afternoon 'since she had never had babies before'. Truth to tell she never did afterwards either!

In the early 50's the Sunday School at Cogges Church near Witney benefited greatly from the help given by students and staff. It was through Miss Long who lived at Cogges and was responsible for the Sunday School that this help continued for many years. 'Auntie' Jackson, Miss Bertha Parker and Miss Morris (later Mrs Habermann) were stalwarts and endeared themselves to the children. It was a touching tribute to 'Auntie' that one of these grown up children was at her Memorial service in 1994. Miss Long recalls too the splendid work done by the Wood twins, Lilian and Rosalie, and Ruth McLeod. Ruth wrote from Brazil, where for nearly 40 years she has been working with the Wycliffe Bible Translators:

> I have especially happy memories of Miss Long, as I helped for two years with the organ and the infants class in the Sunday School at Cogges. I appreciated very much the week-ly preparation classes which she organised for the teachers, and the lovely way in which she led the Sunday School - the atmosphere was so peaceful and spiritual in a way that I had never experienced before in years of Sunday School teaching; I realised that this was the result of Miss Long's own walk with the Lord.

Such was the concern for those and other Sunday School children that a St Michael's camp was organised at Wytham by Miss Morris, who was very experienced with children, to give them a holiday and to continue teaching them about God.

Less than a year later, there was a new venture of faith for the students. This was the opening of a Sunday School at Field Farm, about eight miles south-east of Oxford, an area which has since been developed as the village of Berinsfield. It was a disused RAF Camp where the city council housed homeless families in Nissen huts. It was supposed to be a temporary measure, but some people had already been there eight years, and no Christian work had been done there. In a wonderful way, initial difficulties were overcome, and the children were extraordinarily responsive. So much so that that year three of them applied for the St Michael's camp. But so many children applied from other Sunday Schools and Groups that a second camp was held, under canvas at Sandford. It was the earnest prayer of the camp team that these children might come to know Christ as Saviour and return home as missionaries.

Two years later prayer was answered for this needy area. As a result of a mission led by Church Army workers, a number of the parents of these children showed a real response. That was such an encouragement to the students who worked there, teaching and regularly visiting the children's homes. Following the Mission, a weekly Bible Study and a Sunday evening service were soon being held.

Girl Crusaders

Many students helped on Sunday afternoons at the Oxford Girl Crusaders' Union Class, held at that time in the Northgate Hall. This gave them valuable experience in teaching the Bible to different age groups and in an inter-denominational setting. It was a very mixed group of girls, coming from both church and non-church going homes, private and state schools. For one student, Margaret Norgate, this was the introduction to the movement in which she was ultimately to find her Christian calling. She is currently Assistant Director of the GCU in the London Headquarters. It was a special joy to hold the 1998 London Reunion there, a pleasant venue not far from Buckingham Palace.

Women's Meetings (or Fellowships)

Students were much in demand as speakers at these in both Anglican and Non-conformist churches in and around Oxford; some were as far out as Abingdon, Wolvercote and Thame. Tutorial help was always available for the preparation of talks and supervision given followed by constructive criticism. In those days when women were not usually invited to preach, these opportunities provided a useful foundation for those who, many years later, became deacons or priests and had the responsibility of giving sermons regularly. Visiting these groups was not without incident. Indeed it could be a fraught experience. More than one student remembers the noise of furniture being moved about in the furniture store above the hall during her talk at St Clement's Church. To one it is still remembered as a baptism of fire! She tried to reassure her listeners that she really did not mind the noise overhead, but the

ladies were visibly on edge. Seconds later, she was shocked when a
large tile fell out of the wall with a great crash, making everyone
jump. Shortly afterwards, one member had to be helped out, overcome by so many disturbances. It required an effort of will for the
student not to follow her!

Hospitals

Another form of service which was not an easy one - particularly
for some - was undertaken first in two Oxford Hospitals, the
Churchill and the Wingfield Morris (now the Nuffield
Orthopaedic Centre) in Headington, and later, in the Rivermead
Rehabilitation Centre. In the Wingfield on Sunday evenings, short
services were taken in a couple of the wards, with a varying
response from patients and staff. But on the whole the little teams
were welcomed, and the hymns, prayers and brief messages appreciated. In the same hospital there were also regular visits to the
children's ward on a Sunday morning.

Many years later a number of parish workers were given similar
opportunities in hospitals within their parishes. One former Senior
Student, the Revd Matty McQuillan, who became a full-time
Hospital Chaplain at the University Hospital in Nottingham, has
written about the practical training at St Michael's and in particular, the influence of Deaconess Annette Tatton:

> Dss Annette Tatton taught me so much in Pastoralia lectures
> and Seminars and practical work, and through her ministry
> and on-going care after I left College. When I felt God was
> calling me to minister as a Chaplain to University Hospital -
> a very large acute teaching Hospital - a friend said to me,
> "You will never make a Chaplain, you are much too sensitive,
> you will be hurt, it will be too much for you." But Deaconess
> Tatton had said: "Sensitivity is a gift from God, and it is
> because you are sensitive God has called you. You will be able
> to sit where people sit, weep with them, rejoice with them,
> enter into their suffering."

With that encouragement Matty began her ministry, caring for
the terminally ill and dying, and being with parents whose child
had been in a road accident or who had lost a baby or whose child
was stillborn or brain-damaged. Matty continues "Dss Tatton did
much in preparing me for that shattering and traumatic ministry."

Experience in Schools

Most of those who came to St Michael's for the one year course in Religious Education were experienced teachers, but a few came straight from Teacher Training College. Their intensive study for examinations left little time for teaching practice, but some experience of teaching Scripture, as it was then called, was obtained in local Church of England Primary Schools, and in the South Oxford Secondary School. The latter was a challenge in itself.

Recognising the need for training all students in the skills of working with the young, some specialist lecturers were called in. In the Summer term of 1955, a Youth Leadership Course was run, which included lectures and visits to Youth Centres and Clubs - for example, at Marston and at Littlemore. There was also a rather unusual opportunity to take evening prayers at a nearby Girls' Hostel.

Practising Hospitality

In 1953 Miss Snow gave permission for Miss Morris to organise Open House Sunday Teas for anyone whom students and staff wished to invite. The event was run by a small committee of students, in itself a very useful experience. They trusted the Lord for supplies, no College food being used. Mrs. Habermann writes:

> It was wonderful the way we always had enough of everything. There was a Sunday afternoon when we'd run out of sugar. "Me Mum's sent this, Miss" - and one of the children who came regularly, handed me a bag of sugar.

The Sunday Fellowship, as it was named, was a great success. During the first twelve months there were no fewer than one hundred and nine guests, including twenty-eight from overseas. The first birthday was celebrated in great style, with a special programme called 'The Reason Why' in which the year was reviewed. Students gave testimonies and afterwards interested friends were invited to take copies of Mr Robert Laidlaw's booklet of the same name.

Many of those who came along regularly on Sundays were introduced to Scripture Union Bible Reading notes. Some joined the College on a trip to Dr Billy Graham's final rally at the White City. Sunday Fellowship continued to be a very important outreach into the City of Oxford for St Michael's. Years later in 1966, Anne Dexter (now Punton), Senior Student, wrote in the newsletter:

> Much was learned in the planning of the Sunday Fellowship meetings, especially when the teachers branched out success- fully in arranging a special rally for local children.

These gatherings produced prayer partners for St Michael's, some of whom have continued to be interested to this day. But above all they provided the students with a variety of experience: working on the committee, acting as hostesses, and reaching out to folk of all ages with whom they came into contact during the week. It was an opportunity to show friendship, to return hospitality, to encourage some who were lonely or sad, and some who were inter- ested in enquiring further about the Christian faith, or even their vocation.

Vacations - a widening world

During vacations students found themselves putting into practice what they had learned in a great variety of situations, and far from the supportive family of the College. One remembers standing on a chair in a busy South London High Street one Saturday morning in August, inviting passers-by to pause and listen to the message of the Inter-Varsity Fellowship (now UCCF) Team to which she had been appointed for a week.

Veronica Whinney (Webster) found:

> Going to the Dockland Settlement, prior to it becoming the Mayflower, was very influential in forming my concern for urban renewal of every kind. **Eva Parker** and **Rosemary Harris** were strong members of the team invited by Miss Snow ' to go and see what was needed and try to help in some way'. Broads sailing holidays for mainly sixth form girls and Varsity and Public Schools' summer camps formed much of my vacation work. **Ann Rees** came as Mate to the Broads trip and we had some good times. The leader of the Summer Camp then had a delightful son whose Down's Syndrome had just been diagnosed. I had trained for teaching children with learning difficulties before going to St Mike's so was able to reassure the family that his learning potential could be good

if he was given commonsense guidelines for his general behaviour. He has developed into a delightful individual of great character and his parents say that our meeting was helpful in his early training.

Veronica later returned to teaching children with special needs, including autism, like so many for whom these vacation experiences influenced their careers.

The 1959 newsletter contained an interesting account by Sheilagh Botting of an unusual vacation activity. She says:

> During the Easter vacation six of our students and a team of students from Cambridge went to take part in the campaign at the Thames Refinery of Tate and Lyle Ltd., under the leadership of the Revd David Sheppard (later to become Bishop of Liverpool) and the late Mr Charles Potter.

Factory life to most of the students was something quite new, and to all of them it was a humbling and deepening experience to see God's wonderful way of answering prayer. By the second day of the mission the way was made open for the team to visit all parts of the factory floor. Many questions were asked, the problem of suffering being paramount in people's minds. Some people went to films and meetings and there were those who gave their lives to Christ during the Mission.

Practical experience for what was to follow was provided during vacations by a host of other Christian activities, such as Scripture Union Beach and other Missions, young people's houseparties and camps, run by different organisations and denominations. Some students and members of staff enjoyed College houseparties at the Keswick Convention. For several years others represented St Michael's at the Filey Christian Crusade where there was a good opportunity for making the College known.

Meanwhile, at St Michael's, while students and teaching staff packed their bags and belongings at the end of each term, those responsible for the house and kitchen found their widening world on the home front. Various societies used St Michael's House during vacations for their annual get-togethers for prayer and fellowship, among them C.M.J., B.M.M.F. (now Interserve), SAMS, the Graduates' Fellowship of the I.V.F. and the Student 'Reading' Party run by St Ebbe's Church.

All that has been written in this chapter shows how St Michael's aim was to prepare students for their future work. 'Sharing the faith' was the keynote - whether by going out, or inviting folk in. It has been said that 'import-export' firms thrive on the transmission, not the accumulation of goods: surely this is also true of spiritual truths? Even as they sought to spread the Gospel, students and staff received spiritual blessings themselves, and most of all, constantly proved God's faithfulness to those who trust Him.

CHAPTER 8

The House Next Door
117 Banbury Road

As numbers of students coming to St Michael's grew apace, 119, Banbury Road became too small to cater adequately for the burgeoning family. By 1954, Council and Staff were praying for more accommodation. So, when the house next door, 117, Banbury Road, became vacant, it seemed the answer to their prayers. The moving pamphlet 'Such a candle' written by Miss Snow (see Appendix 2) was distributed widely, in which she reminded readers of the cost of Reformed teaching in Oxford, in the martyrdom of Bishops Cranmer, Latimer and Ridley. She sought financial support for the extension of the College buildings. After all, this was the city where men and women suffered and died for the same Evangelical faith. Slowly but surely gifts came in. The house was bought and the freehold deeds handed over only one day before the first eighteen students moved in on 9th October, 1955. 117 was named Latimer, and 119, Ridley, for very obvious reasons. The big old house had great possibilities, some of which, in time, were realised. Surely no former student or visitor to 117 can fail to have carried away the memory of the beautiful garden. When staff and students returned after the Easter vacation, the purple aubretia by the wall, the yellow laburnums, the deep rose of the Judas tree, colourful rockeries and flower beds formed a picture to remain for ever in the minds of those fortunate enough to see it. Many will remember with deep affection the lawn - despite the labour involved in keeping it cut. It was popular as a lecture room, and a study area for writing essays and doing examination revision.

The garden was not only remembered for flowers - **Evelyn Dunbar-Nasmith's** recollection of 1959:

> Perhaps what some of us will remember most about the garden are the birds. What a wonderful sanctuary for them it is.

The wrens hardly seem to have stopped singing this summer and those who like to think they can distinguish one bird from another claim to have seen goldfinches, nuthatches, woodpeckers, bullfinches, flycatchers and goldcrest to say nothing of the numerous tits and robins which ate out of our hands and came hopping into our bedrooms. Maybe the sweetest sight was five fluffy baby goldcrests sitting in a row on one of the trees in front of Latimer. But the robin that flew into Chapel in the middle of prayers and sat happily on the open window listening to the Bible exposition perhaps signified for us the wonderful peace that should reign between God's creatures. The study of God's Word in such surroundings as these cannot but impress upon us the comprehensiveness and wonder of God's creation.

A number of the ground floor rooms overlooked this lovely garden. The lecture room was one. Another became the Chapel - a simply furnished, quiet room which soon acquired an atmosphere of worship. The Bishop of Oxford, the Revd H. Carpenter, dedicated it on 3rd February, 1956. Morning and Evening Prayer, led by staff and students, Holy Communion Services, Quiet Days, and many more meetings took place in the new Chapel. It became a sanctuary. Many have testified to it as the place where God spoke to them individually with a word of rebuke, of encouragement, of guidance.

The use of 117 eased the accommodation problem but did not solve it. Numbers continued to grow. By 1961 it was clear that some kind of extension to St Michael's was necessary. Both houses were full and some students still had to sleep out. And it was becoming difficult to find suitable rooms near the College. The Chapel could scarcely hold everyone and rooms for lecturing and tutoring were insufficient. The Council of the College, together with Miss Snow, considered the situation. They thought the answer might be an additional building, near 119 linked by a covered way to 117. But how to finance such a project? They decided to make another appeal to former students, staff and Christian friends. In 1962, Miss Snow wrote about it in the annual newsletter, inviting gifts and requesting prayer. Then, unexpectedly, an offer of help came from another quarter. Earlier that year, St Michael's had been inspected by three representatives of the Council of Women's Ministry, the Revd Tom Anscombe, the Revd Martin Parsons and

Miss C. M. Whitbread. They spent three days at St Michael's looking into every department of College life. They reported favourably on the teaching, but considered that the accommodation was limited. Soon after this Miss Snow received a letter from the Churches' Advisory Council for Training for Ministry. They indicated that they might make a grant towards the improvement in the facilities for training women at St Michael's for Ministry in the Church of England.

What an answer to prayer and encouragement to Miss Snow that was. Mr. Kenneth White, the College architect, worked on definite plans, modifying those which had been before the Council earlier on. He now envisaged a new wing to 117, with fifteen study bedrooms, and a new chapel adjacent to the lecture-room, together with general improvements to the house itself. The cost would be in the region of £35,000. By 1964, £2,500 had been received, with the promise of a further £10,000. Then a Christian business man offered £10,000, to match £10,000 if the College could raise that amount. Miss Snow hoped to see work begin on the Extension before her retirement. (This was to take place in December, 1965). However, it did not happen, but on 8th November, 1965 when the entire College travelled to London for her retirement ceremony, the Most Revd Dr Donald Coggan, Archbishop of York, launched the final Extension Appeal.

The Treasurer of the new appeal was Mr Alan Green, staunch supporter of St Michael's and a Churchwarden at St Ebbe's. He worked on matters connected with the Fund with tireless enthusiasm and meticulous accounting.

The Council felt the time had come to build. 22nd March 1966 was an exciting day indeed. The Chaplain, the Revd Keith Weston, led a short service on the building site. Verses from I Chronicles 29 - the account of the building of Solomon's Temple - were read, He prayed that a building would be erected in which all that was done would be in the Lord's Name and for His glory. This prayer has been answered right up to the time of writing.

After this, every member of the College community wrote his or her name on a brick before it was laid out of sight to human eyes, but visible to the Lord in the finished building.

Many individuals worked untiringly on the project for the next twelve months. No one found it easy, living on a building site, but all were excited as they saw the new wing to 117 rising from the ground. In a wonderful way all bills were paid as they were presented.

No debts were incurred. Mr. White, Mr. Sewell the builder, the Chaplain, Miss Jackson, Miss Manners and all staff and students worked as a team giving practical help and advice throughout. Friends came and renovated furniture, curtains and bedcovers - all on a modest budget.

The Dedication of the new Chapel and Wing by the same Bishop of Oxford, the Revd H. Carpenter, who had dedicated the quiet room on 3rd February, 1956, took place on 6th May, 1967 at the annual Garden Party. The Revd John Bournon, Chairman of the Council, Revd John Sertin, Secretary, and other members of the St Michael's Council gathered along with many friends and former students. By October that year, the new building was in full use, and students were able to benefit from the much improved facilities.

However, even while the extension to St Michael's was being built, questions were arising about the future of the College. For a variety of reasons, often personal finance, fewer women applied for places. Other Training Institutions, previously single sex, had opened to women. The Council had to consider various options. Between 1967 and 1968 they put out feelers, about amalgamating with another College with the same aims and ideals. Finally, at a Council Meeting in the spring of 1968, it was decided to close St Michael's in Oxford, sell the buildings, and amalgamate with Dalton House, the BCMS (Bible Churchmen's Missionary Society) Women's Training College at Bristol. This caused great sadness to many, not least to Miss Snow. But, as will be seen in later chapters, she was able to take a very positive view of the decision.

To return to the story of number 117 Banbury Road. Many prayed about the buyers of both houses. Soon University College bought 'Thackley' 119 and its eventual fate is described in chapter 22. A very remarkable thing happened to 117, with its beautiful new wing. With the vision of providing a Christian residential centre for overseas students, the Oxford Overseas Student Housing Association was formed. With private donations, a British Council Grant, and a mortgage from Oxford City Council, it bought 117. That was in 1968. Since then, the same Association has added another extension to 117 (1971), bought and added to 107 Banbury Road (1974, 1986). More recently the original buildings have been extensively improved and modernised, and now the Association can provide accommodation for more than fifty students in single study bedrooms, thirteen married couples and seven families with children.

Over the years, there have been a number of fine Wardens who have cared for these overseas students. Most recently, from 1990 to 1998, Dr John and Mrs Ruth Chambers were in charge, former missionaries with the Overseas Missionary Fellowship. Kept at home, because visas were not granted, they never lost their concern for Indonesian students. In 1997, they heard the call of God to take up a ministry amongst Indonesian students in USA, and prepared to leave the North Oxford Overseas Centre.

Many prayed for a couple to take their place. God answered, and the Revd Tim and Judy Rous became the new Wardens in January 1998. Tim and Judy came from serving for many years with the Anglican Church in Zaire, and they see their appointment to the NOOC as an extension of their work in the Congo. At any one time as many as fifty different nationalities live together at the Centre.

On 30th October, 1993, thanks to the generous hospitality of John and Ruth Chambers, nearly one hundred old students returned to 117 with great joy for the Twenty-fifth Reunion of the Old Students' Fellowship. Many of them had lived in the building and remembered the first Chapel and the garden. Following this event, some ex-members of St Michael's, both staff and students, suggested that a permanent reminder be placed in the house of the fact that St Michael's had once occupied the building; and that it had trained women for full-time work in the world-wide Church of God. Many warmed to this idea, and contributed to the cost of a small brass plaque to be hung in the entrance hall of 117.

Just over two years later on 3rd January, 1996, a little group of old students and staff gathered to dedicate the plaque, which reads:

> St Michael's House
> Theological College for Women
> This building was dedicated to the extension
> of God's Kingdom 1955 - 1968
> "Jesus is Lord" Philippians 2:11.

The Revd Canon Keith Weston (formerly Chaplain) performed the ceremony, spoke briefly and then used these words:

> In the faith of Jesus Christ, our Lord, we dedicate this plaque
> to the glory of God, and in deep thankfulness for all the work

and witness through St Michael's House Staff and students in this place in years gone by. In the Name of the Father, and the Son, and of the Holy Spirit. Amen.

There followed prayers of thanksgiving for all the blessing poured out on so many servants of God in St Michael's; for the provision of the College as a place of training; for the vision and dedication of the founders; for all those called and sent out from the College, to serve God in His Church; for the continuance of the work of St Michael's in the fellowship of Trinity College, Bristol; for the continued dedication of 117, Banbury Road, to the service of God's Kingdom, as the North Oxford Overseas Centre.

Finally, Keith prayed that the plaque would be a silent reminder and signpost for all who seek the Saviour of the world.

What a thrilling story is that of 117 Banbury Road! It points to God's faithfulness to His promise to guide His children. Back in 1968, some said "What a mistake to build an extension when student numbers are falling." But the Lord knew that the building erected through the sacrificial giving of so many would indeed be one in which all that was done would be in His Name and for His glory.

CHAPTER 9

All Work and no Play?

No one studying at St Michael's could complain about being made
dull by too much study - though much study there certainly was.

College tours

Many and varied were the delights on offer to the students to fill
spare time and enlarge their borders. One of the highlights was to
enjoy a tour of various colleges conducted by Miss Spooner, niece
of the famous Dr Spooner whose 'Spoonerisms' (the transposition
of letters in words) circulated around Oxford. We give two exam-
ples, "Sir, you have hissed your mistory lectures, tasted your wine
and you will leave Oxford by the town drain," presumably to a
feckless student. And again, "Madam you are occupewing my pie.
The sexton will sow you to another sheet" to a church member.

To find a more interesting and better informed guide than Miss
Spooner would be hard. And she was so generous with her time.
During one academic year she guided students around New
College, Lincoln, Magdalen, Christ Church, Merton and Wadham
no fewer than six times. She knew what was of particular interest
and yet could relate it to the whole. Thus she would point out how
the empty bases of the unfinished cloisters at Christ Church bore
silent witness to Wolsey's sudden fall from power. And there were
the dining halls, full of interesting details of carving, panelling and
pictures, and yet typical of the early medieval halls where the family would live, eat and sleep on the dais, removed from the rank and
file of retainers and wayfarers. Students on these tours learned of
the development of architecture, the anachronism of Wadham,
built in Gothic style two centuries later than the hey-day of Gothic
Building, and the craftsmanship even in seemingly unimportant
structures such as the lead drainpipes at Magdalen.

Musical evenings

For students spending their days in the somewhat unnatural con-
fines of college life, a visit to the Misses Spooner's home was a real

treat and a refreshing break from daily study. Both sisters were musicians, one played the grand piano and the other the violin. Students were received with great warmth and kindliness. There was always an interval half-way through the musical programme, when home-made scones, jam and tea were served on delicate china. One student almost dropped hers with shock, when she heard a chance remark about its value.

Other evenings away from College were enjoyed in the home of the Revd and Mrs Richard Bowdler. The happy family atmosphere, the coffee and the opportunity to see a 'Fact and Faith' film or listen to a tape recording of a survey of religion in Oxford were much appreciated. Several times, too, students were invited to Wycliffe Hall for a social evening. One such took the form of a 'Soiree Musicale' when a cello soloist and piano accompanist combined with English folk songs to give a pleasant entertainment and refreshments. Not least it provided the opportunity to be introduced to Wycliffe men!

Change - if not rest

New skills were encouraged at St Michael's, and there was considerable excitement and some apprehension when, in 1957, riding was introduced into the curriculum. It was (rightly it proved) considered that to be able to ride a horse would be a valuable asset for a woman going abroad as a missionary. Miss Snow made enquiries, and as a result was able to arrange for the use of horses in Port Meadow, for a few hours a week, at a moderate charge. The Senior Student, Mary Llewellyn, an experienced rider gave tuition, as did Ann Witchalls (Gilchrist) later. Ann writes:

> I had been a keen horse-rider before coming to St Mike's so it fell to me to teach riding to the missionary candidates. I remember how difficult it was encouraging one midwife to ride rhythmically when a horse trots. I kept calling out "Push, Push!" which, of course, was what she called out to patients in the delivery room. She nearly fell off the horse with laughter!!

Mary Cundy also recalls learning to ride from Mary Llewellyn in her second term at the College. The riding gave great pleasure, as well as memorable experience, as will be seen in this extract from the 1958 newsletter, contributed by Jacqueline Stokes:

The Hockey Team …

… and with their Wycliffe opponents.

Students and staff at Parish Workers Conference.

1952 River Picnic.

Students, Fyfield Road, 1951.

Students, 119 Banbury Road, 1952/53.

Staff and Students, 1962.

A green suit may be the approved St Michael's garb, but Port Meadow is more familiar with us in varying shapes and colours of leg covering! The range has included orthodox jodhpurs, (Miss Snow generously gave hers to Mary Cundy), red or tartan jeans, and some things which the archaeologists dug up. Some of us ride for relaxation, but relaxation is not what the horses were prepared to give. They looked peaceful enough on a warm summer's afternoon - with Cirius the piebald yawning, Nonny sleeping and Nimbus merely bored. It was soon discovered, however, that Struth could give a convincing demonstration of the highland fling, if accompanied by bagpipes, and that Nimbus had tendencies to delinquency. This last showed itself in a certain elusiveness when a bridle was produced in his field (though he later improved) and a strong homing instinct; this led to wide divergencies from the path we were following and hasty, undignified return journeys. The efforts of St Michael's to reform him were unavailing. He even threw the Senior Student in the last fortnight of term. Mary Llewellyn brought order into one's inexperienced efforts to control wayward horses. Her welcome weekly tuition meant that progress was made. We would like to thank her for some of the most enjoyable afternoons we have had this term.

But students spent much more time on bicycles than on horses. Some even had to learn to ride a bike when they arrived in Oxford. One such was Jill Palfrey (Hubl). This is her story:

At home I lived at the top of a hill, the highest point in Middlesex, and I'd never had a bicycle. The first few weeks at St Michael's were spent learning to ride one, all around the roads by St Andrew's Church, then out to more distant places helped out and guided by my room mates, Katie Clark and Sheila Pulling. At Christmas my father gave me £5. He said he didn't approve of bicycles but I could spend it as I pleased! I bought a second-hand machine and proudly returned to Oxford.

Another who had to learn the skill was Sophie Morrison and she has remained very grateful:

It was very useful in my teaching days at South Shields, and it gave me courage to learn to drive a car, which has been a great blessing.

Students used their bicycles in all weathers. Dss Poppy Turner remembers a good deal of cycling, often to Woodstock where she loved seeing Blenheim Palace, and sometimes accompanied by 'Auntie' on her 'trike'. The cycle was the usual mode of transport for practical work too. This is a memory of Mary Cundy's:

> Liz Fisher and I used to cycle outside Oxford every week to bring, we were told, "a spiritual influence" into a 'Rock and Roll Club'. I'm not sure how much impact we made, but on the way back we often had fish and chips in a newspaper. Grown up as we were, we were still afraid that Miss Snow might see us.

Felicity Foster-Carter also remembers -

> biking to a lovely 'family' Sunday School in a farm or country house - no buses on Sundays in those days - in the rain.

Perhaps this was at Cogges, near Witney - no small distance to ride.

Games - more relaxation
And then there were the outdoor games. From the earliest days these feature in newsletters. There was a Sports Committee and, at least some years, a Games Captain. Eileen Santon was one who wrote in 1951:

> It is not commonly known that Angels play games, but after having been at St Michael's for a short while, one soon realises that they play both hockey and netball. Netball practices have been going on fairly regularly when the weather has permitted, and towards the end of the Michaelmas Term the hockey enthusiasts started practising for a match against Wycliffe which was held during the last week of the Term.
>
> In November, a netball match was arranged against Wycliffe Hall on our grounds, and, in spite of our tall male opponents in their shorts of various colours we managed to tie with

them, the score being twelve all! After the match both teams tucked into a splendid tea which had been prepared for us.

Three days before the end of term, a hockey match against Wycliffe made a pleasant break from exams and revision. Although the men showed us up by beating us four-nil, I think everyone enjoyed the game and came back to settle down and revise for the next day's exams.

St Michael's teams continued to play in matches against other Oxford teams - Lady Margaret Hall, St Anne's and even the Radcliffe Infirmary (before the building of the John Radcliffe Hospital). Often, it seems, the weather stopped or prevented play, but some matches did take place, like the hilarious netball match played against Wycliffe in 1955 and a hockey match against Keble Scripture Union members. In 1956, the weather was better, and the Senior Students, Peggy Hider and Joan Ecclestone, were able to write about -

the hockey and netball matches against the beef and brawn of Wycliffe, in which St Michael's did gain victories.

With so much study it was important that physical activity should use maximum energy in a minimum of time. The game Jokari did just that, and many tried their hand at it. For those who do not know it, the game involved trying to hit a rubber ball attached to a length of elastic across a rather crumpled piece of tape lying inconspicuously in the dust. When the rubber ball rushes back, the elastic winds many times round the player's unsuspecting neck, providing entertainment for onlookers.

River revels
The Summer Term always brought some sunshine, and with it that delight particularly associated with Oxford and Cambridge, punting. Miss Snow loved water and she soon introduced an annual punting party which had become traditional even by 1954. In the following year Elizabeth Richards, editor of the newsletter, wrote:

Yesterday we were given lovely weather for the river picnic, which we all enjoyed thoroughly, despite the occasional loss of way, punt-pole, or Freckles (Miss Snow's dog).

These outings were not without excitement and the occasional accident. This is the report of what happened in 1962 by the Senior Student, Doreen Begernie:

> Our river picnic was an eventful one with a strong wind and current, which made the punting hard - even, we imagine, for the Clifton student who courageously joined us as a result of having become engaged that week to one of our number. Before we arrived safely back, one potential parish worker took an unexpected dip, and Andy (Freckles' successor) in an attempt to change boats mid-stream, also went in, but fortunately only his hind legs, his front paws nobly being held by Miss Sowdon at great risk to her own safety.

Perhaps this piece written by Eva Parker, full of her wonderful sense of humour, will stir memories of those happy days, on (or in!) the river:

End-of-term River Picnic 1957
Why is it that punting so attracts? Do the deep mysteries of the dark river-water call, or the cool green of the willows and thick rushes soothe - or is it that the hazards of propelling a solid piece of impassable wood packed to capacity with all too passable humanity challenge that part of our nature which normal life ignores? Perhaps, however, for no reason at all, we, in company with Rat, just 'like messing about in boats'.

Messing about in boats - this pleasant occupation, one feels, reveals character. St Michael's appeared yesterday to show three varieties. There are the sedentaries, firmly settled, warmly placid, content to enjoy sun and scenery. Fewer, but more obvious, are the trailers, to whom convention-released hands and feet the water must speak subtle volumes. And lastly the elites - they claim that Venetian blood runs swift and smooth in their veins. The people who can punt surprise one; and so do the people who cannot!

Picture, therefore, eight boats pursuing an up-channel, towards-lunch course. The river banks' heavy mud and rush lining does not preserve them from the occasional battering-ram assault of a snub-nosed vessel; neither are the cool nether-regions of the willow tree world sacrosanct to groups of helpless pole-bereft invaders. Victorious lunch comes at last, however. Stout sausage-rolls, cardboard-flavoured tea, and delightfully sweet-sharp cherries seem to mingle together with hay, blue sky, families of ducks, sunglass-blanked faces, and - thoughts of the future.

Relentless time demands our return. The tidy pick up litter, the comfortable collect cushions, the carelessly abandoned indicate that at present the philosophy of life which really applies is - that you can't sink a punt. Marston Ferry wire is deftly jumped, more poles are left starkly, though temporarily, marooned, and a distinctly zig-zag boat pattern is made over the water's surface, which is already latticed by a slight breeze. Timm's wharf suddenly appears, grey and flat, demanding yet unresponsive. But we, we have been on the river, and some of the magic remains.

In 1957, the excursions on the waterways of Oxford were extended from the Cherwell to the Isis. On Whit Monday Miss Snow's small sailing dinghy 'Redstart' was launched. It was a canvas bottomed boat, bright red in colour, holding two when sailing but four when only rowed. Some students had spent many happy hours sandpapering it in the February sun and painting it in the summer shade.

There was an experienced sailor among the students that year who was willing to instruct others. However, the boat was not entirely river-worthy and it was reported in the 1959 newsletter that 'Father Thames' kept trying to come aboard, either through the bottom or over the side, in spite of efforts to keep him out with an old tin. Unfortunately this little boat did not last very long.

Celebrations

For Miss Snow variety was the spice of life, and she encouraged social events within the College and to these guests were invited. Parties were held on many occasions, for birthdays, for engagements, at Christmas, to welcome or say goodbye to folk - or just for enjoyment and relaxation. They were usually hilarious to judge by accounts in newsletters, with staff and students sharing in the fun and games. One wonders exactly what went on when games called

'Bedtime', 'False and True' and 'Dressing the Potato' were played at the first social evening in 1949. This party was in fact held to say goodbye to Ethel Alfredson, who was returning to Ethiopia to take charge of a rural hospital there.

The annual Christmas Party was eagerly anticipated. Senior Students often referred to these in their reports, always with appreciation of the special food and the ingenuity of the games. Writing in 1963, Joan Botterill says:

> At the party it was fun to see everyone in the common room wearing a hat representing a song - Miss Snow wore 'Riding down to Bangor on the Midnight Train', but it was Rachel Fuller whom the judges chose as the winner with her 'Strawberry Fair'.

Other social events should be mentioned: Guy Fawkes Night when a 'Guy' was burned, hot sausages and a sing song enjoyed round the fire; 'Burns Night' when even Andy sported a tartan bow; Saturday evening times of coffee and relaxation, when Miss Knight encouraged an informal gathering, to listen to records and get mending or knitting done.

There is of course 'a joker in every pack' and St Michael's was no exception. Dss Poppy Turner and her room mate started a "Kulture Klub" (Culture of the "right" sort was definitely encouraged!) The KK was held in their room at the top of the stairs. However, they were asked to remove the notice on the bedroom door as it lowered the tone!

Few could forget those early May mornings in Oxford before breakfast; the Morris dancers, the choir on Magdalen Tower, the blossom, the mist on the river, a general air of festivity; those were magical moments when the students from Banbury Road felt a part of the University scene. Students who preferred to remain in their beds definitely missed something special.

Days Out
From time to time students and staff went off for a day's outing usually in the Trinity term. In 1959 it was to the Severn Wild Fowl Trust at Slimbridge, and Coralie Ive and Shirley Palmer wrote:

> We were shown round the thirty-five acres of land and ponds by a very helpful and informative guide, and saw over

a hundred varieties of British and foreign wild fowl, many of them gaily coloured. It was an outing we shall treasure in our memories and we hope it will not be the last paid by St Michael's to Slimbridge.

It was not, for in 1961 Senior Student, Pat Masterman, reported on -

> the happiness of fellowship together at Slimbridge viewing the Hawaiian geese and various other species.

Outings to Coventry Cathedral and to Stratford are also mentioned in newsletters, partly for the delicious cream teas enjoyed at Banbury on the way home.

However, the last outing from Oxford will never be forgotten by those privileged to be on it. It was in the summer of 1968, when the whole College, students and staff, set out in cars to visit Miss Snow and her sisters in their lovely new home "Forge House", Privett, Hants. It was a superb day and, after stopping for a picnic lunch near Winchester, the party arrived in time for tea and a happy time of fellowship with Dr Eileen, Miss Olive, Dorothy Barter Snow and of course Andy. Although the closure of St Michael's was near, that did not spoil the enjoyment of the day.

Life was never dull

It is fitting to end this chapter with first a quote from Ruth Teeuwen's (Young) report as President of the Social Committee 1956. Her words remained true to the close of St Michael's days in Oxford:

> St Michael's thus continues the still young tradition of striking the happy medium between work and pleasure, and has a quantity of both; believing (whether approved by the powers that be or not!) in quality rather than quantity.

And then one from Gillian Thomas, the last Senior Student in Oxford in 1968:

> Thank God for St Mike's. Many wise lessons imparted, some hard experiences - and exams - encountered, friends made, fun and laughter enjoyed, fellowship, prayer and worship shared.

CHAPTER 10

Billy Graham Crusades

Many of those offering for parish or missionary work in the late 1950's or early sixties had been among the thousands whose lives were deeply influenced for Christ and the Kingdom of God at the Billy Graham Crusades at Harringay and in other parts of the country. They came from every stratum of society, church life and denomination; some who had grown up through the church and others who had previously had little or no connection with any Christian fellowship or knowledge of doctrine.

Two totally different students at St Michael's at the same time in 1958 tell their own stories:

A discovery

Sue Lynn-Allen says:

I found Jesus in 1954 - as a direct result of Billy Graham's momentous crusade at Harringay. I was then 23. What an amazing and unlikely thing to happen to someone like me! To my family, my friends (and myself) this unexpected experience looked so totally 'out of sync' with everything that belonged to my teens and young adult life. Since I was twelve I had only one all absorbing interest in life ... the theatre. Every other possible interest was sooner or later thrown out to make more room for this obsession - theatrical values, skills, ambience and people utterly dominated my waking thoughts and dreams. To me the stage world and 'REAL life' were almost interchangeable terms!

Of course one doesn't expect this kind of tunnel vision to lead to the feet of Christ, and in addition I was undoubtedly alienated from church-goers and religious people. Not that either group crossed my path! Maybe there were some keen

Christians living within a stone's throw of our house in Reigate, but as far as I was concerned they could have been on Mars. Friendship with Christians would not have been an appealing thought. If I'd seriously weighed up the possibility that a young person might 'turn to religion' - but I don't remember thinking about it - it would certainly have looked an unattractive possibility. Some people's spiritual alienation is expressed in protest or arguments with peers. Mine was expressed in utter silence!

At the time I would have described myself as someone who was placidly indifferent about the existence of God, or the identity of Jesus. In hindsight I don't think indifference was the right word.

Our home was full of plays. I read them all avidly, usually over and over again. Yet there was ONE book of plays that I was careful never to open and never to read. The exception? Dorothy Sayer's BBC plays about the life of Christ 'The Man Born to be King'. If I hadn't felt secretly challenged and threatened by this theme I would certainly have studied this series alongside all the other dramatic writings. Why should it worry me if the story was true or untrue so long as the roles were demanding ones to act ... and the plot was a good bit of 'theatre'? I didn't adopt this line and the book remained firmly closed. Why? There was an Inescapable Significance about that central figure and I didn't want to meet Him!

Peace with God
In the spring of '54 a friend of mine - an actor - rang me up. He had an astonishing idea. Could we go together and hear Billy Graham? Why did I say 'Yes'? The outing would be 'different' (we usually went dancing) and the 'entertainment' was free ... but even at this stage I was aware of another motive -

'To love oneself is the beginning of a life long romance' (Oscar Wilde)

The words were truer than even Wilde understood - but what happens to anyone when the 'romance' starts to leave you feeling desperately empty and lonely ...? Lately the sheer futility of life .. the unbearable **pointlessness** of it all had become a suffocating burden I couldn't seem to shake off.

Billy's actual **sermon** was almost double Dutch to me. However, his burning concern spoke volumes. I was also aware of an overwhelming sense of the presence of God in that sports' arena! I knew that He Himself was speaking to me. "When you were twelve you made me a promise at your confirmation - now is your chance to keep it ... come ..." With many others I stumbled my way to the front. Had I understood the heart of the Gospel? Was I ready to accept Jesus into my life? No! There was still a great deal I needed to see.

It was a week or so later that I found myself reading Graham's PEACE WITH GOD. The words that spun out of the page to meet me were these: 'But God commendeth His love toward us, in that, while we were **yet sinners, Christ died for us**'. I was sitting on a No. 13 bus and we were travelling down Fleet Street - but suddenly all that melted away. I could only see Jesus dying for ME. I had virtually ignored Him all my life ... and dared to despise Him although I myself was nothing. How staggering that He cared so much for me. After twenty three years of wasting my life I was at last holding the key to the Riddle of our Existence ... that key was the Person and love of Christ.

Divine Love
How amazing that so much reluctance can be ultimately overcome by divine love ... and the extraordinary message of Calvary! Nothing in the world is equal to that love and that message. My particular memories of 'who I was' and 'how I felt' have been shared here just to make two points. As I look back to 1954 and then allow my mind to skim over around forty years of various kinds of Christian work that followed I feel forced to add to the famous words of Moses and say something like this:

"WHO AM I ... that You should even bother with me?
"WHO AM I .... that I should have been allowed to do the smallest job for You?

It's all like a beautiful dream ... but I don't have to wake up and find it's untrue!

It lasted
In spite of the passing forty years I **still** feel I know just as if it were yesterday, what it feels like to be an outsider in terms of the Christian faith and Christian circles. Even today I vividly recall my point blank antagonism and my total ignorance of the basic teaching of the Gospels. I remember reading St John's Gospel for the first time - the Graham Crusade Office, who were zealous in their follow-up, sent us copies through the post and the truth on every page was like a bomb exploding in my mind. I suppose common sense told me that **other** people knew that this Book had been around for a long time but I had never heard about it and the message it contained was earth shattering and life changing! This understanding of the many who walk through life clutching at their glitzy threadbare gods because no one has introduced them to the one true God has had a big share in shaping my Christian work. It really hasn't mattered whether this work has been in Anglican parishes or national youth work or deputising for missionary work in Central Africa. There are always hangers-on who don't yet speak the language of Zion and who are still dreadfully muddled about the fundamentals of faith. These are the people who stop me in my tracks because I can so easily slip into their shoes.

Another testimony
In that same Crusade, another student, Veronica Whinney (Webster) became a Christian - and that decision was to determine the course of her life.

In Veronica's own words:

We went as a family to Harringay. My Father decided we should hear what this American had to say because he had been made Churchwarden of our local church. He booked the tickets through the family theatre ticket agency. The other main family in the church (never more than twenty people at a service) were not going as they were 'high' Church. I had been to a high Church school and was much affected by the teaching. However, at the Harringay meeting, I was so moved by Billy Graham's appeal after his address that I stood up and said to my Mother "Are you coming?" I went forward and can never describe in words the overwhelming effect upon me as I sensed God's love as if I were the only person in the Arena that night. The counselling that followed was entirely 'superfluous' to that sense of God's presence which stayed with me as a purely intense and personal experience of which I never spoke except to say "I went forward". I thought my Mother went forward to see that I was all right and not on my own.

Years later I asked her why she had, and much to my surprise she said very thoughtfully, "I thought I would regret it all my life if I did not go." Our Vicar was very surprised to get our names from the organisation and decided there was nothing he could do about it, as our family was one of the most regular twice a Sunday when we were not away sailing for the weekend in Summer, though never on the fourth Sunday when my Father read the Lessons in Church! My Mother's faith developed steadily all her life and I went off to my first teaching job at Poole, Dorset, where I found the Evangelical Church of St Mary Longfleet to be more friendly than a high Church I went to first, so I became a Sunday School teacher and Junior Boys' Brigade (Life Boys) leader there. Under Ken Prior's leadership there the work grew and developed and I felt called to train for parish work at St Mike's, which I entered in 1956.

Tribute to St Mike's
As with others Veronica found her time there gave her life a structure and meaning like the 'weft and warp' in Miss Snow's weaving. She formed friendships which have had a profound influence on her life. The Bible Teaching and work for the Diploma of Theology prepared her for writing talks and eventually studying for an M.Ed. at Birmingham University. Many of the things she experienced helped prepare her for her later life as a teacher, mother and clergy wife.

Sheila's story
Sheila Hancock's background was quite different from that of both Sue and Veronica, and involved great sacrifice on the part of her father. She says:

I lived at home with my mother and father and was a book-keeper in a wholesale jewellers and silversmiths' firm in the City of London. In December 1952 my mother died. On the anniversary of her birthday at the end of March, my father and I used to visit the church where my parents had got married, but in 1955 we decided to attend a service in our parish church instead. There we were invited to the television showing of Billy Graham's Kelvin Hall, Good Friday Meeting (April 8th). This was shown on a large screen in the church hall. I went forward, for counselling, but my father didn't; but we both accepted the Lord as our Saviour that night, and continued in fellowship at the church.

Financial needs met
Two years later, after watching the film 'The Unfinished Task' Sheila felt called to missionary work and was eventually accepted to train at St Michael's House. Uncertain of where the Lord was leading, she was not entitled to any grant and her father offered to pay her fees for two years. He was unable to cover the last term, which was paid for by the Daily Prayer Union - a gift repaid in 1965. After working for a year in a parish Sheila eventually completed a Mature Students course at a Teacher Training College, supported by a grant from the local authority. She continued teaching until retirement, always involved - as now - in supporting the local church.

Hallelujah!
These are but three of the many students who passed through St Michael's as a result of the impact made by the Billy Graham Crusades. There were many others who were already committed to supporting the Crusades and were deeply impressed by seeing the awesome power of the Holy Spirit at work in the meetings in a manner previously unimagined. Those who were students at the College at that time were closely linked with the Crusade. Several were counsellors at the three 'hook-ups' in the Town Hall and kept in touch with those they contacted. Some took University and nurse friends to hear Dr Graham speaking at St Aldates and a coach party took students and friends to the final rally at White City. For Joan Garwood the life-changing moment came just before the start of the White City meeting, when she had already sung for three months in the choir and been a counsellor at

Harringay. The choir had been practising the Hallelujah Chorus which they would sing later in the afternoon. Without warning the sound system failed. As she watched Cliff Barrows quietly moving from one microphone to the next, checking the equipment to find the fault, and the thousands already gathered praying as never before, she realised in a totally new revelation that the Holy Spirit was in control and that whatever happened would be used for the glory of God. Long afterwards, while proving the Spirit's power in some very strange situations, she wondered how many more had learned the same lesson on that incredible Saturday at White City. For when the sound came on it seemed as if everyone present touched heaven itself.

Committed to evangelism many former students shared in counselling whenever Dr Billy Graham had campaigns in this country. They spoke in the newsletters of sharing in the relays, or the meetings themselves, in 1961 and again in 1967, and of the great blessing for individuals that those Crusades brought.

It has often been suggested that the results of the various Billy Graham Crusades during the fifties and sixties were over-rated and short-lived. Yet the counselling classes, the choir, the dedication of the Billy Graham Team and much more made an indelible impression on the lives of those who responded. The long-term results are known only to God, but the evidence of the impact they made on thousands world-wide may be judged by the effect the Crusades had on those training at just one College. To God indeed be the glory.

CHAPTER 11

Over the Walls - into Parishes

Between 1950 and 1968 more than a hundred students left Oxford to enter parish work. They had come to St Michael's with vocation tested by a Selection process, carried out by the Council of Women's Ministry in the Church of England - so they knew the call of God on their lives very certainly. Many had already been in contact with the Women's branch of the Church Pastoral Aid Society. Initially called the Ladies' Home Mission Union, later Women's Action, and now Ministry among Women, this Society played a vital role in recruiting women for parish work and supporting them in it. Miss Norah Coggan headed up the LHMU for many years. She also served on the St Michael's Council, until the closure in Oxford. Many a student at St Michael's thanked God for the warm-hearted support Miss Coggan gave, together with her staff at Falcon Court. From an initial approach right through the Selection process and training CPAS Staff prayed for a student, and linked her with a group of LHMU members. They shared her progress, problems and joys in training, and supported her in the early years in a parish. Thousands of pounds were raised by women in the parishes towards the training of students. This financial help continued when they worked in CPAS grant-aided parishes. This prayerful and practical support of men and women in the ministry continues to this day.

Work in the parishes to which women went was immensely varied, challenging and often incredibly taxing. Here are some typical items of news and prayer requests, sent in to the College newsletter in the early days:

> My area for visiting is huge and includes the Ford motor works. I love visiting down there along the endless roads of outwardly monotonous houses, but with such a diversity of people of different races and creeds behind the doors. It's a real thrill to have the Gospel to offer to them - people hawk so many worthless things around these streets.

Life here is absolutely thrilling. It is very tough, materialistic, and we are seeing the Holy Spirit work in many surprising situations and families. I am able to teach Scripture in five day schools and I preach regularly in the Mission Church.

❖ ❖ ❖ ❖ ❖

The Youth Group consists of 75% non-Christians and there is a real need to build up our Christians and to train them to teach others.

❖ ❖ ❖ ❖ ❖

Satan is much on the attack. The old hall is constantly attacked by gangs of youths who smash, slash, and destroy. At night vagrants break in and use the place as a doss-house. The Rectory was broken into - the tape recorder stolen. Yet, one hundred and nine children came along to the Mission.

(From a parish in the North-East)

❖ ❖ ❖ ❖ ❖

Visiting in a temperature of below 20° is a wonderful introduction to the hazards of parish work in winter.

❖ ❖ ❖ ❖ ❖

Parish life is busy but exciting. Home meetings for Bible Study have begun. The Lord is at work, especially among young wives.

❖ ❖ ❖ ❖ ❖

The congregation is fast-dwindling and widespread. Very few from the parish attend church. There are many opportunities to establish good personal relationships with people from all walks of life, including down and outs, prostitutes and others.

Quotes like these show the difficulties facing those in parish ministry do not change. They highlight the need of clergy for constant understanding prayer support.

For the first few years parish workers moved from parish to parish like their curate colleagues. This could be unsettling although it gave a breadth of experience. When a new incumbent arrived they were expected to offer to resign, and sometimes the offer was accepted. Sometimes a break was taken from parish work, to gain a different kind of experience.

Over the years several ex-students were appointed to the staff of CPAS for short or longer periods, so returning 'in kind' so to speak, the help gained from that Society in their own lives. Among these were **Kathleen Shoubridge**, **Sylvia Harding**, **Betty Osborne** and **Mary Kidman** who all did valuable work in this setting. But **Doreen Begernie**, who on leaving St Michael's in 1962 had gone to St Mary's, Islington, felt such a strong call to serve in LHMU that it became almost her life work. She began as the Women's Action Eastern Area Secretary in 1976 and went on to become Head of Ministry among Women from 1979 to her retirement in 1987. On her retirement, the Revd David Bubbers, Chairman, wrote this tribute in 'Together' the magazine of CPAS:

> There will be a sadness at Falcon Court shared by her many friends all over the country in losing a colleague whose personal qualities and work amongst women have been recognised and esteemed by all who have known her. At the same time we all give thanks for the way in which He has enabled her ministry to be so fruitful. She will be missed as a wise counsellor, with a lively sense of humour, and as an accomplished speaker.

In the spring of that year, Doreen was ordained Deacon (she was already a Deaconess) in St Paul's Cathedral, and it gave her special joy as she looked forward to an active retirement in Folkestone. There she was attached to St John's Church where the Revd Harold Harland was vicar. As Honorary Assistant Curate, Doreen's ministry made a deep impression and she was greatly appreciated. Sadly, only a few years into retirement Doreen became ill. In spite of putting up a tremendous fight against cancer, most people knew by the end of 1994 that she did not have long to live. In December that year, in her own church, Doreen was ordained priest by the Archbishop of Canterbury, the Most Revd Dr. George Carey, and the Bishop of Maidstone, the Right Revd Gavin Reid, preached the sermon. At the service he put into words what many felt about the Synod's decision to ordain women to the priesthood:

There is a foolishness about what we are doing today. Here is not some young vigorous candidate with a long life time to offer. Here is someone, very dear to us all, who knows she is far from well. And even with the lights of 'Home' clearly in sight as she journeys on. And yet for her, one Archbishop, two Bishops, many clergy and hundreds of people have gathered because they sense that today something is right. We come, not to confer priesthood but to recognise it.

After Christmas Doreen's condition deteriorated swiftly and she died in hospital on 12th January 1995.

A number of students joined other Christian organisations for varying lengths of time: Children's Special Service Mission (CSSM), Young Women's Christian Association (YWCA), The Cambridge University Mission (CUM), Clerkenwell Medical Mission, the Mayflower Family Centre, the Canadian Sunday School Caravan Mission, Church Society, and the Commonwealth and Continental Church Society. **The Revd Patti Schmiegelow** is currently General Secretary of this Society - now re-named the Inter-Continental Church Society (Intercon). Patti left St Michael's in 1965 and became a parish worker in Cheltenham Parish Church. She writes this about her career:

My two years study at "St Mike's" was foundational and life-changing. I arrived a young Christian with, I discovered, a deep ignorance of the Bible but a developing sense of Christian lifestyle taught by a warm and welcoming London parish and time on the Lee Abbey community.

I remain deeply grateful for the Biblical teaching. It was taught with reverence, prayerfully and practically. I 'fell in love' with the Old Testament and the Hebrew race and my world view totally changed. It was conservative teaching; so what? It gave me a firm rock from which to question and explore. I did not **have** to agree with everything presented.

That was true of all we were taught. That apart, the whole life of the College was geared to prepare us for ministry on the principle that what you are speaks louder than what you say! Occasionally the disciplines seemed stupid and petty but the patience learnt, if it was, must have been of particular benefit to those women who went to serve overseas in bureaucratic countries where paperwork takes a lifetime!

The friendships and the laughter have lasted a long time. We were a close knit community and you had to learn to get on or cope with everyone. But such a community was also immensely supportive. During my last term, my youngest sister was killed in a car crash. My abiding memory of both staff and students was the loving understanding given at that time.

Of course we were all delighted when the time came to leave. That must be surely the sign of a successful training. But in the years that have followed whether in parish or diocesan work; at home or briefly abroad and finally as General Secretary of the Intercontinental Church Society, the lessons learnt particularly in Chapel times have stayed with me. In any major decision for change, I can still see (and hear) Miss Barter Snow in my first term, expounding Deuteronomy, emphasising when the pillar of fire moves, move, if it does not, then stay put. The only problem is to recognise the pillar!

For some, their training and experience led to a totally unexpected change in their career. For example, to Chaplaincy work in H.M. Forces, or in a hospital. **Joan Garwood** tells how it happened to her:

After leaving St Michael's I went to Rainham in Essex as parish worker. The Vicar, the Revd Charles Searle-Barnes, and his wife Virginia, had been missionaries in China, and the three churches, Rainham, Wennington and South Hornchurch under his care, certainly benefited from their experience! I soon realised as I saw the abundance of leaders in the various organisations, that I had been sent there to complete my training as a parish worker. It was a challenging and inspiring three years, at the end of which the Secretary to a small Scottish Mission, the Mission to Mediterranean Garrisons, now Mission to Military Garrisons (MMG), visited South Hornchurch. He spoke at a number of meetings at which I helped him with showing his slides. By this time I was 37, had never been in the Forces, nor worked in a bookshop, and was abysmal in the kitchen, yet I was conscious of the same inward call as I had felt in 1957 when walking home from a young people's fellowship one Sunday evening and the Lord had clearly said: "This is the work you should be doing."

The call was confirmed and after visiting a Selection Committee in Glasgow, I was eventually posted to the Famagusta area in Cyprus for an incredibly interesting and enriching two years.

The Mission worked through its bookshops and canteens, and in their 'spare' time the missionaries ran Sunday Schools, holiday clubs, wives groups, Scripture Union groups and other activities, as well as Sunday afternoon meetings, Rallies and an Easter weekend mission. I shall never forget sitting on an upturned tea urn playing a harmonium in the restored amphitheatre at Salamis and wondering about St Paul!

Although for family and other reasons I came home from Cyprus after my two-year term, what I did not know was that that experience was an introduction to a much longer stretch with the Army. After two and a half years as a parish worker in Deptford, I was amazed to find myself in the Royal Army Chaplains Department, first working on an Army camp in North London, which abounded with young families, and later at the Women's Royal Army Corps Centre at Guildford. At that time all young women recruits entering the British Army (except officer cadets) spent six weeks training at Guildford. Later, this time was extended, and ultimately the Centre closed when it was decided to train men and women together.

Both at the London camp and Guildford, and also at Aldershot - where I worked for two years in tandem with Guildford, so to speak, mainly visiting two Army hospitals - I was involved in many deeply moving incidents. Thirty years later I am still in touch with two - young women at the time - who suffered while their husbands were stationed in London. One lost her baby son through a cot death, and said she would never have another child, but now sends me photographs of her lovely daughter. The other was left by her husband, with four small children, three and four years old and twins of eighteen months, with no home and no money. The journey on the M1 to Yorkshire in a Rent-a-Van packed with furniture given by local Baptists, with the young family following, will for ever remind me of the extremes brought about by adultery and desertion. The couple accompanying the family stayed for a week to decorate the seedy Council house allocated by the local authority to this desperate young woman, who had left the town a few years earlier as a radiant bride. I cried with her!

Because of her relationship with social workers in dealing with family problems in her first posting, Joan studied for a Diploma in Sociology, and was awarded this in 1973. She continues:

Side by side with the regular services, Sunday School, children's clubs, etc. it was very much a one to one work involving visiting homes, workplace, hospitals, and even on several occasions prisons and magistrates' courts. There were also Padre's hours, where there were opportunities to correct some of the more bizarre interpretations of the Christian faith!

A few weeks after my arrival at Guildford in 1973, on Remembrance Sunday morning, with a full church, band, and great expectations, the Chaplain due to take the service failed to arrive. Told, very kindly, by the Commandant to take the service and cut out any sermon or talk, I felt this was impossible - the let-down to everyone present and a great opportunity missed would have been too much to bear. It was the one definitive time in my life when I knew beyond all possible doubt that the Holy Spirit had taken over and given His own message to the several hundred present. I had been very reluctant to go to Guildford, and I realised that I needed some such sign at the outset of my work in that difficult and different situation.

Cliff Richard (Sir) with his manager Bill Latham, very kindly came twice to the London barracks and twice to Guildford, while I was there; he spoke of his faith to packed audiences. On each occasion it seemed as if the Gulf Stream had suddenly been diverted through the Camp, bringing new warmth and openness. His quiet unassuming and so valuable support meant a lot to me in my somewhat isolated situation.

After sixteen years I retired early as my mother was very ill. When she died I was fortunate enough to be able to work with the Revd Bob Gilbert at Westminster Central Hall. Bob had been a Senior Chaplain before retiring, and was then Secretary to the Forces Board of the Methodist Church - a branch of the Home Mission Division of which the Revd Dr Donald English was General Secretary. It was a most rewarding and thoroughly enjoyable ending - lasting eight and a half years - to nearly twenty-six years full-time work with or connected with the Forces. My only regret is that this wonderful mission field amongst our own young men, women and children, is so little known and sometimes so badly misunderstood. I remain closely associated with the Soldiers' and Airmen's Scripture Readers Association, MMG, and Sandes Soldiers' and Airmen's Centres (the Navy have their own missionary societies!).

To conclude I can only echo the words of the hymnwriter - "Who, like me, His praise should sing?"

Hospital visiting was often part and parcel of a parish worker's ministry, usually to members of their churches who were sick and in need of pastoral care. Becoming a full-time Chaplain - or a Chaplain's Assistant - was a much bigger undertaking. **The Revd Matty McQuillan** wrote of her work in Nottingham in 1987:*

My role as a Chaplain differs from other members of the healthcare team. It is a matter of 'being' rather than 'doing'. Being there, to care for patients in the Hospital, also involves caring for their families and caring for the Staff, listening, supporting, understanding, empathising, praying, rejoicing, loving.

---

* Reprinted from *Nursing (the add on Journal of Clinical Nursing)*, Vol. 3, No. 24, M. McQuillan, *"The role of the Chaplain"* © December 1987, by permission of the publisher W.B. Saunders Co. Ltd.

Often on the unit, I also listen to the doctors talking to parents and explaining what is happening. Apparently I am able to reinforce some of what is said and assure parents the doctor is being honest and not giving false hope.

It was at an Ash Wednesday service that I first saw Paul and Helen, the parents of Elizabeth. I was aware they were anxious. Later, I discovered on the oncology ward that Elizabeth was very ill and I knew that being available to that family in the future would be part of my role. My office became a favourite place for Elizabeth to visit between treatments. Twice when the child was in intensive care, I was able to listen to the parents, know their fears and hopes, pray with them for Elizabeth and put into words some of the things they were unable to say, being so full of pain.

A Chaplain also exercises a pastoral ministry on the wards, taking the sacrament of Holy Communion to those too ill to come to the Chapel. Also in my role as Chaplain I may baptise a very sick premature baby or a sick child. It is a joy for a Chaplain to baptise a baby who is well, and to give thanks for the birth.

Now, ten years after writing that, Matty adds this:

I began my ministry as a Chaplain, caring for the terminally ill and dying, both children and adults. Ministering to parents whose child had been in a road accident, or who had lost their baby, or whose child was still born or brain damaged. Bringing care to the families of those who were killed or injured in the Kegworth air accident, and so on. I sat where they sat, bringing the love of God to them in their tragedy and sorrow.

Now more fully retired since October 1997, I see retirement as a gift from God to spend more time in prayer and intercession, rather than organising, administering, and developing new ministry. This is the way my ministry is now developing and one for which I was partly prepared at St Michael's. I give thanks for my time at St Mike's and the preparation through the staff and students for future ministry. Before Ordination to the Priesthood in 1994 our Bishop gave us the opportunity to thank God, in prayer for those who had prepared us for ministry and those to whom we were indebted for that preparation. I gave God thanks for the Staff at St Michael's and especially for Dss Annette Tatton. I do not think she ever imagined she was preparing us for priesting but I felt she shared in that great day of Ordination in May 1994.

Within the Church of England, ex-St Michael's students have achieved remarkable things and risen to positions of influence. Between them, there are Rural Deans, Honorary Canons, Directors of Ordinands, members of the General Synod, and the Crown Appointments Commission; Clergy representatives on School Governing Bodies, and perhaps the highest of all an Archdeacon.

Others have become known as writers and broadcasters. **The Revd Margaret Cundiff** is the author of no fewer than twelve best selling books - one of which, 'Called to be me' up to now has never gone out of print. Margaret would say that she was a fairly unpromising student at St Michael's, being too young really for that kind of training. But her career has been spectacular. She began at only twenty-one years of age in a huge Midlands parish facing a situation and work far beyond her training or experience. Yet, she says,

> I still have friends from those days and it was a crash course in human relationships.

Little did those early parishioners imagine that one day, this very unorthodox 'live-wire', as an ordained minister would be Anglican adviser to Yorkshire Television, Broadcasting Officer for the York Diocese, a member of several august councils and committees, honorary Chaplain at York Minster, and most recently Chaplain to the Mothers' Union in the York Diocese.

Now Margaret, who is wife to Peter, and mother of two grown up children, Julian and Alison, serves as an Associate Minister at St James, Selby, Yorks. Of herself, Margaret says:

> This is the woman who at school was told 'Stop talking, you'll never earn a living by talking.' It just shows how wrong some people can be.

In her life, Margaret has proved over and over again the truth of Paul's words, Phil 4:13

> I can do all things, through Christ, who strengthens me

That is the verse she gives to encourage Mothers Union members in their calling today.

The Revd Sylvia Mutch also celebrated her 21st Birthday, while a student at St Michael's. She achieved fame by being one of the first women to be ordained deacon in England and the very first to be allowed to conduct a wedding:

> I didn't think I would be a priest before I retired (she says) let alone in charge of a parish. In fact I did not hanker after it; it just happened in the way the Lord has pushed me all the time.

The wedding she conducted took place only ten days after her ordination in 1987. It was to be a small midweek ceremony, but the press got wind of it. Thirty five reporters and three television companies turned up to spread the news nation wide!

Today, Sylvia is Rector of Elvington, York, is in charge of three Churches and in 1998 was made a Canon of York Minster, a fitting recognition of the quality of her service.

Many of those who trained at St Michael's went on to enter the Deaconess order. This is not surprising for it seemed to them the only way forward into further ministry in the Anglican Church. Further, the reader will recall that one of the parent-colleges of St Michael's was St Catherine's Deaconess House. The Bishop of London had recognised it in 1927 as a Training College for Deaconesses and Lay-Workers. Only in fact in 1920, at the Lambeth Conference, was the forty-seventh Resolution adopted. It read as follows:

> The time has come when, in the interests of the Church at large, and in particular of the development of the Ministry of Women, the Diaconate of Women should be restored formally and canonically throughout the Anglican communion.

That was welcome news, but, for the next eighteen years, the status and function of a Deaconess was still somewhat unclear. In the 1938 report of St Michael's, Deaconess Hankin, a member of the Trust wrote:

Perplexity about the status and functions of a Deaconess has lightened as the Upper and Lower Houses of Canterbury and the Upper House of York seem to have agreed that the function of deaconesses should include the following:

(1) In case of need, to read the services of Morning and Evening Prayer and the Litany, except those portions reserved to the priest, and to lead in prayer;

(2) To instruct and preach, except during the service of Holy Communion.

Deaconesses were greatly respected within their parishes and in the wider community. They had undergone a further selection process and short period of additional training before Ordination. In 1996, it was estimated that there were six hundred deaconesses and about one hundred lay-workers in the Church of England. Most, but not all of the St Michael's deaconesses chose to be ordained deacons. It seemed to them to be the natural step.

Clergy wives

It is hardly surprising that, working so closely with their male colleagues, many of the St Michael's women married clergymen! At a rough estimate it was between forty and fifty. Trained, especially, in Bible Knowledge and Pastoralia, and with experience, they could give great support to their husbands, as well as being wives and mothers. In at least three cases, these men became Bishops - Pat Harris (m. Valerie Pilbrow) and John Ball (m. Anne Clothier) in the overseas church, and Michael Whinney (m. Veronica Webster) in England. Veronica tells about her engagement to Michael and of God's help and guidance over the years:

Michael proposed the week-end before the Dip. Th. exams - and Liz Cox (Fisher) announced her engagement to Peter. We both passed the exams we took that summer. I left St Mike's to be married to Michael. We set up home in two rooms, kitchen and shared bathroom in the parish where he had been curate for a year. I attended Staff Meetings, Young Wives, helped with Girl Pathfinders, gave devotional talks, led a weekly house Bible Study and started a family. Muriel Pargeter had just left the Parish for a new post having been very active as a much loved Parish worker there. Joan Garwood was welcomed to the staff before we moved to Bermondsey for Michael to be Warden of the Cambridge University Mission. We lived in a flat on the fifth floor with no lift until we moved down to the third floor just before our second baby was born. Joan's mother lived nearby and was a tower of strength to us. The children called her "Guardy" - a combination of "Granny" and "Guardian Angel". We lived in the flat for seven years while our children went to the local school and we had a third baby. When friends from St Mike's came they said it seemed easier for missionaries bringing up families abroad than in an upstairs flat without a lift.

In due course Michael became vicar of the local church and they moved into the Vicarage for seven happy years. It was during the time in South London that Veronica's involvement with autistic children came about. She describes how it happened:

Gwen Mason (ex-St Michael's) became Head Teacher of our local Church School, in Bermondsey where all three children had attended over the years. We much valued Gwen's advice and benefited from her educational expertise at the time. Gwen asked me to help with a boy at the school who had autistic-like behaviour. Funding was found for me to work with him one to one. This was a new area of work for me so I wrote to the National Autistic Society (NAS) for the only available literature at the time. Gwen arranged for ILEA's (Inner London Educational Authority) Deputy Principal Educational Psychologist to see me working with this child and the advice he gave me then has influenced the way I have worked since with children whose behaviour affects their ability to learn.

The Whinneys next move was to Herne Hill, when Michael was made Archdeacon of Southwark. Veronica worked in a Special School where she was in charge of a small unit for children with autism. While there she was granted paid leave to attend an International Conference on Autism in the U.S.A.

Michael became successively Suffragan Bishop of Aston, Diocesan Bishop of Southwell, and Assistant Bishop of Birmingham. Throughout these years, Veronica continued to specialise in her field, spending nine years at Uffculme Special School, where she became Second Deputy Head. She retired from there in 1997. Teaching full-time, Veronica studied part-time and achieved an M.Ed. on her subject 'Facilitating learning for Children with Autism'. A bound copy of her dissertation is kept by Birmingham University. About her time at St Michael's Veronica has written:

> Watching Kath Lefroy (Clark) teach RE in a mainstream school and going to Mrs Habermann's Sunday School lesson preparation classes have been useful for some of my work in teaching children with complex learning difficulties and Autism. Sunday afternoon Fellowship Meetings prepared me for the hospitality we were able to offer over the years in parish, Archdeaconry and Diocese.

A former clergy wife who pays a warm tribute to St Michael's is (Mrs) **Delphine Hine**. This is her story:

> When it was known that my husband Rupert was to go to Oak Hill Theological College, our Parish Worker at St Clements, Oxford (Win Impett - ex-St Michael's) suggested that I get in touch with St Michael's with a view to **training** to be a Clergy wife. I found myself on a lovely summer's evening walking in the garden of St Michael's with Dss Annette Tatton, chatting about many things including a possible course for a clergy wife.
>
> So I came up to St Michael's as a day student in the Autumn of 1961. I was to pay six guineas a term. I attended a variety of lectures - Old and New Testament, Pastoralia, Worship, and Church History. It was a very happy year, meeting with women of all ages and from all walks of life, all there because they felt that God was calling them into a life of fuller service for Him.
>
> One evening during the summer term, Mrs Stella Gough spoke to those of us who were to be specially involved in Parish life: she gave some motherly help and advice - but it was not all serious - we had some good laughs over coffee.

During my time there, I found that I was expecting a baby. Since we had had many disappointments over eight years, we were cocooned in prayer which was a wonderful experience. And Esther Faith arrived safely on September 20th 1962.

When Delphine's husband finished his training, he served his title in Southall, moving from there to Tunbridge Wells and finally to All Saints, Farmborough near Bath. Here, unexpectedly in 1984, Rupert died, leaving Delphine with three lovely daughters, Esther, Judith and Paula who was still at school. Rupert's funeral was one of tremendous joy and thanksgiving, and Delphine testifies to God's faithfulness in helping them to rebuild their lives. They moved to Lower Weston, where Delphine became very involved in the parish.

She concludes:

The Lord has been gracious and good in so many ways and I thank and praise Him for it - to God be the glory, AMEN.

Because the whole of our country is divided into parishes, theoretically every man, woman and child could be reached with the Gospel, through men and women in the ministry of the Anglican Church. What a challenge to prayer that is for those in that ministry, and for those whom the Lord would call.

Open your eyes and look at the fields. They are ripe for harvest. Ask the Lord of the harvest therefore to send out workers into His harvest field. (John 4:35; Luke 2:2).

CHAPTER 12

Women's Ministry in the Church of England

It was not until 1987 after years of agonising debate and often inertia, the Church of England passed legislation permitting women to become deacons. It was another five years before General Synod voted, in 1992, for women to be ordained to the priesthood. For many this was the culmination of years of fulfilling ministry, but for some women there would still be frustration because of the limits within which they were allowed to exercise that ministry.

Many of those who trained for parish work at St Michael's were unaware, at the time, of the difficulties that lay ahead for women in the accredited ministry of the Church of England. Women's ordination was not a burning issue. There was no hint of campaigning for it, such as surfaced in the 1970's with the formation of the Movement for Women's Ordination. Some, however, realised that in responding to God's call they would meet with attitudes in both clergy and laity that would be difficult. They needed all of God's sustaining grace to cope with the problems. In this chapter and the next two former students write frankly of the experiences in their ministry:

Getting on with the job
Mavis Bexon (Student of St Michael's 1962-64)

My pathway to St Michael's

It was while I worked as a librarian that I felt I should be doing more to bring the Gospel to the uninitiated. I was reading Numbers 32 from my pocket Bible as I sat in the staff room at my tea break. It was the part where the Israelites are to cross over Jordan and fight for the land on the other side. Two and a half tribes had a lot of cattle and wanted to stay where they were because the pasture was good. Moses explained that if they did not all go into the fight together none of them would possess the promised land.

113

Was God talking to me? If I did not leave the comfort of home would there be those who would never get into the kingdom of heaven? I looked again at the Authorised Version I was reading at the time: "Why sit ye here while your brethren go to war?", I read further down. As I was sitting with my feet up on the table at the time that was it. Within hours I was visiting my vicar and sending for Bible College prospectuses.

I went to a missionary training College then did eleven months as a voluntary worker in my home church. It was there that I realised God wanted me to be a missionary in my own country. It was later I read again Numbers 32 and saw that Moses promised the two and a half tribes that if they entered the war they would be allowed to return to the pasture they had claimed for their cattle. In Joshua 12 this happened. The Church of England required me to go to the Selection centre and then do some Anglican training, which was how I ended up at St Michael's House in 1962. There were those who thought their time there was tough. They had left jobs, often with positions of responsibility, to go to a college which had such a regimented day. There were times to get up with official prayers, lectures that could not be missed, practical work in some of the churches and a time by which the doors were locked at night. No television and little opportunity for any social life outside the college. But to me, who had been to a missionary training college, life was easy. At least we could make tea and coffee in our bed-rooms. We could invite guests and, when I shared a downstairs bedroom in my second term, I realised it was very easy to let people into the building after lights out!

There were two things that Miss Snow said that I remember above all others. One was when I had to have a one-to-one chat with her. She said: "We are not here to change people's lives. Just to train them for ministry." What a relief! My missionary training college had been the very opposite. The other thing was after there had been a few arguments going on about how much evangelicals should stand up and be counted. How far should we compromise about things that probably did not matter too much? Miss Snow said: "Things are not always black and white. But don't be too hasty to make up your mind. The world would be a very dull place if it were all a murky sort of grey." Being a black and white person myself I have kept in my mind's eye that dull greyness to stop me accepting things I do not need to accept and hold back from giving in to conformity.

A Missionary at home

My first job was in Carlton, Nottinghamshire, the county I originally came from, though in a part previously unknown to me. St Paul's is a large parish with mixed housing, old and new, detached and terraced. There was a council estate a mile or two away from the parish church which the Rector felt needed special attention. A mission hall had been erected the year before I arrived and a work had started which I was asked to follow up.

In those days money was not forthcoming for accommodation. The rectory was huge and the curate's house had been owned by the church for many a decade. I had a flat in the rectory which was a twenty minute uphill cycle ride from the mission hall. Recently I went to the celebration of the thirty-fifth anniversary of the hall and was glad to learn that the present minister is living on the estate. A much better arrangement.

It was some time before I realised that it was not obligatory to go round with a happy face all the time when cycling uphill in the rain! Here I was ambassador for Christ, wanting anyone who saw me to know I was available for spiritual help in their time of need.

To tell the truth I was pretty tired. We kept long hours. With evening meetings and youth clubs it might have been thought advisable to have a latish start to the day. But no, in the sixties Christian workers seemed to think that one prayer before breakfast was worth ten afterwards. I have never been my best in the early morning and one day I staggered into the dark, cold church to meet with my colleagues. "It's foggy outside" was the only thing I could think of saying. One look at my face and the obvious reply came, "It's foggy inside". This did not make me pull my socks up but caused me surreptitiously to push the bottom of my pyjama trousers back under my skirt.

The Rector was ahead of his time with no discrimination against women and I did all the law would allow. I was responsible for the services at the mission hall and the many activities that went on during the week. There was great backing from the small group of worshippers already gathered and we did a lot of outreach with more enthusiasm than know-how. We saw people come to the Lord and, with very meagre resources, made an impact on the community.

There was a great deal of fun also. Our most successful Harvest Supper was with the assistance of the mobile chippy. The owner brought the van to our window and we passed hot plates out to be returned filled with fish, chips and peas. The fun the Christians had together flowed over into the community and probably attracted more people than any direct evangelism.

The end of the world
If you do not know where Barrow-in-Furness is you may be forgiven. Nobody goes through Barrow unless they want to end up in the sea! It is on the end of a peninsula and understandably was fairly insular though I expect mobility has changed things somewhat since the late sixties.

Women workers were not given removal allowances as curates and vicars were. When my next appointment took me to Barrow-in-Furness I had just enough money to pay for the hire of a van. This was driven by friends from Carlton with the bits of furniture I had collected, mostly with the help of a church member who was a dealer in scrap. I still use the wash-hand stand he gave me as a dressing table. Antiques Roadshow eat your heart out!

St Mark's, Barrow, was already a thriving church with an established work going on. There was a healthy young people's work and most of my time was spent on this, along with the curate, Chris Idle, who wrote then and has continued to write some of the best modern hymns we have in our books.

Barrow is a ship-building town and our parish consisted mainly of terraced housing. Most people had some connection with the shipyard, and mealtimes on the whole, were a safe bet because they fitted in with the yard's routine. Because of the great dependency upon the shipyard for jobs parents seemed inclined to give their children the best education possible in order to give them a choice they had never had. A lot of the youngsters we were involved with went to college or university and never came back.

This seemed frustrating at times and we used to say to each other what good leaders they would have made if only they would return. But those who would have made good leaders in Barrow did in fact make good leaders wherever they went. It took me some time to realise the obvious truth that **The Church** is bigger than the parish church I happened to be working in!

I had exchanged my push-bike for a moped and was able to get up to the Lake District on my days off but I was very homesick. It was four months before the vicar allowed me to go home and that was only because it was Christmas. For those four months I did not meet anyone I had known before going to Barrow. Later family and friends visited me but it was not an easy journey and had to be deliberate.

My house had been for the Verger when he had been employed full-time by the church. It was surrounded on three sides by church halls so it was dark and damp. It opened straight on to the pavement and I was scared stiff when passing drunks knocked on my door as I lay in bed. One night a man knocked persistently and I was quivering in the dark until I heard two other men say what they would do to the knocker if he did not disappear pronto. I looked through the curtains and it was two men who lived on the opposite side of the road - father and son-in-law. After this we became friendly and it was Ben (the older man) and his daughter who helped me cover the glossy painted walls (the whole house was decorated like a bathroom) with wallpaper we had bought in the sales.

Later on I was able to exchange my moped for an old car. A 1956 A30. Ben was as excited as I was and filled it with petrol for my 'maiden voyage'. We donned our best clothes and went out for a run, Ben treating us to a meal into the bargain. The last time I saw him, when I was visiting for the church's centenary, Ben had had a stroke. But I hope he understood when I tried to tell him how much I had appreciated his friendship, for he died soon afterwards.

Into the Pool

It was a cultural shock to move from Barrow to Liverpool. Far from being at the end of the world, Liverpool was the centre. I moved there in 1970 and the euphoria of the sixties was still about. I had been almost three years in Carlton, almost five in Barrow and I was to spend seven in Liverpool.

The Beacon Group had been set up by the Bishop of Liverpool. Nine parishes had been put together along with Shrewsbury House, a mission of Shrewsbury school. They were to be worked as one unit by a large team of church and community workers. The area was not large and the church buildings had been close together. When Bishop Ryle had been Bishop of Liverpool it was as if every time a pub went up on one corner of the street a church was put on the other. Eventually there was to be one church building, but in 1970 there were three.

I had first visited Everton to see a college friend - Olivia Abbay. She had gone straight from St Michael's House to work in the Beacon Group. Terraced housing had been pulled down and every direction the eye turned it was met with a tower block. There were more high-rise flats for the area than in any other part of Britain. On my journey to find Olivia's flat I passed graffiti announcing in six-foot letters 'Billy is a bastard' to be countered by 'Down with the Pope'. I was to learn later of the rivalry between the extreme Protestants (with William of Orange as their hero) and the Roman Catholics. The first question many people asked when they met you was were you catholic or protestant. When on one occasion I replied I was neither, I was just a Christian, a puzzled reply came, "I've never heard of that before".

On my visit to Olivia, as I parked the car a boy of seven or eight came up to me. "Mind yer car, miss?", he asked. I said , "No thank you", but dared him to harm it as his eyes met mine. When I repeated the story to Olivia she said it was a protection racket and I should have paid him. I had understood that but nevertheless felt it right to challenge him and that my car would be all right. It was. When Olivia left Everton I took her place.

There were four clergy, one of whom was Eddie Neale, and me plus various youth and community workers. As we were all of similar age and experience there was no Vicar and the constitution allowed us to select our own leader annually. The social needs were enormous and the team had already put into practice suggestions later made in the 'Faith in the City' report which came out in 1985. The group had started in 1963 and it was well in advance of contemporary thinking and eyed suspiciously by other evangelicals who thought they had 'sold out to the social gospel' - a saying I was to hear repeated many times in the following years.

Where lack of choice of work had made Barrovians the more vigilant in education and training the same thing in Liverpool brought the opposite reaction. It was more 'today we live, tomorrow we may die.' It gave them a flippant attitude towards life and a quick repartee which produced the Arthur Askeys and Ken Dodds and many other comedians down the years.

My entry into Evertonian life began with a lesson in specific prayer. I had chosen to live in a high-rise flat and my oldest sister and her husband helped me to move in. I did not think they would be very happy about my new environment so I asked God to make the sun shine on removal day working on the principle that the sun makes everything appear at its best. The removal took place on the Bank Holiday when caretakers had not been on duty since the previous Friday. The rubbish chutes were overflowing, corridors covered in dog dirt and the lifts full of vomit and urine after the Saturday night spree. The sun poured down mercilessly and the stench of the corridors and lifts had to be experienced to be believed. My brother-in-law never did eat a meal in the flat all the time I lived there.

It was noisy living in the flats. Not only from feet above your head as you lay in bed or shouting from next door, but the plumbing was such that every time the lavatory was flushed the noise went down the whole of that column. The only way I could cope was in trusting that God does indeed supply our every need and I accepted whatever sleep I could get with thanks.

There were frightening times also as the time when a prostitute lived next door to me. My door was knocked on by mistake but I knew the same protection I had known in Barrow. As I lay cowering a voice called out, "If you don't get away from that door I'll throw you over the balcony."

One of the jobs I inherited from Eddie Neale when he went as religious adviser to Radio Merseyside was the pensioners' holiday. I was the only one who got tired on these occasions. The pensioners would be out before breakfast and not in bed until long after the day had ended in order to get as much enjoyment out of the holiday as possible. One night I was called out of bed by some women who thought their friend had had a stroke. But I knew the symptoms by now and recognised the smell. "She's drunk," I said. "Let's get her to bed." It was a story that was related year after year that I the 'innocent' had diagnosed where hardened drinkers had failed. The fact that the hardened drinkers were muddle-headed at the time did not occur to them.

There were spiritual results of a different nature though. Each morning began with a Bible reading, a short talk and prayer and some of the older people did come into a new faith. One year when I led the confirmation classes out of the twelve candidates six of them were senior citizens. They joined in the discussions with refreshing honesty. One day we were talking about love and forgiveness and one woman volunteered, "I never liked my husband even before we were married." The obvious question was then, "Why did you marry him?" "To spite him". Where do you go from there? Scouses do not bear grudges as I discovered when I found three boys trying to break into the church with a battering ram. Quick as lightning I bashed their heads together (those were the days!) and they were so humiliated I cannot repeat the suggestions of what they were going to do to me. But when I met them later on in the day they called out with their usual friendship, "Eyup, Mave!" Nineteen years after the event I had a 'phone call from one of them. "I thought you'd like to know I've become a Christian," he said. I asked him lots of questions. I wanted to be sure we were both talking about the same thing! After all these years he knew I would be thrilled to bits to hear the news and he cared enough to want me to be thrilled.

Recently I went out to Australia to take part in the wedding of a girl I had been godmother to in Liverpool. Her mother, Dorothy, I had known when she was sixteen. On Olivia's recommendation she had come to a Pathfinder camp I was leading when I was still in Barrow. Dorothy will be fifty next year and her mother is one of the people who used to go on the pensioners' holiday. There are twelve of the family out in Australia. Some of them I had not known but with the others I have kept up a friendship all these years.

When the priesting of women came in I had a call from Everton. The P.C.C. were anxious that I should be the first woman to celebrate communion in their church. I had left Liverpool in 1977 and this was 1994. Such long lasting loyalties and affections are the 'rich tapestries of life'.

Robin Hood Country

It was hard to leave Liverpool but I got to the stage when I felt I was putting Liverpool before God and eventually I joined Eddie Neale in Nottingham; he had moved there after leaving Radio Merseyside. The parish consisted of three council estates at the time. Later we were to take in more. Eddie had gone there to build up a team ministry of whom I was the first recruit. Ted Lyons, who had become a Christian at the Mayflower Centre when David Sheppard was the warden, was to join us a year later.

We decided the best way to work was for each of us to be responsible for the church in the area in which we lived. I lived in a flat over the doctor's and next door to the community centre in Top Valley. It was in this parish I took my first funeral. I visited the widow of the dead man and her brother-in-law was there. He said to the widow, "I don't know whether you understand what this young lady is saying," (I was forty-six at the time!) "She is going to take the funeral service." "You can't do that," she informed me. I told her I could and I would, to which she responded, "Poor old

Bert. Second best in life and second best in death." They were both to apologise after the service.

The church was a dual purpose building and as such left much to be desired. But we had a parish mission which ended in a week of evangelism and many people with no church background became Christians. I had been called to missionary work in my own country and saw it working out in my own town. Some who had trained with me and gone abroad as missionaries were forbidden to proselytise. They did nursing or teaching or housekeeping but were denied evangelism, while I had all the freedom in the world to lead people to the Lord. What a privilege.

Where Liverpool's problems were mostly stealing, Top Valley's were more often of an emotional nature. It took me some time before I learned to say "no" to a woman who would ring me up any time of day or night in a depressed state. She would say that if I did not go round to see her she would commit suicide. A wise friend told me to say, "Then you'll just have to do it." What of the risk? The same friend told me that I could not be responsible and she was right. In the end each person is responsible for him or herself. After nine years in Top Valley I was worn out and yet it was with reluctance that I went to Oakwood.

Great oaks from little acorns grow

Oakwood was a vast private housing estate being built in Derby. There was no graffiti. Nobody sitting on the doorstep talking. The gardens and houses were neat and tidy. After my first visit I wrote to say I could not work there. But the letter would not get posted. I wrote another letter expressing my doubts at the same time realising that was where I had to go next.

It was quite different from my other experiences. The diocese bought me a house to live in and there was no public building at all. We cheered when we got our first post box! There were about ten thousand people in Oakwood and it is still being built. Many Christians had moved into the area. It was a case initially of getting them together. We started with a weekly prayer and Bible study in my house. Then a Baptism was arranged and, as it had been fixed for Pentecost, I decided that, rather than have it in the parish church, I would have it in my house. We moved all the furniture and got over sixty people into my sitting room.

That was the beginning of public worship. We attracted a lot of publicity. A church in a home. A woman 'Vicar'. We just grew and grew. A convent on the edge of Oakwood had been sold by the Roman Catholics to the Church of England and the Community of the Holy Name invited us to have our Sunday morning service in their chapel which we did for the next few years. I still had mothers and toddlers, keep fit, Bible Club, 'vestry' hour, Baptism and Confirmation classes, committee meetings and Bible study groups in my home. I did not do things any differently from the way I had done them before and yet, spiritually, it was easy. This was just the work of the Holy Spirit bringing people into the church.

We had members of the fellowship gifted in every way you can possibly imagine. So different from the rest of my ministry and somehow I felt God was presenting this as a gift after the hard times I had had. He was also, I believe, preparing me for retirement.

Our biggest problems were getting land for a church building. This happened before I left and our estate became a parish in its own right. Two years after my retirement I went to the opening of the church. Our problems had been of an ecumenical nature. All denominations worked and worshipped together in my home and the convent but when it came to buying land and making ours an official ecumenical church the hierarchy became involved. The tortuous meetings that became the order of the day made me decide very firmly that I would retire at sixty.

Members of the congregation were surprised. We had the land. Did I not want to see it through? I had been involved in the building of a new church in Everton and it had not really been my thing. I am not much into buildings, necessary as this one was. I was reading in my Bible and what I read confirmed my feelings. It was when Moses came to the promised land. The general idea is that he was prevented from going into the land as a punishment. I believe God was being kind. Moses had that hard forty years of bringing the tribes from Egypt to Canaan. There was to be a harder time to come when they had to go in and fight for the land. I believe God was telling Moses he had done his bit and was due for a rest. And now, with all the legalities still to be thrashed out, God was letting me off the hook as He had done with Moses all those years ago. People tell me the Oakwood church has 200 to its morning services and it seems to be thriving in all ways. That is fantastic.

Barchester Towers

After much searching I settled in retirement in this lovely market town of Southwell. Pretty well everybody here has some connection with one church or another. The Minster is in the centre and as I walked down the path I realised why so many people on hearing of my retirement home asked me, "Have you read Barchester Towers?" I believe God has given me a nice place to live, not as a reward for living in a flat with mice running over the bed at night, as in Carlton or in a dark damp house in Barrow, a high-rise flat in Liverpool or a flat next door to the community centre in Top Valley. Not as a reward. Just as a love token. Out of His generosity He has given me an attractive final (I think!) resting place. And Oakwood, where I had an attractive house, was preparation.

Working in a parish situation you feel responsible for everyone around you. At first I felt free of this. My neighbour was not my responsibility. But this false sense soon disappeared. As a Christian I am involved with those around me.

Being ordained has given me freedom to help out in churches where there is a need. I have been involved with two interregnums and could right now work every Sunday if I were so inclined. Before I was priested I could spend a whole day hunting for a priest to do the appropriate pieces in a communion service. My role has changed from being the hunter to the hunted. I rarely say no to church wardens searching for a priest because I know what a difficult job they have to fill up that rota of services.

Although I have strongly defended people's rights in Liverpool and Top Valley sometimes in quite a militant fashion, I have never campaigned for women's ministry. I never belonged to the Movement for the Ordination of Women. But I did take every opportunity that came up. Any opening for ministry I grasped with both hands and I was never afraid to go into a situation where male clergy were prejudiced against my gender. I just carried on with the job as if it were the most natural thing in the world, which it was to me.

And again I think of Miss Snow and St Michael's. Miss Snow said that the suffragettes had their place and certainly the position of women and the vote needed to be brought to everybody's attention. But what got them the vote in the end was what happened during the war. They did the jobs of the men who were in the Forces. It could be seen that they were not decorative beings sitting at home without any knowledge or understanding of the world outside. Their capabilities were shown in what they did. And so it has been with women's ministry. There have been those who have been upfront with organisations like M.O.W. There have been others who have got on very efficiently with the job, showing they can do it. I hope those reaping the benefits today of what some of us went through realise this. For me getting on with the job was what ministry was about. If in doing this I helped to make women's ministry credible for those in the future that is an added and very welcome bonus.

Hearing of the Synod Vote - 1992

As I was retired, I could give the full day to it. In the morning the debate was on the radio and in the afternoon on the television. I saw and heard every argument. And very good they were too. It was a very good debate. Not emotional. Well reasoned. All aspects covered. Theological, social, matters of truth and justice. Then the voting. As the results were announced and numbers for and against read out I was frantically trying to work out whether there was a two thirds majority and decided there was not when I heard the words: 'That is more than two thirds in favour and so the motion is carried.' I was stunned. The General Synod had agreed to the priesting of women. Why had I watched it on my own? There should have been a celebration. Why did I not record those brilliant speeches for posterity? The reason I was alone and not recording was because I never expected in a million years that it would go through. The person I should have naturally rung up was one of the people before me on the screen. There sat Eddie Neale. We had worked together in West Everton, Liverpool, then Bestwood, Nottingham. Eddie had managed somehow to get himself on to the General Synod and there was no doubt which way his vote would go.

And soon Eddie was the first person to ring me to say how pleased he was. I wonder what Dorothy Barter Snow would have thought? She had been the Principal at St Michael's when I did my training there. A woman ahead of her time in her thinking she probably would not have been surprised and she would certainly have been pleased. We were soon meeting with the Bishop. Another nostalgic thought. Patrick Harris was my diocesan Bishop but when I was a student at St Mike's he had been in his first curacy at St Ebbe's, Oxford. He had married a contemporary student, Valerie Pilbrow, and here we were over thirty years later sharing this amazing shift in the Church of England.

We already knew that women up to seventy years of age, even if retired, could be ordained if they were thought suitable. And so plans for interviews, retreats and services were put into motion.

I had been through the lot! In 1963 I was licensed to St Paul's, Carlton, Nottingham, as a 'lady worker'. By the time I moved to Barrow-in-Furness I was a 'Parish Worker'! In Top Valley, Bestwood, Nottingham, I was ordained deaconess and at Oakwood, Derby, ordained a deacon. Different names for basically the same job. A minister in the Church of England.

I knew that but nobody else did. When I worked at Barrow I was, for some time, the only woman minister in the Carlisle diocese and I appeared on no list so I was not invited to or involved in anything outside the parish. I had a one-woman crusade to get myself into the diocesan directory and the editor finally conceded, "I'll put you with the social workers." I told him for the umpteenth time I should be in my parish entry alongside the vicar and curate. I was not a social worker but a minister. "There's no such thing as a woman minister," he replied. We have come a long way since then. But I suppose it is not very surprising that I was one of very few from my college year who stuck parish work out until retirement. You had to have a very clear calling if you could get on with the job while a large part of the Church of England were unaware of your existence!

The reason ordination was important was that it gave us the wherewithal to do our job to the full. In my first parish I was looking after a mission hall on a council estate and the difference it would have made in building up the congregation if I could have led communion services and performed weddings would have been enormous. To build a fellowship and then take it to the parish church, twenty minutes away, for communion, which should have been our central service was not helpful.

In Liverpool I had the unofficial title of Team Vicar given by the Bishop because we were a team of ministers who were similar in both age and experience. But still I could prepare people for marriage and not do the service. In the absence of my male colleagues we could not have communion.

There had been painful divisions between clergy and 'lay'. When I went to meetings with my four fellow clergy from the Liverpool team we were split up straight away into house of clergy and the house of laity. They were together with fellow ministers and I was 'lay' with people in secular jobs. Was there any other profession in which qualified people were considered 'lay'? This was changed when women's ordination to the Diaconate came in in 1987. We were also allowed to take weddings which was a great help but communion was still the big hold up.

I was ordained deacon in Derby cathedral where, for my last paid ministry job, I had been instrumental in planting a church. Ordination not only meant receiving a title (Reverend) with which everyone in the land was familiar so nobody would have an excuse for confusing me with a social worker; it also gave my ministry recognition by the church at large. As we went into the vestry after the service to receive official documents, the Bishop (Cyril Bowles, since retired) said he and his legal advisers had looked thoroughly into what they could put on my licence. "I would like to make it 'priest-in-charge'," he said, "but the nearest I can get is 'deacon-in-charge' of the church on Oakwood." Seven years later he could have done: many of my friends are now Vicars or Rectors, Canons or Rural Deans: one, Judith Rose has even 'hit the ecclesiastical glass ceiling' and become an Archdeacon! Her story follows mine.

CHAPTER 13

Developments in Women's Ministry
Judith Rose

(Student of St Michael's 1964-66)

During the last thirty years there have been dramatic developments in the ministry of women in the Church of England. When I was a student at St Michael's House I was blissfully unaware of the changes that were likely to affect me in the years ahead. As I look back I realise now that my story runs parallel to many of the developments which have given much greater opportunities for women to use their God given gifts and experiences in the service of God and his church.

Unexpected discrimination
As a child I do not remember being treated in a special way because I was a girl. I suppose I learned to think of myself as a person who happened to be female. My chosen profession was farming, which is very largely a man's world, and women who enter it do so on the same terms as men, which always seemed quite reasonable to me. It was not until many years later that I was conscious of meeting discrimination because I was a woman. Sadly, I met that discrimination in the church when I found that my abilities and experience were an embarrassment to the church because I was a woman. I still think of myself primarily as a person who is grateful to God for being female. It amazes me even now, that in the eyes of some people in the church, my femininity is more important than my personality and the bundle of gifts and experiences that has made me the person that I am.

Insistent call
It was in the early 60s that, as a committed Christian, I began to want to serve God in some form of Christian ministry. Having an

127

agricultural background, I thought it would be exciting and useful to become an agricultural missionary. God had very different plans for me. At the time, I was working for the Ministry of Agriculture in Cornwall. I came to realise that God was saying 'no' to missionary work, but my attention was drawn to serving in the ministry of the Church of England. In those days, for women this meant becoming a parish worker. This did not sound a very exciting prospect for someone in her twenties. I had never actually met a parish worker, there weren't any in the Truro diocese in those days. I certainly did not want to become one of them, but the call was insistent and eventually I found myself accepted for training. As soon as I had responded to this call, which I believe came from God, I found my attitude changed and I began to look forward to the future. I have never regretted that decision.

Training for parish work

In the early 60s women were selected for training in a way similar to clergy, except that the selection conferences were for women only. The training likewise was similar although men and women trained separately. There were three colleges at which women were trained for parish work, namely Gilmour House in London, Dalton House in Bristol and St Michael's House. Although I was a committed Christian I did not know what sort of Christian I was! I didn't even realise that there were Anglo-Catholics and Evangelicals. I visited all three colleges. I thought that my leanings were probably in the Anglo-Catholic direction, so to correct any imbalance thought that I ought to go to an evangelical college. Having grown up near Bristol, I decided on Oxford. I suppose God worked through this rather pragmatic thought process. I arrived at St Michael's House with my trunk and bicycle for the Autumn Term of 1964. There were only three entrants that year for parish worker training. The other students were training to be missionaries or were teachers for a certificate in Religious Knowledge.

As I had two years for my training, I decided to get as much out of it as possible. As well as the parish worker qualification of an Inter-Diocesan Certificate, I also studied for a London University Diploma in Theology. I found it a great privilege to have two years in which to study the Bible. I became excited about Biblical theology, thanks to some superb lectures, especially those given by Peggy Knight on the Old Testament. As well as studying theology, we were given a training in pastoral ministry, which I believe was more thorough than the training given to clergy because it included pastoral placements. I remember preparing talks for women's meetings and Sunday school lessons, but cannot remember any sermon preparation, or even expecting that I would ever preach. Parish workers had a very limited liturgical role. I don't think we ever discussed the ordination of women. It was not an issue - at least not for me.

'Cardinal Wolsey'
In 1966, I became parish worker in a large parish in Swindon. The staff consisted of the vicar, two curates and myself. I visited endlessly on my bicycle, I prepared girls for confirmation and I supervised the Sunday School. I was given £10 per year to cover my expenses. I wore a maroon gown and cap when I helped with services and was nick-named "Cardinal Wolsey". My incumbent insisted that the staff were known by their surnames so I was Miss Rose, or "Rosie"! I had been there for more than a year when I was asked to speak at a family service. This I did only very occasionally at first, but my preaching career had started.

I spent five busy but happy years in that parish. The role of women in the church must have been a growing issue, but I was untouched by it. I boasted proudly to Canon Geoffrey Paul, who was later to be my Bishop at Bradford, that I would always be happy to take the role of an assistant. With greater wisdom or foresight he replied, "You wait, my girl, your views will change."

The joy of theological study
My quest for theology remained, and in 1971 I went to London Bible College to study for an external London Bachelor of Divinity degree. I did not know where it would lead but I enjoyed a further two years' study. It was while there that the issue of women's roles in the church began to impinge upon me. I knew I had been called into the ministry and had had five years parish experience. It was an arrogant eighteen-year-old who challenged my vocation. He said that God would not call a woman into leadership roles because this was forbidden in the Scripture. He acknowledged that God could have used me by saying, "God can use anything - he once used the jawbone of an ass." It was not very tactful, but at least it made me think. I, too, wanted to live by scriptural principles so concluded that the ordination of women must be wrong, and yet I was sure of my vocation. I thought this meant remaining an assistant to a man.

By the time I left London Bible College, I had laid a sound foundation for my future ministry. I had done five years in a good training parish, and had learned much about pastoral ministry. I had also acquired a working knowledge of theology. These two dimensions prepared me well for the next phase.

A developing ministry

In 1973, I was appointed as parish worker to St George's Church, Leeds. Again I joined a staff of three clergymen. I was now a graduate in theology and, as it happened, was better qualified theologically than any of my three colleagues. The congregation had been told this so had great expectations before I even arrived. I often wonder if I measured up to their initial expectations, especially as I am only five feet tall. I am sure that both stature and gender condition our initial assessment of people much more than we are aware. Paper qualifications are, of course, no guarantee that a Christian minister will be effective, and I, like any other, had to prove my worth as time went by.

I remained at St George's Church for a total of seven-and-a-half years. They were probably the most formative years of my ministry, as latent gifts began to develop. I was asked to preach about once a month which I enjoyed and found very stimulating, especially because the large congregation was so receptive and, at times, critical. The staff team was also stimulating and many principles were thrashed out together and policy decided. Over the years, various projects were worked through one at a time, for example, lay pastoral elders, all-age instruction for Sunday morning services, a telephone ministry and an evangelistic training programme.

It was a great thrill to be sent by the church to study some large and growing churches in America. What impressed me was the American Sunday School which catered for the whole church membership. As a result, I became involved in setting up something similar in the church in Leeds. Through that, I learned a great deal about the principles of adult education and developed my teaching skills with adults. I had the opportunity to try and enthuse others with my own love of biblical theology. One of the greatest rewards for me has been to see young Christians grow in their faith and in their ability to understand it, articulate it and put it into practice.

As part of the leadership team, I often found myself taking the chair at meetings, and doing so quite naturally. I began to realise that I had leadership gifts, and started thinking about appropriate styles of leadership for a church. It seemed to me that one of the important aspects of being a leader was first to seek God's vision for that church, which means a lot of knee work. Then to convey that vision to the church so that it catches the vision and owns it. Then to work with the church in seeking to fulfil that common vision. The challenge was to put the theory into practice.

The ordination of women debate

In 1975, the question of the ordination of women came before General Synod. In preparation for that the issue was debated at parish and deanery level. Being a woman in Christian ministry, I was asked for my views and the reasons for holding them. I began by saying that I was opposed to the ordination of women because I believed Scripture forbade women to hold authority over men. In seeking to defend my position, I was now compelled to think more deeply about it, to explore the Scriptures, and read what others had written. I came to realise it was not an issue that could be answered by a few proof texts. It touched significant doctrines such as creation, the Fall, the Incarnation, redemption and the gifts of the Spirit. I came to believe that to be true to the whole of Scripture, I had to change my views and support the ordination of women. This also made more sense of my own vocation and my growing awareness of the gifts of teaching and leadership that I was increasingly exercising.

It was about this time that I became a deaconess. In part, I did this for the benefit of those who did not not know what a parish worker was. To have an ecclesiastical title like 'deaconess' helped to define my role. I was also ready for my lifelong commitment to Christian ministry to be recognised. A parish worker only has the title as long as she is employed, but to be a deaconess was to enter an order of ministry for life. So in 1976 I became a deaconess. Looking back on it now, that is probably when I should have been made a deacon had that been possible. A deaconess is in orders but remains a lay person. I had continually to remind enquirers that a deaconess is not a female deacon, and is not in Holy Orders, (nor yet in "Unholy Orders"!)

General Synod - House of Laity

1975 was also the year when the General Synod elections were held and, much to my surprise, I was elected to the House of Laity representing Ripon diocese. My maiden speech in 1976 was about the diaconate. I was re-elected again in 1980. I learned a great deal through my membership of General Synod. The background material kept me abreast of the current issues, and I became more aware of the structures of the Church of England, as well as getting to know some of the notable figures in the church.

Around about 1980, I began to be aware of the need for senior posts for women in the church. By this time, I was also the diocesan lay ministry adviser, responsible for deaconesses and parish workers in the diocese, and for women enquiring about the ministry. I wrote a brief paper for the Diocesan Board of Ministry about the lack of openings for women with experience, but the issue was not taken seriously. I had also been appointed to the Vocation and Training Committee of the Church Pastoral Aid Society and under their auspices did some limited research on senior posts for women. The results were noted, but nothing was done. No one seemed to have any answers or to have the will to find answers. It was ten years later before the church began to address the issue, and then only after women were ordained to the diaconate. It seems that while women remained laity, the church did not really take them seriously.

This became a significant issue for me personally after I had been in the ministry about twelve years. I had enjoyed my work and had learned a great deal. I had thought carefully about how a church should be led and pastored to enable its members to develop their own ministry and outreach. I had served a long and useful apprenticeship and I was now ready to spread my wings, make my own decisions and take responsibility for my own success or failures. It was time to move on. The problem was finding a job that would use my gifts and experience. Had I been a man, I would have had the opportunity to become the vicar of a parish, but I was a woman and could not be ordained priest.

I was also concerned about my motives for wanting more responsibility. Was this selfishness and 'thinking of myself more highly than I ought to think'? Was I becoming ambitious in a way that was inappropriate for someone in Christian ministry? Christian ministry is by definition about service. This lay behind comments which were often heard in church circles in those days about "these ambitious women who are seeking status"! I noted that such comments were never heard when men curates were wanting to be vicars. For men it was the fulfilment of a vocation, but for women it was called ambition. In a Christian study group to which I belonged we decided that ambition was wrong if it meant self-preferment at the expense of others, but that it could be right if it were a matter of seeking to develop and use to the full God-given potential in a way that was helpful rather than harmful to others. As far as I could discern my own motives, that was what I wanted to do.

Time to move - but where?
And so the search for a new appointment began. I followed up numerous openings. Some resulted in interviews which took me to at least eight different dioceses. Some jobs would have offered me less scope than I already had. At other interviews I sensed that I had more experience and initiative than the vicar, and knew that that could lead to difficult relationships. Nothing seemed to open up for me. I began to think seriously that I would have to leave the ministry. I considered joining the Methodist Church who did allow women to become ministers, but it did not seem to be the right reason for changing denominations. This was quite a dark period for me; there seemed to be no way forward, and yet neither had God released me from my vocation.

Chaplain to Bradford Cathedral.
Eventually, I was invited to join the staff of Bradford Cathedral. Bradford is a parish church cathedral with a large regular eclectic congregation. The provost decided to appoint a chaplain to the cathedral, whose responsibility was to be "vicar" to the regular congregation. I understood that the plan was worked out in principle without the congregation being told that the post might be filled by a woman. I was the first woman minister to join the staff of the cathedral. I later heard of one member of the congregation who, when she heard of my appointment, had serious doubts about whether she would be able to receive communion from me. Three months later she wondered what she had been worried about. One of the greatest compliments that I received was from someone who, after she had experienced my ministry for about six months, told me that when I went to the pulpit to preach she could now forget that I was a woman, and just listen to what I had to say. I was delighted. The word of God had become more important than the messenger. I had responsibility for overseeing all aspects of the congregational life in the cathedral. This included home study groups, young people and children's work, fellowship, pastoral care

and outreach, together with a teaching and preaching ministry. I spent nearly five years at Bradford Cathedral. The job was demanding and stimulating, but cathedrals are not the easiest places in which to work. However, the same question presented itself to me. Where do I go from here?

Minister of a Church in Rochester Diocese

Again I applied for numerous jobs; again I thought about joining the Methodists, and actually walked to the nearby Methodist church and knocked on the minister's door. In the providence of God, he was out. In 1985, I moved to Rochester diocese to work on a large housing estate in the parish of South Gillingham. The parish had four congregations served by three full-time clergy. I became the minister responsible for St Paul's Church on Parkwood. This was the largest of the four areas of the parish (with a population of 10 - 12,000), but had no Anglican church building. The congregation had been in existence for about ten years, and at that time consisted of about twelve families who attended fairly regularly. My brief was to build up the church on the estate. The base of operation was two terraced houses. One was the minister's house and in the other was a chapel which seated about thirty people.

The parish was run as if it were a team ministry, although it did not have that legal status. The vicar was a good team leader and allowed me to develop my own ministry, which included responsibility for adult education across the whole parish, so I found myself in a new but stimulating situation. Soon after I arrived, I was asked by the bishop to be responsible for reader training in the diocese, alongside my work in the parish. This I did for two years; it was probably very important for me at the time as it gave me further responsibility and was demanding in a different way from the routine work of the parish. It also enabled me to learn about the diocese and to meet people throughout the whole area.

From Deaconess to Deacon

In 1987 the Church of England passed legislation permitting women to become deacons. This was a significant step because it meant that for the first time women could enter Holy Orders, and as such be entitled to be called "Reverend". Those of us who were deaconesses were invited to be ordained deacon. For many this was the cause of great rejoicing. Large celebrations were planned for the first ordinations of women to the diaconate. My own feelings were very different. I had seen myself, for many years, as not only a deacon, but as a full member of the clergy team. I knew that, technically, I was not a priest and respected the restrictions that were laid upon me. I worked within those limitations but, for the most part, what I did was the same as my clergy colleagues. The churches in which I had worked had for many years ceased to talk about "the clergy" but rather about the "church staff", of which I was one.

They treated me as if I were already ordained. The congregation at Parkwood, for which I was responsible, spoke of me as their vicar. Indeed, on one occasion, one member introduced me to her friends as "our priest". When I was asked in the ordination service if I felt called to be a deacon in the church of God, I wanted to reply, "Yes, I did ten years ago, but I've developed into a role more akin to that of a priest in the intervening years." For me, being made a deacon was not a great occasion. It was a very painful and humiliating event. It did not seem to mark a change for me personally. Rather I felt that it was the church that had changed, and was catching up with where I had been some years previously. I was ordained deacon in Rochester Cathedral in May 1987.

Being a deacon, rather than a deaconess, had one practical effect. Deacons are clergy in the Church of England, and are by virtue of this, registrars, and can conduct marriage services. As I was on the staff of a very large parish, I soon found myself taking weddings. Within three-and-a-half years, I had married nearly 100 couples.

Apart from weddings, the actual work that I did as a deacon was no different from what I had done as a deaconess. For that matter, it was not very different from what I had done as a parish worker. It was my experience over the years that had changed my role. I had, by now, had hands laid on me three times. I was commissioned as a parish worker, ten years later made a deaconess, and about ten years after that made a deacon, yet I was still not a "proper" vicar and still could not preside at the Communion Service, or be appointed as vicar of a parish. There were times when this was frustrating. It was certainly inconvenient, and most of the time seemed to me and to those among whom I worked to be sheer nonsense. I was, of course, very well aware of all the theological arguments and knew that this was more than just a pragmatic issue. The fact was that I had to live with the situation every day of my ministry. In practice, I found that the job was very demanding and offered tremendous opportunities. I was so grateful to be doing something that I enjoyed and found fulfilling.

Rural Dean - a 'first' for a woman

Although becoming deacons did not greatly affect the actual work that we did, it did have an enormous psychological effect on the church. This was much greater than I had expected. Once women were clergy, they had to be taken much more seriously, certainly by male clergy, which is a sad reflection on lay ministry.

Being a deacon had one very significant effect for me, in that it led to my being appointed Rural Dean of Gillingham. After consulting the incumbents of the deanery who proposed my name, the bishop was advised by his lawyers that it was legally possible for a deacon to be a rural dean. I was the first woman in the Church of England to hold that position, a post which I held for two-and-a-half years and I enjoyed the role very much indeed. It was to the credit of incumbents with whom I had worked that neither had any difficulty in accepting me as their rural dean. In deanery matters I had the main responsibility, and in parish matters the incumbent had responsibility. It may sound impossible in theory, but in practice it worked very well indeed.

General Synod - House of Clergy

In 1987 I was returned to General Synod by the Deacons of Canterbury Province, and in 1990 and in 1995 was elected to represent the clergy of Rochester diocese.

I worked for nearly five years on the Parkwood Estate. During this time the need for a church building became more evident and eventually, after much prayer and considerable negotiation by the diocese, a site in the centre of the estate was acquired and plans for a new church building put in hand.

Bishop's Chaplain

In 1990, Bishop Michael Turnbull, who was then Bishop of Rochester, appointed me as his personal residential chaplain. It was a big decision to leave parochial ministry, which I had enjoyed so much, but I knew from experience that posts of responsibility for women who were deacons were not readily available. As well as being the Bishop's Personal Chaplain I also became the Diocesan Deacon, Bishop's Press Officer and Associate Diocesan Director of Ordinands. I was part of the Bishop's senior staff and so present at his staff meetings.

Marriage - definitely a plus!

After less than a year in post as Bishop's Chaplain, I married my husband, David Gwyer, who was a widower with two teenage daughters. Only with David's support have I been able to cope with the further responsibilities that have come my way.

I served as Chaplain to the Bishop from 1990-95 during the years when the ordination of women to the priesthood was one of the most notable issues facing the church. I was on General Synod when the decisive vote was taken in 1992. I was then involved in diocesan plans for the first ordinations in Rochester Cathedral in May 1994. Much has been written about this elsewhere which I will not repeat. One of the things of which I began to be aware as time went on was that the inner anger and frustration disappeared.

After I been Bishop's Chaplain for over four years, I began to feel that I should move on. This was about the time when Bishop Michael Nazir-Ali became Bishop of Rochester, and was in part to allow the new Bishop to build his own team around him. Due to my age, I realised that I would probably have one more job before retirement. Now that I was eligible to become an incumbent, this was something David and I thought about very seriously.

Archdeacon - another 'first'

As I look back, I note that often I have been in positions which have been pushing against expectations or the legislation that determined the ministry of women in the Church of England. I was in effect a team vicar while still a deaconess and a rural dean when the lawyers disagreed about whether the office could be held by a deacon. So it was with my appointment as archdeacon. There was a proposal on the table to make a minor amendment to the qualification for an archdeacon, from being six years in priests orders, to that of a priest who had been six years in holy orders. This amendment made it possible to appoint as an archdeacon someone like me who had less than two years in priests orders. In September 1995 I was appointed as acting Archdeacon, and once the law had been changed commissioned as the Archdeacon of Tonbridge in February 1996. I was the first woman in the Church of England to be made an archdeacon. I count it a privilege to hold such a responsibility which I enjoy enormously. In this work I am able to use so much of the experience that I have gained in the past. I particularly enjoy pastoral care of the clergy and their families, my involvement in appointments, and helping to give vision and confidence to

parishes, clergy and lay leaders in their ministry and in the procla-
mation of the Gospel. As part of the senior staff team in the diocese
I am influential in the structures and policy-making, so that the
church is better able to fulfil its mission. As a senior ordained
woman often I am able to press for the continued development in
the ministry of women and their integration, so that the whole ministry of the church can be enriched and become more effective.

In Retrospect
As I look back over thirty years in the ministry of the church, I
realise how far the ministry of women has developed. For me they
have been exciting and fulfilling years, although not always easy. I
have been privileged to be active while many changes have taken
place, and have sometimes been in pioneer situations. Little did I
realise what lay ahead when in 1964 I entered the doors of St
Michael's House. I remain grateful for the foundations that were
laid there and for the way the Lord has led since those days.

CHAPTER 14

Over the Walls - into Education

The Education Act of 1944 required that Religious Instruction (Christian) should be given in all state schools, and Christian assemblies held. Christians rejoiced, but the ruling created a problem for many Head teachers. In primary schools particularly, relatively few teachers were either qualified or willing to teach the Bible. Teacher training for primary teachers lasted only two years, with little time for Religious Education, although it was given much more attention in the Church Colleges. To meet the need, the Ministry of Education set up Teachers' Supplementary Courses in 'Divinity' - generally of one year's length. Teachers were released from schools and given grants to study these courses at 'recognised' colleges. St Michael's obtained recognition and, until three year courses for teachers were introduced, about eighty women came to study for London or Cambridge qualifications in theology. They had to work very hard to achieve their goal in one year, but most succeeded. Wonderful doors of opportunity opened to them, to teach Scripture (later Religious Instruction / Religious Education / Humanities) in all types of school in this country - and even abroad.

A few women came straight from their two-year course at Training College. One such was **Jill Palfrey**, St Michael's Old Students Fellowship Secretary. She has taught R.E. for many years. She tells her story:

> I started at St Michael's in 1956, fresh from teacher training college.
>
> I joined the train at Paddington together with several other students, most of whom seemed to be parish workers in their green uniforms. Those uniforms filled me with horror. It was worse than school. The hats, the lace up shoes, and everyone seemed so much older than me!

When we arrived there was worse to come - lights out at 10.30 p.m! Even then it seemed incredible. But I was not a rebellious type and soon settled down to consider the good things about life at St Michael's.

I'd never lived (for more than two weeks at 'camp') in a Christian environment. It was great to be able to read the Bible, to pray, to discuss my faith with other Christians, to go to as many Christian activities as I liked, without anyone wondering if I was still sane!

I was taking the London Diploma in Theology in one year, so it meant hard work, but I enjoyed that. I often went to Pusey Library and worked there all day, with a short break for the OICCU (Oxford Inter-Collegiate Christian Union) daily prayer meeting in the middle. Then back to college for the evening meal.

My year at St Michael's went all too fast. I made many good friends both in college and in the University. I gained my Dip. Theol. and found a job teaching Scripture.

I went to Oxford quite critical of much in the Church of England. I enjoyed worship at St Ebbe's Church, but attending the Bishop Jewel Society meetings made me decide that, rather than criticise the Church of England from the outside, I'd throw in my lot, work in it and pray for it. I've remained in the C. of E. ever since and have served God in it as a Reader for the last 25 years.

Now when I think back to St Michael's so many images flash through my mind: the smell of Miss Snow's old dog (the one before Andy); going out to the Bible class at Cogges in 'Victoria' - a large old-fashioned car bought to transport some of Queen's College hockey team; punting on the Isis; hats for church; Miss Morris speaking in chapel one morning on the word "My times are in Thy hand". Those words have encouraged me many times since as I've married and had two sons; I've taught Scripture in several schools; worked in the church and spent hours on mundane jobs in the house and garden.

When I stopped teaching to have my first child in 1971 I took on the job of being Secretary to the Old St Michael's Students' Fellowship. It is now 1997 - and I'm still there! It's always thrilling to receive news from old students and hear what God is doing, through them, throughout the world. It's even better to meet them in person at Reunions (or some other quite unsuspected place!) and hear from them direct.

Now my boys are grown up, I'm back teaching Scripture again, half time, and hope to be able to continue for a few more years using the qualifications I gained at St Michael's.

From the schools, teachers wrote back to College with items of news and prayer requests. They reveal both the opportunities and the problems being faced:

- pray for the Scripture Union group and a newly formed Bible Study and prayer group among the Staff.

- teaching senior girls in a Secondary Modern School, thankful for experience and training - able to speak of the Master to the Head and Deputy Head.

- three girls at my school were converted through the Greater London Crusade - I have started a little Bible Study Group with them meeting once a week in the dinner hour.

The requests were urgent and honest:

- a tough Secondary Modern School in Manchester - my special needs are for wisdom and firmness in handling discipline problems. Pray for the children who just seem to tolerate an RI lesson.

- life in School gets no easier: correcting work is a nightmare; but on the other side the response of girls to the Christian Union is encouraging and the numbers who come from the Sixth Form alone, rejoice my heart - but Scripture gets the last place on the time table!

- It's a battle to influence girls against their home background.

- I have to cope with a difficult form this year.

- a difficult task in a new Comprehensive School! - my life is closely watched by non-Christian Staff.

- in a large Comprehensive School - many mixed races, living in crowded conditions, unusual problems have often to be faced at school.

- a Class of between thirty and forty, five year olds - many are West Indians or Cypriots.

The influence of these teachers was incalculable. Often they also put their talents and experience to use in their local Churches, running Sunday Schools, Youth Groups and Pathfinder Classes. They were sowing the seed of the Word in thousands of young hearts and minds. Only God knows what that accomplished in the years that lay ahead. Even in their own time, some were encouraged to see the beginning of a spiritual harvest:

- praise for great encouragement in the Christian Union - a crowd went to Camp and several found the Saviour there.

- teaching Scripture and Music - the Lord has blessed the Scripture Union - membership grown to over one hundred - blessed the Scripture lessons. I would not have believed it possible for there to be so much opportunity to speak of Christ as Saviour and Lord - what a joy it is to be a Scripture teacher!

- school work has been very encouraging. Many pupils are seeking the truth and peace which only Christ can give.

- I am beginning to find more opportunities for dealing with the questions that most teenagers have about the Christian faith.

- teaching is an increasing joy and the opportunities for evangelising are certainly unique.

- praise for the growth of the Christian Society - Some girls have been converted at school - some at Camps and others have found Christ through Tom Rees Rallies.

In due course, a number of the teachers had even greater influence as Heads and Deputy Heads in day schools or as House-mistresses in a Boarding School:

> - There are both joys and sorrows - a joy is that we have a weekly Scripture Meeting before bed-time called the 'Pyjama Club' - and I took a school party to Bavaria last year.

> - Assistant House-mistress - responsible for the pastoral care of girls in my house, and teaching R.E.

While most continued to teach in primary or secondary schools, a few went for varying lengths of time into college work - as lecturers or tutors. Several joined the staff of other Bible Colleges such as Mount Hermon, Ridgelands, Romsey House, Cranmer Hall, Crowther Hall and St Michael's itself. A few became lecturers at Teacher Training Colleges - teaching the future teachers - a fulfilling and important role.

The influence of St Michael's teachers spread abroad too. Some of those young women who had come to give domestic help in the College and to improve their English, were to become teachers in their own countries. They too have kept in touch through the prayer fellowship and sent in their requests for prayer. These came from Germany:

> - pray for my Scripture lessons.

> - I am teaching Scripture, Latin and English. Please pray for the older girls who do not seem interested in Scripture and for the 15 year old boys who are just as difficult as in England.

> - I am teaching theology at Bonn University to students who are to become Scripture Teachers.

"One generation will commend your works to another; they will tell of your mighty acts." So wrote the Psalmist, and that is what many St Michael's teachers went overseas to do - in schools, colleges and other educational establishments in many different countries. A list of these is printed in Appendix 5. It is impressive, but probably not exhaustive. It is included to show the amazing way in which many of these former students influenced Christian education throughout the world where doors were open.

Mary Cawthorne (Bogg) came to St Michael's for a one-year course in 1955. She gained the London CRK to enable her to be a 'Scripture Specialist' in a secondary school. At the time she also thought she would be a clergy wife but, traumatically, that relationship ended during the year, causing her considerable distress. God had other plans for her life, and looking back Mary wrote in the 1996 newsletter:

> - after leaving St Michael's I taught RE for thirteen years in secondary schools, then, served as deputy Head and Head of a school, while caring for my father, and my invalid mother, paralysed after a stroke. The Lord revolutionised my life and released me to marry Michael Cawthorne and serve with him in a Muslim village in the North West Frontier Province of Pakistan from 1971-91 - latterly with C.M.S.

The story of Michael and Mary's incredible life has been written by Helena Rogers in her book 'Reaching for the Crescent Moon' (or 'Adventuring with God in Pakistan'), published in 1995. [See Appendix 4].

Mary could not have known what was ahead of her, when in 1969 Michael, a science teacher whom she had appointed to her staff, asked her to marry him. They had already worked together closely, both professionally and as Christians, having a concern for the conversion of their pupils. But Michael had made it clear that he thought marriage was not God's will for him. Mary, however, prayed a lot about their relationship and it was not altogether a surprise when, at 4.30 a.m. one morning, she heard Michael proposing to her over the telephone. He spoke excitedly:

> "Mary, it's me. I believe the Lord wants me to marry you, how do you feel about that?"

All Mary could say was:

> " It's ... it's wonderful."

This somewhat unusual proposal was but the introduction to a way of life hitherto unknown to a Head Mistress of a Kent school. Within two years Mary and Mike and their first child Ruth were on their way to Pakistan, travelling overland in an old Saab with

The Library at 119 Banbury Road.

Missionary Outreach.

The Chapel of St. Michael and All Angels. (Dedicated 3rd February 1956.)

Opening of New Wing – 117 Banbury Road. (6th May 1967.)

Architect's plan for extension of 117 Banbury Road.

The Principals at Filey.

"The Girls in Green" with Miss Snow.

camping equipment and a supply of Scriptures and Christian literature in other languages. It was a miracle (the first of many) that
they reached Peshawar safely. But to them it was proof of the faithfulness of God - such as He had shown Abraham and Sarah when
they had set out for an unknown country in obedience to Him.

For twelve years, Mike and Mary lived by faith independent of
any Mission. They brought up their two daughters, often faced
danger, illness and hunger, and because they believed their call was
to serve the Pathan people, they chose to live alongside them in a
tribal village. Conditions were primitive. The small mud-brick
house had no electricity, gas or running water. Outside their door
were stinking open sewers. And Mary had to observe Purdah,
spending much time in seclusion. Even when outside the home she
must behave as a good Muslim woman, always walking behind
Mike, only speaking when she was spoken to, and wearing modest
Pakistani dress. Such restrictions she gladly accepted for the Lord's
sake. Michael mastered Pushtu, the local language, and Mary
Urdu.

At the same time, both became 'tent-makers' taking every opportunity of using their teaching experience and skills. Their input into
education was really remarkable.

For several years they were both able to teach English to the
boys at the University Public School. When in due course the
authorities decided to open a junior and kindergarten department,
it was Mary who was asked to supervise it and help train the young
Pakistani lady teachers in English Teaching Methods.

Another door opened when a general in charge of the large army
training centre at Kohat - about two and a half hours' journey over
the mountains from Peshawar, was minded to set up a nursery for
children of his personnel. Hearing of Mary's expertise he commanded the Principal of the Public School to release Mary for two
days a week for a term, to instruct the Army wives on how to teach
little ones. The Principal had to comply, so on Tuesdays and
Thursdays Mary was escorted to and from Kohat, having to start
at crack of dawn. She enjoyed her time there very much and at the
end of the term was presented with a fine silver plate as a mark of
appreciation.

In the remaining years Mary and Mike continued in different
educational spheres. Mary was asked to set up and be Principal of
a new Public School for children of police officers; she was made
an honorary member of the police force with the exalted rank of

Superintendent. She held that position until they went home for a long leave in 1986. On their return her work changed again. Now a CMS partner she found herself overseeing five schools for poor Christians, which were financed and run by a Finnish Mission. She also helped occasionally at the prestigious Edwardes High School (Michael was then Head Master of the English-speaking section) and Elizabeth High School. Some time earlier, this Mission and the Dutch Reformed Church had started a much needed Christian Training College in Lahore. Inevitably Mary and a very well qualified friend Mrs Talal-Peters were asked to run some training courses for the students. They grasped this opportunity with enthusiasm knowing that most of the teaching methods at the time were antiquated - learning by heart, rather than understanding, was very common. They were able to introduce teachers to better methods, through refresher courses and supervision of teaching practice.

From 1991, Mary needed to remain in England for the sake of her father and her two daughters (her mother had died in 1978). Mike continued to head up the Razmak Cadet College until December 1997 when he returned to England. Now both have 'retired' to England but continue to serve the Lord as and where He leads. They look back with thankfulness to the way they saw God at work during those years and they rejoice in the knowledge that there is now an indigenous church in that village where they lived - nothing short of a miracle.

Wyn Cornish was one of the first teacher students who began the course in 1949. She too was called to teach overseas. Now in retirement, in Oxford, she has reflected on what happened to her after leaving St Michael's:

> For about five years I continued teaching in the UK, but was now able to specialise in RE teaching alongside English and history. Then God confirmed what I believe was His call to teach overseas, and in 1956 I went out to the then Northern Rhodesia with the Methodist Missionary Society, to teach in the country's leading school for African girls. Seven years later I was moved to the Southern Province to open a new secondary boarding school for girls; this was just before independence and amalgamation with the United Church of Zambia. WHAT a privilege it was to be out there at such an exciting and formative time in the nation's history. Those fif-

teen and a half years in Zambia have, I think, been the most rewarding and enriching of my life.

Wyn has stressed what those years abroad meant to her - but - in 1997, an event took place in Zambia which revealed what an enduring impression she and other Christian teachers made on the many schoolgirls who passed through their schools. She wrote about it in these words:

Last May (1997) a friend and former colleague and I spent nearly a month in Zambia. It was twenty-five years since I had left the country and of course there were many changes - regress rather than progress - sad to see. The country has endless problems, not least AIDS and water shortage. There is a desperate poverty and debts to the World Bank and IMF had led to the near collapse of free education and health care and much of the infrastructure.

But what a welcome lay in store for the two of us! Sixty-six old pupils from my two schools (and my friend's one school) were at the airport with bouquets of red roses - now a useful export from Zambia, and after being whisked into a VIP lounge by smiling airport officials we found it was to be VIP treatment all the way. After a TV interview on our first full day we found we had become TV stars. Even the curio sellers at Victoria Falls recognised us. So for almost four weeks we sampled the delights - and difficulties - of being on the receiving end. Former pupils, now mothers and many of them grandmothers, entertained us and planned our programmes. Many of them, and their husbands, hold top posts, but how glad we were to find a fair number heavily involved in voluntary social and caring activities.

We returned home utterly exhausted for every moment of our stay had been planned and by ever so many people - especially old girls (probably about two hundred) and church leaders, and not just once but many times.

Teaching in another country, culture, climate and language brought its own peculiar difficulties. Sometimes teachers had to live through dangerous political situations. They created emergencies for teachers and pupils. Often conditions of work proved less than satisfactory too. A selection of news items illustrates some of these circumstances well:

- pray about difficulties in adjusting to school, learning a new language, and teaching Punjabi girls from a Muslim background.

- I'm teaching Science in Hindi - a language I can only just read!

- training teachers - pray that those being trained may be spiritually alive and prove faithful. (Ethiopia)

- the children speak many languages and come from many different backgrounds. (Jerusalem)

... school has grown - we have doubled our numbers in two years. Need for greater spiritual impact amongst children and staff. (Chile)

- dreadful aftermath of civil war - did not start school again until November - constant battles - shooting and unrest for 6 months - have worked extra months and few holidays to make up for lost time. Praise the Lord that not one of our pupils or staff was injured or killed.

- the members of Staff living at the College during the emergency were drawn together in closer fellowship - evening devotions in the dim light of our imperfectly blacked-out room - using torches to see our hymn books. (Pakistan)

- pray for strength and patience in hot summer months - for wisdom in planning classes and schemes of work - that the Holy Spirit may do a mighty work. (S. America)

- pray much - the Christian background of most of the girls is negligible - after school days unless they are converted many will have no other contact with the Church - I superintend a Sunday School for two hundred and fifty refugee boys and girls on the roof of a seven-storey building. (Hong Kong)

- learning Persian, pray for the girls - one hundred and twenty of them as they hear the Word of God. (Teheran)

- it's not a beautiful, nor a friendly city, but it is a needy place - teaching in a newly started school. (Paraguay)

- pray these fine young people may be challenged by the present (political) situation to lives of dedication and service and a seeking after truth and righteousness. (Africa)

- at Gindiri - a good way of learning the language is having to give instructions in Hausa as to how to build a pig-sty! (Nigeria)

- social and political upheavals unsettle the girls, but many faced up to their fears and yielded to God. (Africa)

- many old girls of the school hold positions of professional responsibility in addition to being wives and mothers. Pray the school prayer for them "that we may be Christian not in name only but in deed and in truth." (Nigeria)

Often these overseas teachers faced another kind of emergency. Relatives at home, usually parents, became old or ill and in need of care. They had to give up their work to respond to this need and come home, often because of their single status, to care for their relatives. But their dedication to their calling was such that when the emergency was over they were back picking up the threads of the work again wherever possible.

One of the earliest prospectuses of St Michael's informs its readers:

There is at the present time a demand for Christian women with a personal knowledge of Jesus Christ and with a teaching vocation to undertake some of the work of Christian education both in this country and overseas. Divinity mistresses are needed in schools and there are also diocesan and other branches of Christian education open to women who are called of God to undertake such work.

James points out that to be a teacher is a solemn responsibility ("We who teach will be judged more severely" 3:1). A Christian teacher is well aware of this which is what makes the job more demanding than ever. Dependence on the Holy Spirit to equip and enable - something constantly stressed in the college - was vital. This is the testimony of many of the ex-students who were/are in the profession.

The need for Christian teachers today is greater than ever, both in this country and in colleges and universities all over the world. So this chapter draws to a close with a quotation from Miss Snow's 'In Memoriam' for **Anne Morgan** in the 1966 newsletter. Anne was the first former student and teacher to die while on active service:

> Anne Morgan was one of the earliest students. She came to see me soon after the College re-opened in 1948. Her heart was set on Africa, in which country God called her to work and teach at Arua, Uganda. We at St Michael's followed Anne's career with much prayerful interest - her school difficulties - the shortage of staff - the joys and sorrows of the work.
>
> During her last furlough, Anne came to St Michael's and told us something of her work and the need for more teachers. Now at the comparatively early age of forty-eight, Anne has been called to leave her work. Where are the teachers for whom she pleaded in her life time? His work remains to be done. Anne obeyed the call. "Who follows in her train?"

One of Anne's colleagues wrote about her funeral in Arua. A brief quotation is a fitting description of Anne's influence during the fifteen years she served in Uganda:

> Colleagues, black and white, carried Anne's body to the Church. The simple service was led by the African Pastors, one the Archdeacon, the other the Rural Dean. The Lesson was first read by the Mission Doctor, then in Lugbara, by one of her "boys" now a Headmaster. Anne had always prayed constantly for those she taught to read the Bible.
>
> More than five hundred gathered to pay tribute to her memory.
>
> A dear African brother, now a high Official in the West Nile administration, gave an inspiring message on the

"Resurrection victory of Jesus" (I Corinthians 15: 51-58) in (as he said) "the English which Miss Morgan taught me."

It is surely to the glory of God that so many women underwent their theological training for teaching of one kind or another at St Michael's. But even more important than the theological qualifications they gained, was that they left with an awareness that they were Christ's servants. Wherever they were they would have the opportunity of being His witnesses to their colleagues, to parents, to others in the community, or country in which they were to work.

CHAPTER 15

Into the World - South America

During the twenty years in Oxford, more than one hundred and forty former students left this country to serve Christ abroad. They went to more than twenty countries; they learned between them at least twenty-five new languages; they served in more than thirty different Christian societies or organisations; some went independently of any. Many remained single, others married and brought up families abroad.

To write about each one would fill many books, so here we can only recount the stories of what happened to a small representative number. We regret that so many have to be left out and we trust readers will understand. Fortunately, some have written books themselves, in which they describe experiences, truthfully and humbly, in difficult even dangerous situations, when faith was severely tested and they saw little fruit for their labours. But they testify to the faithfulness and grace of God which kept them faithful to their calling.

- to South America
Probably more former students went to South America with SAMS (South American Mission Society) than to any other single country, except India, with BMMF (Interserve). The first to go to South America were **Jocelyn Padbury** and **Dorothea Wedgwood** (Clarke). They arrived in **Paraguay** early in 1958, soon to be followed by **Kathleen Clark** (the Revd K. Lefroy) in December of that year, bound for **Chile**.

'Thea', a nurse, expected her missionary career to be in medicine, as it was to begin with. At Makthlawaiya, a remote spot in Chaco, she ran a small dispensary and with Jocelyn started a school, and a Sunday School for Paraguayan and Indian children. The school grew and by 1960 there were thirty one enrolled, including eleven boarders and five language groups. With some practical help, Thea (it is recorded in a newsletter) was able to be released from cooking and mending, to share in the teaching.

So she was launched into education, and within a couple of years, now based in Asuncion, was led to start a kindergarten school, which, she could not have foreseen, would have a great future. Indeed 'large doors open on small hinges.' Thea tells what happened:

> There was to be a Billy Graham Crusade and we set out to visit homes, twice before and twice after the Crusade. People were not at that time allowed to read the Bible for themselves. As we visited, we found more and more parents asking for their children to be taught English. They were rather hoping for an 'Eton' or 'Harrow' in Paraguay! So I began, with just six little children, aged four years, in the vestry behind the church. Year by year a fresh grade was added both up and down - and a teacher of Spanish joined the Staff.

In another SAMS centre, Concepcion, Jocelyn Padbury and Glenys Williams (also ex-St Michael's, who reached Paraguay in 1961) had founded a small school which flourished like St Andrews. But one of their prayer requests in the early days was for the parents who removed their children when they began to show interest in their Scripture lessons.

After a few years, Jocelyn and Glenys joined Thea in Asuncion, and together for seven years they developed the school and it gained recognition by the Paraguayan Ministry of Education. The Official Inauguration of the St Andrew's Kindergarten took place in 1967.

Their prayer booklet sent out during this time reveals what a remarkable vision they had. We quote from it:

> - Christian education is the introduction of the child to the Living Christ

> - introduction of the child to the Living Christ is most surely effected when dedicated Christian teachers encourage him/her to develop to the full his mental, physical and spiritual powers.

> - parents, teachers and ministers work together for the phys-ical, intellectual and spiritual well-being and development of

the child. Each has his contribution to make in understanding the child and helping him/her on the path to developing an integrated personality.

The school was bi-lingual, forty-five per cent English and fifty-five per cent Spanish speaking. The motto chosen by them was:

Ex amore sapientia
(out of love comes wisdom)

The meaning for a Christian school is clear - it remains the motto of St Andrew's today.

From that beginning, St Andrew's College, Asuncion, did indeed become the 'Eton' of Paraguay. Today, it is a leading Christian educational institution, with its students going to University, and most recently taking the examinations of the International Baccalaureate Diploma. Out of it too is evolving a Christian Education Faculty for the training of Teachers. The school has benefited greatly from the dedicated leadership of Miss Eileen Murphy, Head Mistress for some twelve years.

In 1988, excellent new buildings were opened and Thea had the joy of being present to celebrate the twenty-fifth Anniversary of the founding of the School.

Thea retired from Paraguay in 1974 but not to a life of ease. The Lord gave her 'something to do' in many different countries. She took Bibles to Hungary, Yugoslavia and Egypt, and made other 'useful' trips to Egypt, to Nepal, Kashmir and Australia. She says:

Listening to God, and doing what He tells you to do, is the most important thing, although it may be surprising.

In November 1987, Thea married Dr Rupert Clarke, a retired surgeon who had served with OMF for forty-eight years in China, Indonesia and South Thailand. They enjoyed four and a half happy years, until Rupert's 'Home-call' in 1992. At that time, not wavering in her faith, Thea wrote:

Life is full of 'ifs' but it doesn't worry me. My heavenly Father has the way ahead planned and he'll reveal each step as I need to know.

The **Revd Kathleen Lefroy (Clark)** arrived in Chile in 1958. Temuco was then the centre of the SAMS Chilean work and soon she was hard at it, learning Spanish, house-keeping at the Mission House and even learning to play the accordion. Not long after this she was appointed to the staff of Quepe Bible Institute where most of the students were men, not used to study. She gained much joy in seeing the face of a student light up as some new truth from God's Word went home to his heart. She wrote:

> We praise the Lord for His hand upon the 1960 session. Four students completed the three-year course and are now out in service in different places.

This teaching was Kathleen's work for six months of the year. The other half she was out, helping with Bible Teaching in country churches, and teaching at camps and conferences.

Kathleen was also one of the writing team, in South America together with Elizabeth Richards which developed a course of programmed Bible Study known as SEAN. The initials stand for Seminary by Extension to All Nations. The studies are now produced in more than ninety languages, and one hundred and thirty countries. Kathleen is still Chair of the International Board of Trustees.

Her prayer request was:

> Please cry unto the Lord, that the Gospel we deliver may not be in word only but in power and in the Holy Spirit and in much assurance.

After twenty years in Chile, Kathleen returned to England and served on the home staff of SAMS as Personnel Secretary. At the same time she cared for her elderly parents. There were other changes ahead of her. After she was ordained into the Church of England she married the Revd John Lefroy, who was the widowed husband of former student Sally Blacking. Kathleen and John shared a fruitful ministry at Holy Trinity Church, Eastbourne, until John's death in 1998. Kathleen continues in a pastoral and teaching role, and in her involvement with SAMS (she is Vice-President). From time to time she has been able to return to South America. After one visit she had this to say:

> I had the immense joy and privilege of returning for two months to South America, and seeing many dear brothers and

sisters in Chile, as well as Peru, Bolivia, Paraguay and Brazil - some old St Mike's among them!

Another who served in a different way in South America was **Felicity Bentley-Taylor (Houghton)**, part of whose story is told in an earlier chapter. Having been born to missionary parents in north China, Felicity was nine when her whole family was taken into an internment camp under Japanese control for the remainder of the war. At that time she says;

> I asked my father what regions of the world were unevange-lised. The only part of his reply that stuck in my mind was his mention of South America. From that time on I grew up with the thought: "When I'm the right age, I'm going to be a mis-sionary in South America."

Later on Felicity had to consider whether that childhood desire laid any obligation on her as an adult, or could be laid aside and forgotten. On her 24th birthday, when Felicity was in her second year of teaching, her mother wrote a Bible reference on a card: Proverbs 4:25,26. The words "Let thine eyes look right on, and let thine eyelids look straight before thee", took on a specific meaning for her:

> I knew then that I was not free to choose another path than the one that had already been shown me. To go back on that was not to go back on a dream of mine, but on a call from God.

The next step for Felicity was to leave her teaching post and find a place where she could be trained for becoming a missionary. She entered St Michael's House in the autumn of 1958 on a two-year course. Before she returned for her second term, a generous friend paid for her to attend a conference of the South American Mission Society. This led to further contact with the Society and to her acceptance as a candidate. In September 1960, Felicity embarked in Liverpool on a ship bound for Valparaiso, Chile.

Her first term of service was difficult and yet useful. Gradually God steered her into what was to be her life's work: laying the foundations and then building up a student movement which in the course of time became affiliated to the International Fellowship of Evangelical Students.

Felicity left a healthy and vigorous movement with its own leadership in Chile in 1981, and the following year moved to Bolivia. There she and two colleagues were the pioneers whose vision, labours and prayers brought into being the Bolivian student movement, sister to the one in Chile, and also affiliated to the IFES.

In 1994, Felicity was preparing to retire. As the year advanced, she discovered that God had prepared a husband and a home in England for her. She married David Bentley-Taylor six weeks after her return from Bolivia. David had first seen her in China, and in the course of a varied missionary career had worked for eight fruitful years with the IFES. Now David and Felicity serve the Lord together in Herefordshire.

Of those who went overseas three are known to have died on 'active service'. **Anne Morgan's** life and death in Uganda have already been described in Chapter 14 and we tell of **Muriel Gideon**, Head Mistress of Queen Elizabeth High School, Peshawar in the next chapter. The third was **Fiona Ross** whose death in 1978, in South America was the saddest and most shocking, humanly speaking. She was at Buenos Aires Airport to meet a missionary arriving from Australia. A fast moving car hit her as she was crossing the road, knocking her unconscious. She died in hospital a few hours later.

Fiona had been at St Michael's from 1964-1966, in both Miss Snow's and Miss Cooke's time. Staff and students remembered her lovely personality, her care of them as College nurse, and her complete certainty of her missionary call. A SAMS candidate, she sailed for South America in February 1967, and she was soon to become involved in the training of Indian nurses in the Argentine Chaco. For the 1977 St Michael's newsletter she had written about her work:

> May 1st last year ('76) I have been seconded by SAMS to Nurses Christian Fellowship International. TEAR Fund is supporting NCFI in its Vocational Outreach here in Argentina. I was home on furlough last year and was greatly privileged to see Miss Snow at one of the Reunions. Little did I know that I would not see her again. I received news of her having gone to be with her Lord and Master quite sometime afterwards. However, I would like to add a word of tribute to that great lady. She was an inspiration to all who knew her and even today as I have just received the October 76

Newsletter and read her letter she has inspired and encouraged me to "continue putting myself at the disposal of our Lord and Saviour." When I remember Miss Snow and her life I am encouraged to believe God's Victory in and Control of our lives. Miss Snow was a living testimony to that truth. May her life continue to be an inspiration to all of us as we struggle in a world which is ruled by the Prince of Darkness and who never lets up in trying to pull us into that darkness, but praise God Jesus tells us "I am the Light of the World" John 9:5.

In one of Tear Fund's magazines, it was written of Fiona:

Tear Fund's sponsorship of Fiona began seven years ago during her work among the Indians in the Argentinian Chaco with the South American Missionary Society. In 1976, Fiona moved to join the Nurses Christian Fellowship based in Buenos Aires. Her aim was to promote interest among the Argentinians in nursing as a career. Her work involved travelling to schools, churches and colleges to organise vocational training programmes on nursing.

Fiona's motivation stemmed from her belief that "the future of any medical work such as is being done in the Chaco depends on national staff but unless young people seeking a profession and those already in the profession are motivated by a Christ given vision, there is little hope for the continuation of medical programmes using expatriate missionary teams."

And in the SAMS magazine, this tribute to which all who knew her would have assented:

Perhaps two qualities in her life stand out. First her generosity. Fiona was always giving whether it was care and compassion to a sick Indian lying in poverty, time to a lonely Argentinian nurse, or fellow missionary, who needed encouragement and someone to turn to, or hospitality to anyone who needed it. Furthermore a significant number of children are going to miss one of their favourite 'aunts'. Second, her joy. Fiona was full of fun and laughter. She has now entered the joy of her Lord forever.

We extend our deepest sympathy to her parents and family and thank God for the privilege of knowing and loving Fiona and working with her for the extension of His Kingdom in South America.

Her great friends, the Cremers who sent out her prayer-letter added this:

There will surely be many who will rejoice in glory, one day, because of her life of service.

And her parents wrote:

The days don't lessen the pain for us here. Her final home-coming from Argentina will remain in all our hearts 'til we ourselves join her. We can only try to meet each day as Fiona would wish.

To us she was so precious and never gave us a moment's worry as she knew from a very early age that her life's work was to be for her Lord and Master.

The Falklands crisis in 1983 brought a big change in the lives of **Lynn (Fletcher)** and **(the Revd) Charles Barr-Johnston**, who were missionaries in Northern Argentina. Lynn, a nurse had been doing medical work amongst the Chaco Indians since 1966. It fell to her in 1969 to nurse Charles, when he was in hospital suffering from pneumonia. Their friendship developed, and they were married in Juarez, South America in 1970.

Throughout the seventies they were based first at Juarez then Formosa, having the pastoral oversight of the two congregations two hundred and ninety miles apart. Their children, Nicholas and Susan attended the local Spanish School, but Lynn taught them English subjects at home. As life became unsafe in Argentina, the Executive Council of SAMS asked them to move to Asuncion in Paraguay and here they settled permanently, they thought. The children went to an American Christian School and Charles and Lynn still bent on Mission began church planting. Lynn wrote in 1986:

Praise God for nine people recently confirmed: land has been bought and there are plans to build a Church.

It was at this time that Charles developed a voice problem that was to trouble him for a number of years, but his evangelistic teaching and training work did not lessen. Nor did they spare themselves on their deputation visits to churches. Also, from Paraguay, Charles continued with his pastoral oversight of the pastors in North Argentina.

In 1987, they saw the fruits of their labours in the dedication of a new church in Villa Guarini, a suburb of Asuncion. On April 17th that year the Revd John Ellison, the new Bishop of Paraguay, was consecrated in the Church.

They continued to work in Paraguay in the eighties building up the believers and encouraging them in evangelistic outreach. As they grew up, Nicholas and Susan had to leave home and pursue their higher education in this country living in Leamington in the home of Charles' father. That this was such a success, enabling them both to go on to University, Nicholas to Cambridge and Susan to Durham, is a great tribute to Charles and Lynn's parenting.

This is not the end of the story. 1993 saw Lynn and Charles back in Argentina, once more in Juarez, working especially on an evangelistic course of a SEAN type. Lynn wrote from Formosa:

Pray for those who profess conversion that they may go on to read their Bibles and see the importance of worship. Pray for the training of pastors and ministers.

Charles and Lynn have a great testimony to God's enabling grace. Over so many years, through trials of illness and bereavement, they have been privileged to see a harvest of souls, churches planted and pastors trained. And they have trusted God for their children in the long periods of separation, seeing them now happy in their chosen professions, Nicholas an Accountant, Susan a Biology Teacher.

For the first time, they are requesting prayer for:

- the young people in the Church now leaving home to go to University (a thing unthought of by their parents).

Of this couple, the words of Mark 16:20 seem completely true:

"Then the disciples went out and preached everywhere, and the Lord worked with them"

Friendships begun in Oxford could have long consequences. For **Valerie Pilbrow**, a parish worker student it led to marriage to the **Revd Patrick Harris**, curate at St Ebbe's when Valerie was at St Michael's in 1962. Valerie left College for the parish of Morden, with her heart on overseas mission. She applied to SAMS, was accepted and by 1966 was in Asuncion, Paraguay, learning Spanish and bound for Argentina. There was much rejoicing amongst her friends when in November 1967 her engagement to Pat Harris was announced, he being now in South America too. Their wedding took place at Algarrobal in the Argentine Chaco in July 1968.

Only a few years later, in 1973, Pat was appointed Bishop of the new diocese of Northern Argentina. In the years that followed Valerie was kept very busy as Pat's supportive wife and the mother of their three children. They were a family united in the desire that in their open home Jesus would be glorified. All were happy and engaged in the many Christian activities in the church and diocese.

But a new ministry in this country was ahead. It was not without some sadness, yet with the certainty of God's leading that, in 1980, they returned to England, to the parish of Kirkheaton nr Huddersfield. It was the best move for the family, especially for their son, David. Their interest in world mission was as strong as ever, both were utterly devoted to evangelism. It was not long before Pat received a joint invitation from the General Synod and the Anglican Missionary Societies, to become Secretary for Partnership for World Mission. He accepted this opportunity to bring the vision of world mission more to the centre of the church. They moved to Reading where they had a supportive role in Greyfriars Church and the children had good opportunities to further their education.

This settled period was to last only two and a half years. The 'pillar of cloud' moved again. Patrick was to have an even greater opportunity of exercising his evangelistic and pastoral gifts. In 1988, he was appointed Bishop of Southwell, the very large diocese only created in 1884 and comprising the county of Notts and a little bit of South Yorks.

Based in Southwell with two of their grown up children settled, Valerie and Pat have exercised a wonderful ministry for more than ten years. David, their twenty-seven year old son, who has some learning difficulties still lives at home. In Valerie's words:

> We work with so many fine people, lay and ordained. Work and pressures are plentiful.

In 1998, Pat was diagnosed with a bone marrow complication. Nearing his sixty-fifth birthday, he gave notice of his retirement for April 1999,

His wife Valerie (in the public gallery) attended their last General Synod, and heard the warm tribute to them, spoken by Archbishop George Carey. He recalled that Patrick, although only ten years at Southwell, had been in Episcopal orders longer than any other member of the House of Bishops. Referring to Pat's love of cricket, he said that such a long innings was entirely appropriate. He spoke too of the large part Valerie had played in Pat's ministry, first in South America and then in this country. One of the things that had endeared Pat to his 'flock' in Southwell was also his love of football and his support for Notts Forest:

On a recent Good Friday, Pat stood in Nottingham's Old Market Square during an open-air ecumenical service and preached, not in his cope and mitre but in his Forest scarf ... he spoke about Jesus, our substitute on the Cross.

In June 1998, a Service was held in Southwell Cathedral for the Harrises to celebrate, with family and friends, twenty-five years as Bishop. It was a truly joyful occasion and appropriate that Bishop Bill Flagg who ordained Pat in Argentina, should be asked to preach. He spoke of Pat and Valerie's commitment, of their compassion and concern for people that had characterised all their ministry. He said:

> In Argentina the indigenous people had named their Bishop as the one who comes and sits down beside us and makes us feel good.

As President of SAMS, and well known throughout the Christian world, Patrick and Valerie will continue to have the prayers of many, many people, and not least the St Michael's family, as they enter retirement. We do indeed praise God for their long and fruitful ministry.

"Two are better than one, because they have a good return for their work." Ecclesiastes 4:9.

There could be no better illustration of this truth than the inspiring story of two former students, **Ruth McLeod** and **Valerie Mitchell**, who first met in Brazil, and became partners in translation.

As a student, Ruth witnessed the removal of St Michael's from the old site at 1, Fyfield Road to 119, Banbury Road. In her editorial of the 1953 newsletter, she made reference to this welcome event and then wrote:

> None of us knows what the future holds, but looking back upon the year we can re-echo the words of Joshua "The Lord has done great things for us whereof we are glad" and can say with assurance as we look towards the future "He is able to do exceeding abundantly above all that we ask or think."

Little did Ruth know that forty years later, in Brazil in 1993, she would witness the dedication of the Half New Testament in the Xavante language, in which she and Valerie and others had been involved.

After leaving St Michael's, Ruth's preparation for work with Wycliffe Bible Translators involved a preliminary course in linguistics, and a year at the London School of Oriental and African Studies. She finally left for the mission field in 1957, arriving in Brazil the following year after three months at the Wycliffe Jungle Training Camp in Mexico, and more linguistics in the USA.

At about this time, Valerie Mitchell was studying at St Michael's. As Ruth's name came up on the Chapel prayer rota, she heard about Wycliffe Bible Translators for the first time. Hearing more about the mission and its work, she felt God wanted her to be involved in Bible translation. A year later she applied to the Society and was accepted. She left England in February 1960 for Jungle Camp, followed by a second linguistics course in the USA, and arrived in Brazil in November. She wrote about Jungle Camp where Wycliffe recruits received training to prepare them for working in isolated or jungle areas, building rustic houses, manoeuvring wobbly canoes, swimming, hiking, receiving a basic medical course, cooking on a mud stove:

Our survival hike gave us the opportunity of putting our newly gained knowledge to the test. The survival hike lasted for more than a day, so individually and without any help we had to erect a shelter which would serve as protection both from weather and from animals. In these we each spent the night alone. The final expedition (of the whole training course) involved sailing down the river on balsa rafts which we had made together in groups. This journey took us to a little air-strip where we camped for a few days before being flown out to civilisation again.

Some of us might not have survived such a test. But both Ruth and Valerie did. Ruth, having been to Jungle Camp two years earlier, was by now working in the State of Mato Grosso, among the Xavante Indians, only recently pacified by the Indian Protection Service. She and her fellow missionary needed much patience in learning the hitherto unwritten language, preparing an alphabet, discovering the complex grammatical structure of Xavante (i.e. how the language worked), and gaining an understanding of the culture - all essential for Bible translation. A literacy programme was essential also. Six men were the first to learn to read and write. It was exciting to see their enthusiasm, and to receive little messages on scraps of paper from time to time. Ruth wrote back to college:

> Pray with us that one day soon we may be able to answer the questions about eternal things which the people sometimes ask. At this stage all we can say to them is that when we know more of the language, we will explain.

Ruth and her companion soon encountered the inevitable difficulties in translation. Beginning work on the Creation story they could find no word adequate for 'God'. However, they pressed on using every means to master the language including tape-recordings of Xavante people talking about every-day things. Ruth's prayer request in 1961 was:

> Please continue to pray for us as we work on towards the goal of giving to the Xavante people the Word of God in the only language they can understand.

God answered that prayer very wonderfully, for year by year translation proceeded. Along with the first draft translation of

Mark's Gospel, collecting of data for a future dictionary and grammar continued. And there was more to encourage her. Returning from leave in 1965 Ruth rejoiced to find that:

> There has been a real turning to the Lord of the majority of the village. The old spirit dances have ceased and in their place, meetings are held for praise and prayer and testimony.

In the following year the first baptisms took place, and now prayer was asked for the weekly Bible teaching of the Xavante Christian leaders, as well as for the literacy and translation work.

In the meantime, and up to 1973, Valerie had been working in two other Indian tribes. One of these was very isolated and in dense jungle about 400 miles north of the Wycliffe Centre in Cuiaba, State capital of Mato Grosso and geographical centre of South America. During this time she had several bouts of malaria, and eventually, after a particularly severe attack, her doctor in Cuiaba strongly advised her not to return to that area.

The St Michael's family prayed hard for Valerie. She recovered and clearly this was the Lord's doing. In 1973 she was assigned to the Xavante tribe to join Ruth, whose colleague had married and left Wycliffe, and so their partnership in the work began - one which was to last to this day.

In 1976, Ruth faced a need in England. Her father having died, her very elderly mother needed her care, and Ruth came home to look after her. But she brought her work with her and for the next eighteen years, with Valerie's help, was able to continue translating, going to Brazil for short periods every two years to retain her permanent visa and to do further translation checking. It is a lovely story of friendship and dedication to the Lord's work. As translation proceeded, the news items were exciting:

- 1972 - just finished Titus - great interest in the village in Bible teaching

- 1977 - "Aspects of Xavante" grammar book published

- 1980 - Valerie helping to check Luke

- 1981 - completion of work in Ephesians

- 1982 - Ruth - a two month visit to Brazil to get 1 Timothy checked

- 1985 - The Xavante-Portuguese Dictionary published

- 1991 - Ruth and Valerie back to Brazil for short visit - further checking of Scripture

- 1993 - Ruth to Brazil - involved in the distribution in several Xavante villages of newly-published half New Testament. Valerie in UK caring for Mrs McLeod

- 1995 - Ruth and Valerie return to Brazil - Valerie with a new permanent visa, miraculously granted after the loss of her original visa through a prolonged stay in England due to illness.

- 1998 - Revision of James

- 1999 - More translation and revision.

With the help of a second translation team assigned ten years ago, the whole New Testament is now nearing completion. Some parts of the Old Testament have also been translated, and more is in progress.

Ruth's mother died in 1994 at the wonderful age of ninety-eight and a half after many years of loving care. Readers will no doubt agree that this is a remarkable story, and praise God for the faithfulness of Ruth and Valerie. We pray on for them as they continue to serve the Xavante people together.

Today the young Xavante church, with its indigenous leaders, has congregations in a number of villages, and some Xavante are studying at Bible College. Like churches world-wide, the Xavante church faces problems of various kinds. The people need prayer that as they receive more of the Scriptures in their own tongue, the Holy Spirit will continue to change lives. That, surely, is the goal of every missionary, and the whole point of translating the Word of God.

CHAPTER 16

Into the World - Israel and Africa

From the early days a strong link was forged between St Michael's and the Church's Ministry among Jewish People (CMJ). The first of seven or more students who served with this Society in Israel and other countries was **Ursula Jones** (Nehab)

to Israel - land of promise
Ursula entered St Michael's in 1949, soon after its re-opening. She had begun her nursing training, but had heard God's call to full-time service with CMJ, and that had brought her to St Michael's. Ursula's family had emigrated to Jerusalem from Berlin in 1936, during the rise of Nazism. Ursula has written about this period in their lives:

> My father was an architect and an engineer. He brought an irrigation patent to Israel, which meant that he was soon on the immigration quota list. Visas into Palestine were already being restricted. My mother, sister and I soon followed. I sometimes wonder how different our fate would have been had we stayed on. I was nine at the time and so began my 'love affair' with Israel.

Ursula's father was a liberal Jew, and her mother a nominal Christian. In Jerusalem Christ Church became Ursula's spiritual home and the ministry of Canon Hugh Jones a great strength to her and her sister Ruth. Both were confirmed at Christ Church in February 1947, not long before Israel became a State in May 1948.

At St Michael's Ursula's heart was set on mission and her call to Israel clear. Her sales of work to finance mission held in the sitting-room at Fyfield Road were precursors of more ambitious efforts held annually in the years that followed.

As editor of the 1951 newsletter Ursula wrote:

It is a great privilege for me to send this second copy of our Newsletter on its way to let you know more about our life and activities here at St Michael's.

We welcomed some new students for the Michaelmas Term and had to say goodbye to others, but we have never lost the happy family spirit which we enjoy here. It unites us all because we all love and acknowledge the same Master and Lord. As we look into the future, often so mysteriously veiled to our human eyes, may I leave the following words with you, which have come home to me with a new and deeper meaning recently:

"I will instruct thee, and teach thee in the way which thou shalt go; I will guide thee with mine eye." Proverbs 32:8

Ursula returned to Israel to become secretary to Hugh Jones. Their relationship deepened and in April 1953 they were married at St Paul's, Jerusalem. Together, in the Church and in their home, they had a wonderful ministry, greatly appreciated by the congregation and visitors to Jerusalem. They were blessed with two daughters, Anne and Rhoda. Ursula wrote back for prayer:

- busy with preparations for an Annual Sale of Work in Jerusalem, and the special opportunities for hospitality that Christmas affords - please pray that all who come may find Jesus.

Ursula kept in close touch with Miss Snow, who shared her love for Israel. She often returned to the College, sometimes as a guest speaker.

Sadly Hugh developed a serious illness and died in 1964. In 1965, Ursula and the two children came to England. Then began a second period of outstanding ministry at CMJ HQ. She was, over the years, Personal Assistant to the General Director and Assistant Home Secretary. She continued to lead tours to Israel. In the seventies she described her work as 'so varied, there is never a dull moment in the office'.

On her retirement in 1992, after forty years service to the Society, the following tribute to her, was printed in 'Shalom', C.M.J's magazine:

'What will we miss at HQ now that Ursula is not here?' - The ladies point of view at the meetings of the executive staff. The informed background to life in Israel. The knowledge of our supporters which no computer can give us. The apparently tireless worker, thumping away at a typewriter, churning out letter after letter. No word processor for Ursula. The warm welcome for anyone coming into the offices and a cup of tea, and all the Christmas cookies, but, above all, the concerned prayer for the staff, the finances and the witness of CMJ.

In active retirement, Ursula keeps her links with CMJ and friends from St Michael's days, and enjoys her role as grandmother to her two grand-children.

- to Israel and South Africa
Janette Ross was another CMJ candidate who studied at St Michael's 1961-2. Already a graduate and with social work experience, Janette took the Cambridge Diploma in Theology and also gained her I.D.C. (Inter-Diocesan Certificate) with Distinction. (She did not know then that, many years later in South Africa, this would qualify her for ordination.)

In 1963, Janette left for Israel, studied Hebrew (Yverit) in Tel Aviv, a language in which she became totally at home, enabling her to work in Israel for twenty-six years. An excerpt from the 1986 newsletter gives an insight into her work:

> I would appreciate prayer for a basic (Bible Study) course I have to prepare for older people who are new in faith, or, longer in faith but without much background teaching. We are increasingly thankful for continuing growth in the congregation.

Janette spent thirty-three years in Israel, with a very varied ministry in which her many gifts were used. She was concerned for Arab as well as Jew and during that time made many good friends amongst them. It came as a surprise to her when, in 1989, she was asked by the Council of CMJ to go to Johannesburg and pioneer a work amongst the Jews there. With her heart in Israel it was a difficult decision to make. However, with the prayer support of her many friends and confidence in the Lord's guidance she left for South Africa in 1989. Of the years in Israel, her friends Laura and Ronald Adeney wrote this in an issue of 'Shalom':

In Tel Aviv, at Immanuel House, Janette's linguistic and musical gifts were a great asset to the work. She cared deeply for people, welcomed them to her home, Jew and Arab, rich and poor, mentally stable or not. She loved them with the love of Christ and visited, first on a moped, later by car, bringing comfort and joy, often just at the right moment. Sensitivity to the Lord's promptings was fundamental to her ministry. By many, Janette was not seen as 'foreign'. This was particularly true in the young peoples 'Camp' programmes in which she was greatly involved. Her warm, caring nature and love of fun led the campers to love her and through her, the Lord.

It was a tremendous wrench for Janette to leave Israel, but in South Africa she has made many new friends and seen the Lord at work in a troubled country in many ways. There have been personal tests and problems in which she has known the Lord's enabling. Now ordained, and officially (but not actually) retired by CMJ, Janette continues to serve God in the parish of St Luke, Orchards, Johannesburg, developing 'Messiah's People' which is the South African 'Wing' of CMJ. She has travelled extensively all over South Africa, into other African countries, and taken Shoresh tours to Israel. She constantly praises God for protecting her in all her journeys. In an article entitled 'Thirty-four years down the line' Janette wrote:

> I thank God for all of you, who, over the years have prayed for and supported me personally. Without your fellowship I would not have been able to stay in the work - first in Israel - and then in South Africa. And I thank the Lord Who cares (from the beginning of the year) even unto the end of - not just the year, but the span of ministry and of life.

to Africa - the 'small woman'

Is it always women who are physically small who display specially great courage when the need arises? Certainly in missionary annals many of those who have done great things for God have been small in stature.

Thus wrote Canon Alan Neech of BCMS, in a foreword to 'Ruth's Story' the account of **Ruth Stranex's** experiences in **Uganda** as a missionary nurse. She was arrested, imprisoned and deported in 1975.

Ruth had grown up in South Africa, to which her parents had emigrated. She found herself at St Michael's in 1963 and has written this about it:

> I've said nothing about the call to missionary work. There is little to say as the conviction grew on me as I grew up. Some time was spent in traditional Women's Missionary Training College in England. I found the time of value in learning to stand on my own feet without the props of home. The College was left with the impression that "all South Africans are wild"(!) The Principal (i.e. Miss Snow) filled in a questionnaire when I applied to the Bible Churchmen's Missionary Society. I happened to see it when being interviewed "Qualities of leadership? Not outstanding."

In 1964, Ruth flew from Johannesburg to Nairobi, Kenya, en route for Amudat Hospital, Uganda. She comments:

> No miracle took place in mid-air to change me into the superior being that missionaries are sometimes made out to be. I was the same Ruth who was not outstanding, who would somehow fit into a difficult situation. I knew that God, who had called me, was great enough to be trusted.

Year by year Ruth wrote back to St Michael's requesting prayer. This, in 1971, revealed her work load:

> Work increases while staff decreases i.e. sister of O.P. and Theatre, Lecturer of Govt assisted nurses. Relief Sister for wards, "Mama" of ten girls in small hostel for schoolgirls and they fight; Parish Worker when time available (no pastor now) builder of mud huts at cheap rates. I never was much good at anything. It is amazing what you can do when you must, and God is in control.

But her requests did not touch her deepest needs. For example, as a single woman in an African Society, where until you were married, whatever age you were, you remained a 'misichana, a girl'.

She writes frankly in her book, especially of the fear which at different times could grip her heart and threaten to choke her:

> One night about a year after arriving in Amudat, the two dogs broke into a frenzy of barking. I woke up with a start. I lay still under the mosquito net, my heart thumping loudly. My whole body was tense and alert. Lilian (her Senior Missionary) was away so there was no one to call, CRASH! The sound of shattering glass broke the silence and turned the dogs on again. I broke into a cold sweat ...

In His mercy the Lord gave Ruth sleep that night even after this terrifying experience. It was next morning that she discovered the evidence of it having been a leopard driven by its hunger from the cold hills and hoping for a meal of dog flesh. It was only the first of many occasions when she experienced great fear and proved that God can control it.

From 1972 the situation for foreigners in Uganda became serious, yet Ruth returned from home leave in 1974 keen to take up again her work in Amudat. The crisis for her came in 1975 when a group of Government officials came to the hospital, searched her house and then declared, "You must go and pack your bags and come away with us." She felt the worst was happening and fear rose up inside her almost choking her. Worse was to come. Soon she was locked in a filthy cell at the Central Police Station. In its far corners were a crude sink and a toilet sunk into the floor which accounted for the awful stench. Ruth wrote:

> I lay on the bed board. I read a book, I read my Bible. I jumped every time someone came to the door or rattled the lock. I caught a faint glimmer of what it must be like in a Communist prison: the loneliness, the uncertainty, the fear. Those prisoners have no friends as I had whom I knew were doing their utmost to obtain my release.

After four terrible days and nights, the false charges against Ruth were dropped and she was allowed to return to the hospital, but not for long. Only ten days later without explanation she was re-arrested, kept under guard, and then handed a deportation order and a ticket to England. Within hours she was put on a Boeing 707 bound for London together with an Asian and a missionary of another Society.

Although Ruth did not know it at the time, like Peter in Acts 12, thousands of Christians were praying for her in her imprisonment.

Chains of prayer were held throughout the night: Sunday Schools prayed. Families in African countries and in Britain gathered together and prayed.

It was very hard for Ruth, taken away so suddenly from the work and people she loved, and for a while she was greatly traumatised. However, once a missionary, always a missionary, and by September 1976, Ruth was out in **Tanzania**, in charge of Murgwanza Hospital, still serving with BCMS and facing many more demands on her, but thankfully with no risk of arrest and deportation. Ruth was to stay in Tanzania for fourteen years, during which time God led her out of hospital work, and into a pastoral and evangelistic ministry in the Diocese of Victoria, a truly enormous one, which bordered Kenya, Uganda, Ruanda and Burundi.

At first it was in rural primary schools, teaching the Bible to as many as sixty children at a time, and with virtually no equipment, not even a chair. Travelling by foot, she taught and preached in scattered churches. As time went on, with a burden for the need of teaching pastors and church workers, Ruth was able to set up a cassette ministry, and became its co-ordinator for three dioceses; she reported in 1988 that more than a thousand people were studying the Bible through this ministry, many hearing the Gospel for the first time in this way. Thanks to 'Feed the Minds' a Suzuki jeep was provided for her in 1986, enabling her to reach far more scattered communities.

In 1989 Ruth was led to leave Tanzania and BCMS, after twenty-five years service. But it was not to retire. With her heart still in mission, since then, Ruth has been serving in a tough urban-priority area in the North of England, Hartlepool. Now supported by the Church Urban Fund, she is sponsored by All Saints, Stranton, involved in house groups, a school, a youth club, a community centre. She writes of this work:

> There is little to show for our efforts. We have planted a church and relationships are beginning to develop.
>
> It is an even harder jungle than it was in Africa.

Ruth's official title is Community Development Worker in an inner city parish of Stranton. It is an area where three years ago virtually nobody went to Church. Also she continues to keep her links with Crosslinks as a member of its Advisory Group for the North of England.

Paul's words in 1 Corinthians 15:58 seem apt:

> "Always give yourselves fully to the work of the Lord, because you know that your labour in the Lord is not in vain."

CHAPTER 17

Into the World - India, Nepal and Pakistan

In all, something like thirty students heard and responded to God's call, to work in these countries, many with BMMF (now Interserve). In 1954, from the United Field Conference of the Mission at Lucknow, a letter was sent to all home churches, which included this sentence:

> We felt a solemn conviction that the constraint of God was on us to advance.

The letter called for thirty-six new missionaries to reach the field by 1960, the first twelve being needed within the next two years. The response to this appeal was immediate and world-wide. Recruits came from UK, Eire, Canada, New Zealand, Barbados and Germany. Amongst the first twelve were St Michael's women: **Ruth Neve** (India), **Dorothy Davies** (Diggens) (India) and **Mary Cundy** (Nepal) and amongst the next twenty-four, **Edith Mullins** (Gooding) (India) **Ann Cooper** (Pakistan), **Margaret Wilson** (Pakistan), **Betty Cox** (Pakistan) and **Sheila Nixon** (India).

Ethel Raddon was in this group too, appointed to the Paton Memorial Children's Home in Manmad, West India. Later, in 1965, she came to St Michael's for a short time and returned to India to take up the great responsibility of leadership of the Christian Writing Institute at Nasik, where Indian Christian writers were trained. Her work in Christian education took her to the USA, where, after obtaining a Doctorate she was made Director of the Learning Technology Dept at Nova University, Florida.

- first stop India
India is the seventh largest country in the world and the second most populous: a country with many ethnic and cultural groups

and where about sixteen hundred languages and dialects are spoken. A vivid description follows of what missionary work was like soon after India gained its independence in 1947.

Margaret Wardell tells her story:
I left university in 1950 with a Degree in Geography and went to teach in a school in the Midlands. In 1954 I went to teach in the West Indies where I became a Christian in 1957. In 1960 I felt God was calling me to be a missionary though I had no idea where he wanted me to serve. I knew nothing about how to go about pursuing my intention. At first I did not even know one needed special training. However that gradually dawned on me and eventually I arrived at St Michael's in October 1960. I stayed until 1962. Those two years were among the happiest of my entire life. I learned so much from the staff, other students and the Lord himself. I did take the Diploma in Theology but the vital factor in my life was learning to walk more closely with the Lord. To my surprise, within a few weeks of arriving at the college, God showed me that he wanted me in India. Eventually he led me to apply to the Bible and Medical Missionary Fellowship, now called Interserve.

I was accepted and sailed for India on October 20th, 1962. From Bombay, where we landed, I was put in the care of Mary Cundy (also an ex-St Michael's student) for the two-day train journey to north India. I found the new country I could see from the train window fascinating. My destination was Allahabad, where I started language study. I was unable to complete the year's course, as after four months I was suddenly needed to teach children of missionaries at Woodstock school in the foothills of the Himalayas. The school was mainly staffed by Americans and followed an American curriculum. While still learning to live in one foreign culture I had to learn to do so in a second, American. I actually found this harder than adapting to India. The school was planning a course for those of their students who were from the Commonwealth and needed different teaching from the majority who were headed for further education in the USA. I was to set up the Commonwealth course.

I only stayed there for four terms when I was replaced by another missionary newcomer who had just fully completed her language study. In those days two years language study was compulsory for everyone, wherever you were going to serve. I returned to the study I had had to interrupt. At the end of my first complete year I went to a small market town about 50 miles east of Delhi on the vast Ganges plain, where BMMF had a centre for village evangelistic work. There I studied language part time as was usual in the second year and joined in the work of the centre. We had a school for village girls on the mission compound and also work in the surrounding villages. Sometimes we travelled daily to the nearby ones by tonga (a horse drawn vehicle for two passengers) - my companion was usually one of our Indian Bible teachers.

After completing my language study successfully I stayed on at the village centre, continuing to visit nearby villages daily, but also sometimes camping on the outskirts of villages further away, in the cooler weather. The mission also had permanent houses in three villages where we spent a month at a time teaching and ministering to the local women. Staying in one of those houses totally surrounded by a village atmosphere was the highlight of my life. I loved it.

In the area in which we worked there had been mass movements into Christianity from Hinduism in the 1920's and 30's. Now the children and grandchildren of those converts needed teaching. Most of them were illiterate so couldn't study the Bible for themselves. Some knew little about the faith into which their parents or grandparents had entered so eagerly, except that they were Christians and not Hindus. We did Bible teaching with as many visual aids as we had the resources for, so far from anywhere where ready produced ones were available. We also ran a small dispensary where we treated mild complaints such as headaches or worms and mixed the dried milk which malnourished children came to drink daily. We never let them take the milk home because probably some less needy member of the family would then drink it.

Indian village women are simple but shrewd and, most of them, keen to be taught. Even today I can visualise a group of them sitting round listening eagerly to a Bible story. Jesus taught by means of stories so often, didn't he? It is still a most effective way of teaching in the East today. But the learning wasn't one sided. I learned much from the village people too. One day an elderly lady called Badamo, meaning "almond", came into our courtyard. She squatted in front of me, as most Indian people do, and began to tell me about all the Christian workers she had known come to the village. She was very generous in her comments. She made no criticisms such as, "She never understood our language properly," or, "So and so was stingy with the dried milk." But she came to one person and she stopped for a moment and then said, "She didn't love us, all the rest loved us but she didn't love us." Her words have remained with me for life. It isn't whether you wear the local dress, speak the language well or provide for their bodily needs that matters the most, it's the love you show people you work with that really counts. I carry Almond's word with me even today.

In 1967 I returned to Britain for leave but was unable to return to India because of a health problem. So in 1968 BMMF seconded me, as a parish worker, to St John's church, Southall in West London. At least 60% of the population there is Asian and I was to have particular responsibility for reaching out to them. I remained there until my retirement in 1985. Those 17 years were filled with a huge variety of experiences. Some I wouldn't have been able to cope with without knowing at first hand the culture of north India from where most of the Asians came. Some West Indians also lived in the parish. I was bitterly disappointed not to be able to return to India but couldn't help seeing the hand of God in what had happened. The two biggest ethnic minority groups in Britain are Jamaicans and Indians and I had worked in both countries. Plenty of people had worked in one or the other country but I have yet to find anyone who has worked in both, rather than just gone for a holiday.

In Southall I continued teaching women, many of whom were from the sort of village background of which I had experience. But I was also involved with teenage Asian girls growing up with a foot in two cultures, Asian at home and British at school. The pressures on them were sometimes beyond belief. They were confused as they struggled to find a personal identity. One point of conflict is the arranged marriage system which their parents take for granted. Some girls are still happy to accept a bridegroom brought from India whom they have never met before. One unmarried Indian friend of mine, over 40 years old, said, "I would rather my parents chose my partner for me. After all they have lived longer than me so they must know best." Others, however, on coming into conflict with a system of choice which their parents have never known, want choice for themselves. There are many other matters which give rise to conflict too. When parents are very bound in the traditional views, young people sometimes opt out in extreme ways. I had to minister to one family where a boy had poured petrol over himself and burnt himself to death rather than accept an arranged marriage. No doubt he had secretly formed an attachment to some other girl, though his parents either did not know this or did not want to know. They certainly denied that he had. To do otherwise would be to lose face. Not losing face is critically important in Asian culture.

In St John's church I played my part in the usual activities of the church, helping to lead services as well as preaching and overseeing the Sunday school. But most of my weekdays were spent visiting.

In 1985 I retired and came to live in Witney, 10 miles west of Oxford. I joined Cogges church in which I had first gained practical experience when at St Michael's. I used to take Auntie J and one or two other students there on Sundays, to teach the young people, as I was privileged to have a car.

Ever since 1962 I have been writing articles for magazines spasmodically. In 1978 my vicar in Southall felt I had the potential to do more of this nature, so I started to do what I had time for during the busyness of parish life. I even wrote the agony column for an English language magazine for Asians (mainly young people) for six months!

I felt the Lord would lead me to do more writing when I had retired so on arrival in Witney I began to work through a correspondence course in creative writing. From there I went on to make writing a major part of my life. I have now written, or shared with others in writing, five books, all out of the experience I have gained through my life overseas and in Southall.

[Margaret's fifth book was published in 1998, and is listed, with the others, in Appendix 4].

- to India - a different story
Ann Witchalls (Gilchrist) trained as a parish worker at St Mike's 1958/60 even though a few years before she had felt strongly called to serve overseas. She describes how she and Brian served the Lord together at the Christian Medical College and Hospital Vellore, South India. Their engagement was a testing time, involving a separation that would probably not be demanded today:

> For some time I had been friendly with one of the young men from the youth fellowship in my home church. However, Brian did not feel particularly called to the foreign Mission Field as I had been. He wanted to go into the ordained ministry. He was turned down by CACTM being told that he should seek to serve the Lord as an engineer. "Missionary

Societies are crying out for engineers," he was told. So he applied to CMS and was accepted for service at Vellore. We got engaged the day he was accepted! But CMS asked us to wait until Brian had been in India for a year before we got married, saying it would put an unfair strain on a new marriage in a new situation if we married before either of us had been to India. So Brian left for South India - I undertook another year's training at the CMS Training College. This twelve months' separation was not easy. However, the end of the year found me going out to India, carrying my wedding dress, my wedding ring - and the refrigerator. Brian and I were married three weeks after I arrived.

We spent the next twenty years serving in the Christian Medical College Hospital, Vellore, South India. I did a variety of jobs, mostly pastoral work with the medical students - leading Bible study classes, helping to run the Sunday School and holiday clubs for the children. We had responsibility for the many visitors who came to the hospital. I produced quite a lot of the hospital's promotional material.

Ann and Brian had two sons, both of whom had most of their education in Hebron School, India, on whose executive committee Ann served. Then in 1983 they returned, as a family to England, to complete that education. Ann continues:

It was wonderful how God undertook, bringing Brian's current work to an end just at the right time, bringing other of our friends at the hospital back to England at the same time. Even our pets died of natural causes in the twelve months preceding our return.

Back in England, Brian continues his work as a hospital engineer: Ann is a career counsellor with the Ministry of Defence and a non-stipendiary lay worker in her village church in Wiltshire with three clergy, reaching folk in nine other churches. A most thrilling fact is that Nigel their eldest son is back in Vellore, working as an air-conditioning engineer in the very department his father set up twenty years ago. Jeremy is a physiotherapist in Australia. The family had a wonderful reunion at Vellore in 1997.

- to Nepal - the roof of the world

After the death of her mother in 1955, **Mary Cundy**, a Medical Social Worker in Reading was surprised how often the newly open-to-foreigners country of **Nepal** kept appearing in different parts of her life. She went to help in the summer at a Guide camp in Wales. While there she remembered that a colleague she had worked with, but not seen for years, was a Medical Social Worker at Rhyl hospital. She decided to invite her to supper. Knowing nothing of what had been happening to Mary, she said:

> It's interesting that you should get in touch with me now, as a friend of mine, Dr Evans, has just been on an expedition in Nepal. I thought of you and felt you would be much more use there than me as you are a Christian and I am not.

Mary, hearing this, began to wonder if God had a purpose for her in Nepal.

When she got home before going to church the next Sunday, she knelt down and asked God to speak to her by name.

In the second Bible reading came the words 'I count all things but loss'. Mary felt as if God directly was asking her if she was prepared to count all things but loss - and that she wasn't prepared to!

Later the preacher said his text was 'For my sake' taken from Mark 10:29 "There is no one who has left house, or brothers or sisters or mother or father or children or lands 'for my sake' and the Gospel." It was as if God linked the two and said 'Mary, are you prepared to leave all for my sake?' By the end of the sermon she knew she had to go to Nepal. Mary was accepted by Interserve, and advised to go to St Michael's for two terms to see if people could live with her. She sailed for Nepal in January 1957.

When Mary set foot in Nepal in 1957, there were practically no indigenous Christians. When she retired in 1990, the church in that country was the second fastest growing in Asia, so greatly had God answered the prayers of many, many people. Mary's two books 'So great a God' and 'Better than the Witch-doctor' (see Appendix 4) describe vividly what she experienced and witnessed during her thirty-three years in Nepal. Individuals who were converted, often underwent terrible persecution. No direct evangelism was allowed in the Hindu kingdom. Yet, God's kingdom continued to grow.

For many years Mary ran a small dispensary, high up in the foot-hills of the Himalayas above Pokhara. It was eight hours trek (and climb) from the nearest village in the valley, a rural settlement. Living conditions were primitive and Mary, oftentimes only assisted by a dedicated but unqualified Nepali helper, was expected to be doctor, surgeon, even vet at times. Her testimony is quite simply to God's faithfulness.

Mary has continued to keep in touch with many individuals in Nepal, including those who were children when she was there, and who are now making good as Christians in their careers. She has returned a number of times to help and encourage them in their Christian lives. And, although her stay at St Michael's was short, she has always maintained a close relationship with the College. In 1967, she was the representative speaker for the old students at the opening of the new wing at 117 on the Day of Prayer and Gifts.

- to Pakistan - tent-making and partnership

It may seem surprising that Christian teachers and nurses were able to work in the Islamic Republic of **Pakistan**. But that is exactly what a number of students did and some were appointed to important positions in institutions. **Anne Cooper** became Director of Nursing Training for Pakistan, **Dorothy Boswell**, Deputy Principal of Kinnaird College. Anne and Dorothy were close friends, often going on holiday together. Dorothy retired to England in 1975 after nearly twenty years' teaching, to live in London with her sister Margaret. She continued to take a lively interest in Interserve, and to keep in touch with St Michael's and Pakistani friends right up to her death in 1998. At that time, Anne wrote this about her:

> Her students remember her as an excellent teacher, and her fellow missionaries were grateful for her outstanding stability of faith and of personality, always calm in a crisis, always ready to discuss problems, always able to produce a soothing cup of tea. When I visited her, a few days before she died, she prayed and thanked God for the joy of Christian fellowship.

Anne herself continues to be busy, studying and writing, in her retirement, in Manchester.

When **Phyllis Tring** was a student at St Michael's in 1959, she was already an experienced English teacher, with a definite call to serve God abroad. She believed then and throughout her life in the value of Christians working in secular jobs:

It gives one an identity - an understandable reason for being there. I feel that people need a secular job if they are to make contact with people.

Her first assignment under BMMF was to teach English and Scripture at Kinnaird High School (Pakistan), and to work with the Pakistani teachers. By 1962 she had passed her second Urdu examination but wrote about other problems:

> The failure of an old well has been a great trial: water has had to be pumped from the Municipal Supply - but God is sending money to pay for the Boring of a new well and we hope this can be made soon.

At first teaching of Scripture to all students was permitted, but after Phyllis returned from leave in 1967 (having completed a TEFL - Teaching English as a Foreign Language - course at Leeds University) she was only allowed to teach the Bible to girls from the Christian community. This, she found was more effective because the teaching could be more challenging and direct. Some of the girls came to real faith and their lives were changed.

After nearly ten years in Pakistan, Phyllis began to feel she should move on, but where? Just at that time the Mission asked her if she would be willing to go to Iran. She felt at once that that was the right thing. So, after helping a new Pakistani Principal settle into the school, she came home on leave, just before Christmas 1970, visiting Damavand College, Tehran, on the way. She was to join the staff there after her leave. She describes her time there:

> After my leave that was where I went. Damavand College was a Liberal Arts College upgraded from a school which had been started by a United Presbyterian missionary. It was a secular college, or it could not have given degrees, but there was a large number of Christians on the staff and faculty. For the first four years I was the only English person among the Americans and Iranians, but they were welcoming and the difference in accent was usually a matter for interest or for good-natured teasing. I taught second year students Communication Skills, Introduction to Literature and some years a course called Ancient Myth and Epic. I grew fond of my students and my work. Although I was told that politics

and religion should not be discussed in the classroom, I did find I could answer the questions which arose especially in the myths course.

Phyllis was seconded and supported initially by BMMF but later became a Field Partner, employed by the College. She always regarded the teaching itself as her main ministry, rejoicing to see the young Iranian women opening up to new ideas, but she also ran a Bible Study for Christian students, and managed to find time each morning to pray with the Christians, sometimes one or two, at other times as many as could fit into her office. Even with a growing threat of unrest and revolution in the country, they saw other new Christians joining them.

> One, a Korean woman, turned from Buddhism to the Lord and was welcomed and helped by the Iranian students, particularly one Armenian who travelled across Tehran to get her a Korean Bible.

Early in 1979, after the Shah had left the country, the College was closed for five months. For a while the staff hoped it would reopen and faculty meetings were held each month. But, as Phyllis and others realised, there was little future for an English Medium Women's College in Iran, and Phyllis left the country in February 1979, on the last RAF flight. She says:

> It was a grief to leave, but we had had ten years in which to educate these women and encourage them to use their own minds, and to ask questions.

At that time, it is estimated that about three million Iranians fled the country, of which some ten thousand came to England, where Christians among them continued to worship together, especially in London.

For Phyllis there were more adventures ahead. First, she gained an M.A. in Linguistics and English Language, at Leeds. Then, although she says she was not very keen (!) she agreed to go to the Lebanon Evangelical School in Tyre, again at the somewhat tentative invitation of the BMMF. Lebanon was in the throes of civil war, but, bravely, she went. It was 1981. Here she helped untrained teachers and wrote teacher's notes for English lessons for all the

Junior School. She also ran a course for teachers in Beirut, being there at the time of the Israeli invasion and siege of West Beirut. The Lord protected her when, at one point, she was caught in the cross-fire of the different factions but not hit. Her courage shows in these words:

> I'm afraid that bullets and bombs will continue to be part of my daily life here in Beirut. They hinder some things but not the work of the Holy Spirit.

After two difficult years, Phyllis was appointed an Interserve Consultant on English teaching in the Middle East, based at the International office, in Nicosia, Cyprus. Here she worked until February 1992 when she retired after thirty-nine years with Interserve. This last uprooting after thirty-years out of the U.K. was not easy for her. At the end of that year she shared her feelings in a prayer letter. We are reminded of the need to pray for returning missionaries to their home country:

> Being in England just shows more and more need for prayer. If I weren't a Christian I would say it is depressing here with so much unemployment and such low moral standards, but I can see God working in my home church and in other places. Sometimes I feel very ignorant about life here, a bit like Rip van Winkle, especially about things that have been on television. What's most important is that I know this is the place where God wants me now, and I'm content to stay.

Apart from a return visit to Cyprus in 1995, Phyllis has stayed in Worthing, very active in her church in spite of some health problems. In 'Widening Horizons' the story of Interserve, Katherine Makower wrote of Phyllis:

> This small and unassuming and rather frail lady had been in two of the toughest Spots of the 1970's and 80's. She had certainly made contact with people for Him.

It is what she continues to do in 1999 and we thank God for her.

CHAPTER 18

Into the World - Further East

It is likely that **Ruth Teeuwen (Young)** was the only student at St Michael's who had been one of Miss Snow's pupils at Clarendon School. She was not very interested in Biology, but did want to teach Scripture, and that is what brought her to Oxford.

Ruth recalls that taking chapel was quite an ordeal for most students, and required much preparation, but afterwards a student always received words of encouragement from Miss Snow. She does not forget one encounter with Miss Snow, whom she describes as a 'down-to-earth' Principal:

> We had strict rules regarding being back at College at night. One night I was late, so climbed the fire escape and landed in another student's room, who let me in and I got back to my room safely and unnoticed, I presumed! However, next morning I was duly summoned to Miss Snow's room and given a mild reprimand, and dismissed with a smiling Miss Snow calling after me, "Ruth, I was young once too!"

Her time at St Michael's shaped and prepared Ruth first for six years of teaching in England, and then for pioneer missionary work.

- to Indonesia
Ruth married Jacques Teeuwen, a Dutchman, in 1958, and together they offered to the Regions Beyond Missionary Union - for work in New Guinea (now Indonesia). With preparation and deputation and support raising, it was not until 1961 that they were able to leave (USA) for that country. They arrived in Hollandia in September that year with their first child Priscilla who, Ruth observed, was a baby born for pioneering and making discoveries! In fact, they discovered the people were very friendly, in spite of looking savage:

> Outwardly they seem so fierce with pig tusks etc. through
> their noses. Pray for us that we will be able to get hold of their
> language quickly to be able to help them.

Soon they were seeing great blessing and wrote in 1963 from
Irian Basat:

> Ist April, sixteen native Christians were baptised. Some three
> thousand Ndani had gathered. We wish every one of you
> could have seen the candidates. I believe there was not one
> who had not had at least one finger or one piece of ear
> chopped off, a vivid reminder of their past bondage to the
> powers of darkness.

God continued to bless their ministry. Throughout 1977, they
witnessed many conversions and baptisms. A Bible School was
established. Some of those graduating after three years, returned to
their villages to teach their own people; others went as missionaries to other parts of the island.

Then, with their four children, Ruth and Jacques were called
back to the Netherlands where and from which in the years that
have followed they have exercised a Bible-teaching Ministry, particularly in Eastern Europe. They have worked independently, and
also in association with Torchbearers and the European Christian
Mission. They have organised Camps and Conferences, and this
very year plan to be present at Mission '99, a European Youth
Congress, which will, it is believed, be attended by some 7,000
young people.

One of their special joys now is that all four children and their
families are engaged in Christian mission in different countries.

- to Malaysia and the Philippines - God rules and over-rules
Gillian Hunt went to St Michael's in 1958 to be better prepared to
teach older girls in a Girl Crusader Class, and emerged in 1960
with a definite Missionary call:

> Gradually, during my last year at Bible College, a vague sus-
> picion turned into a growing conviction that God really did
> want me to become a missionary. And to my amazement, I
> discovered that this was no longer the hardest thing I could
> think He might ask of me - I really wanted to do it for Him.

Gillian did not find living in St Michael's easy. In her book she writes:

> From a distance, studying at Bible College had seemed a great idea. Only when I got there did I discover what a rebel I was. I found the discipline irksome, and fretted under what seemed petty rules. It took me a long time to recognise these things as part of God's sandpapering to rub off our rough corners, in His continual process of polishing us so that we might reflect the beauty of Christ.

Gillian was accepted by CIM (later renamed the Overseas Missionary Fellowship), and sailed for Singapore in 1961, bound for Malaya (as it was then). Orientation and acclimatisation began at once; learning to keep healthy and happy in the heat involved drinking vast quantities of water, a sip at a time, taking extra salt on one's food and getting used to an afternoon siesta. Language learning - for Gillian it was Hokkien Chinese - took up six hours of the day, struggling to get the tongue round unfamiliar sounds and to remember and recognise what had been learnt the day before.

Gillian has told the story of her twenty three years with OMF in her book 'All the pieces fit'. With an appealing frankness she reveals the doubts, questions and certainties which she experienced during her years in Malaysia and the Philippines. Over and over again she testifies to the way God enabled her to cope. He brought her through a health breakdown, gave her grace to switch from teaching in Malaysia to tribal work in the Philippines, and to learn yet another language, Tagalog.

At one point she describes how, in Malaya a court case brought against her (unjustly) for careless driving, was dismissed. But the fact that it was brought at all led to her obtaining a Visit Pass which she badly needed. Gillian saw God's care and over-ruling in it all. As she walked from the court:

> Once again I was walking on air. The case was over. I was cleared. And I had a Visit Pass to the end of the school year. Every bit of it had been God's doing.

Just as she had been very certain about God's call to be a missionary when the time came, she was just as sure it was time to come home and be near to her ageing parents. Confirmation of the rightness of this came to OMF too. Gillian relates what happened shortly before her leave in England was due: it refers to an interview with the OMF Superintendent for Mindoro (Philippines):

> After a while a request came from Dave for me to go and see him again. He said, "Gillian, at its last meeting the Mindoro Field Council talked over what other situation we could put you into to use your teaching gifts, but we couldn't see any new opening for you on this island. I've also discussed it with the other Superintendents to see what there is in other areas of OMF work in the Philippines. But I'm afraid that we can't find anything that appears to be just the right slot for you at the moment. This would seem to endorse the idea that you should stay at home when you return to the UK."

> My first reaction was to feel very hurt. It was all very well for them to say that I had real gifts in teaching, and then to tell me that they had nothing for me to do. However, the feeling of rejection was only momentary. Wasn't I the one who had first brought up the subject of staying at home? From that moment, I accepted God's will with complete peace, surprising even myself that I could view so calmly the prospect of severing official links with the OMF after so many happy years in Asia.

Back in England, Gillian spent many months writing the book, to which we referred above, before teaching English as a foreign language, and caring for her parents. One surprising job that came her way was in Reading jail, teaching English to foreign drug-smugglers who had been picked up at Heathrow. Of Gillian it would be said, she has never had an opportunity to get into a rut!

- to Japan - land of the rising sun
Three students, **Kathleen Cotton**, **June Griffiths** (Hetherington) and **Maire Johnston** were called to work in Japan - one of the hardest mission fields. Kathleen was at St Michael's from 1959 - 61 training for parish work. After three years in Tooting Parish, in 1965 she left for Japan, to serve with the Japan Evangelistic Band, having had a short period of further training at Emmanuel College, Birkenhead. Kathleen fell in love with Japan, the country and the

people, from the start. After two years language study she was sent to Minoshima on the island of Kobe. Soon she was deeply involved in visiting, taking Bible Classes, Sunday School, and in her contact with many people improving her Japanese. One of her prayer requests was:

> - please pray we may become more burdened for Japan where the doors are wide open for evangelism - pray for freshness and vision - there are many obstacles that keep the people of Japan from believing.

For ten years Kathleen took every opportunity for sharing the Gospel, but then suffered illness for which she needed long sick leave. This led in due course to her emigrating to New Zealand to join her family there. Except for short visits she was not able to return to her work in Japan, although always open to the possibility. She remained faithful to her calling in New Zealand, where she died in 1999 after battling with cancer for a number of years.

June Griffiths (Hetherington) also trained for parish work and left St Michael's in 1963 for the parish of St Mark's, Barrow-in-Furness. There she met her future husband, David Griffiths, the curate, and also received her call to Japan. St Mark's was a church with a vision for Mission. June wrote:

> Three evangelistic week-ends are planned for this year: a men's weekend: a women's weekend and a family week-end. I have the main responsibility for the women's week-end and would value your prayers for that.

While June was at Barrow, both her parents died and she was granted some leave to cope with the bereavement and support her younger sister. There followed her application to the China Inland Mission (now OMF) which was accepted, and she sailed for Singapore in March 1966. By September she was in Sapporo, learning Japanese which, like many others, she did not find easy. She wrote of her engagement to David who was already with OMF in Japan. They were married in June 1967 and were soon serving the Lord together in Sapporo, chiefly amongst pupils at Fuzoko High School. A typical prayer request was:

- we held a Youth Squash in February to which sixty-five young Japanese came. Pray for quicker progress in language study.

In the years that followed, the work amongst High School students continued, alongside English Bible Classes, much home visiting, and even a Christian bookstall in a big Departmental Store. They were often saddened by a shallow interest in the Gospel, and a reluctance to get too involved in Christian things. Two children, Ben and Bronwen, were born to them, and June was kept very busy in the home, in addition to keeping up her many contacts with people.

Gradually over a period of time, June and David were led to leave Japan for a new sphere of work in the Philippines. Ben and Bronwen were being educated at Faith Academy in Manila, which necessitated fairly frequent visits. It was not surprising that, after a leave in Wales in 1986, they left for the Philippines where they still serve today.

Dave wrote in a prayer letter:

- of all the Student parties I preached at, this challenged me during the question time, "When you meet Jesus Christ after death, Kuya Dave, what will you be most ashamed of?" That, from a very godly student who had been asked the same question in 1995, and his walk with God had changed as a result.

June works with the Japanese Church in Manila, where she rejoices to see the Lord at work. In a recent prayer letter she was praising God for an Evangelistic Concert held in February 1999 attended by three hundred people, mostly Japanese, with about thirty Filipinos or foreigners. Weekly meetings are held on Saturdays for children. The Church itself has only twenty-five members and June asks for their ongoing witness amongst other Japanese in Manila. She especially needs prayer support in her visiting and talking with women seeking to answer their questions and lead them to faith in Christ.

June and David are grandparents now to Bronwen's twin sons. Their son Ben is back in Japan, teaching and responsible for setting up an English teaching programme in Primary Schools. We praise God for June and David and for His grace which has kept them faithful to His call for more than thirty years.

Maire Johnston was working in television in London on drama serials and camera scripts, when she became aware of a call to overseas missionary service. She was worshipping at All Soul's Church, Langham Place, at the time.

The change to St Michael's, the study of Greek and Theology, could not have been greater. Due largely (so she says) to the help of Miss Peggy Knight, Maire obtained her Diploma in Theology in five terms and in 1965 she went out to Singapore. In her words:

> I'm still very conscious of the Lord's timing, of when He led me to study at St Mike's and that of my application to OMF International - and indeed all the movements thereafter - to Singapore for the Orientation course, and thence to Japan.

Maire had a wide ministry in Japan for nearly fifteen years. At Sapporo and Asahikawa on Hokkaido, the northernmost island; and at Hachimohe, Hirosaki and Tokyo on Honshu.

Much of her work was amongst students, young people and housewives, with national student organisations and their affiliated Christian Unions in colleges and universities. She would lead Bible Studies with diverse groups: university staff, married folk, school teachers, and foreign students from other countries of S.E. Asia on scholarships in Japan. Within one Japanese Church she was able to assist pastors, with baptism classes, counselling and preaching. Getting alongside young people involved sporting and cultural activities. From the first attempts to try out language in shops and on transport, or to master dialect, Maire mastered Japanese to great fluency.

She fully expected to remain in Japan until retirement but that was not to be. In 1979 after three terms of service, for health reasons she was not able to return to the field. Once again she was to prove God's timing. He led her to use her gifts and experience in Japan in this country.

First, she was able to achieve a Master's Degree in Linguistics, centred around current analysis of the Japanese grammar system. This led on to lecturing in Japanese studies and teaching Japanese to students on university courses, and to business people. She became a speaker representative for the Japanese Embassy in London, invited to give talks to business companies and management associations: to take orientation courses for business staff being sent to Japan, needing help to understand cultural and psychological factors in conducting negotiations. It has been truly said that the Lord never wastes His servants' time or talents.

Maire has been able to make a four month return visit to the country to which she was called, and maintains close links with many Japanese friends in Japan and elsewhere. In her active retirement she remains involved with All Souls, her sending and supporting Church.

CHAPTER 19

Into The World - Here, There and Everywhere

And here we take the line of the writer to the Hebrews, "what more can we say? - for we do not have time to tell about "

- Christine Clarke (Day) and her husband **Peter** who for more than thirty years have served the Lord in Argentina with CMJ. They sailed for Buenos Aires in January 1965 to work with Jewish people amongst whom were few Christian workers. Today there are more than four hundred thousand Jewish people in Argentina, mostly Ashkenazi, European immigrants, the majority living in Buenos Aires. Christine's 'call' came in 1956, through visiting a Bible Come to Life Exhibition. For Peter it was during a CMJ Youth weekend at St Michael's in 1958.

After they became CMJ candidates, they accepted CMJ's invitation to enter a country not before entered by CMJ. Peter and Christine have found that the most effective form of evangelism is personal work, friendship and doing regular Bible Studies with individuals, listening, being patient, getting involved in other people's lives. Studying alongside people has been an important part of their ministry. It helps to authenticate the message. Peter has been finishing a Master's degree in Jewish Studies, alongside teaching in the Rabbinical Seminary. Christine has developed the training side of the Diocesan Counselling Service. During the Falklands War, Peter was in a Class at the Seminary, and at a time when all minorities and especially the Jewish one felt threatened, his presence led to a great feeling of solidarity.

Although they are now associate missionaries of CMJ, officially retired their lives are as busy as ever, their ministry in Buenos Aires continues.

- Lyn Hodges, a student in 1961, who served with the European Missionary Fellowship at Metz in France from 1966 to 1983, only giving up that work to return to England to help her elderly parents. Lyn's teaching of children and young people, pastoral work with women and others, bore much fruit. She saw prayer answered in the establishment of a daughter church at Krutange, with its own pastor, and a full-time worker to the Christian bookshop at the evangelical church at Metz.

- Anne Ball (Clothier), who trained for parish work 1959/60 and sailed for Kenya in February 1963, with her husband John and one year old daughter Mary, to serve with BCMS in the Diocese of Nakuru. For the next sixteen years they remained in Kenya, serving with the Anglican Church, at diocesan and provincial level. They saw much blessing in youth and Sunday School work, and later, for John in particular, literature and publishing. By 1972 a Diocesan Literature Centre had been set up and was opened by Archbishop Donald Coggan. They were blessed with two sons, Philip and David; they together with Mary attended Christian boarding schools in Kenya and England. The publishing work became Uzima Press, based in Nairobi. John prepared African staff who took on the leadership and then moved on to become vicar of Karen on the outskirts of Nairobi.

In 1979, at the invitation of BCMS they returned to England where John joined the home staff. In 1981, John was appointed General Secretary of the Mission (now renamed Crosslinks) a job to which he brought his many gifts and experience. It involved a great deal of travelling, so Anne settled into parish life in Sidcup, serving on the PCC and becoming a Lay-Reader. By the time they had been married for over thirty years, they might have retired to a less demanding life. But no, God had other things in store for them.

Seeing the invitation to become Assistant Bishop in the Diocese of Central Tanganyika as God's next place, they left for Tanzania in late 1995. January 14th 1996 saw John consecrated as Bishop to serve alongside Bishop Mdimi Mhogolo, based in Dodoma. Truly God is the God of surprises. There they still serve, after an incredibly busy three years. Their work schedule is often unbelievable as the following extract from a 1999 prayer letter shows:

CONFIRMATION CUTTINGS

Twelve different sermons, Anne speaking on prayer, large crowds, many services outside; always very hot, much sweat, large sales of New Testaments.

Twenty-one different beds, generous hospitality, fifty-six meals of rice and meat, washing by moonlight, long discussions, encouraging stories of evangelism, happy Christians singing and drumming all night (thankfully, not always!) early mornings.

Fifty-six services, processions of choirs to welcome us, large crowds, two thousand seven hundred and eighty-eight confirmation candidates, 68% of whom were females, some excellent choirs, thousands of children.

Two thousand, eight hundred and twenty-eight kilometres, roads badly potholed due to the floods, huge clouds of dust, very dirty hair.

And John and Anne keep up their writing. Anne has helped in production of books for the women's groups and teaching seminars; John, books of sermon outlines and catechists courses. He has also been working on a new book of confirmation lessons and parish Bible Studies. He serves on the board of Central Tanganyika Press, the Anglican Publishing House in Tanzania, which publishes Christian books mostly in Swahili.

People in central Tanganyika have suffered great hardship due to three successive years of famine. Many have benefited from the generous response of friends and supporters to the Diocesan Famine Appeal - money channelled through Crosslinks and other agencies. Students who had not been able to pay their fees, have continued their studies at Msalato Bible College; College staff who would not have been paid because parishes have not been able to bring in their quotas, have received their salaries; families of students, left at home have had enough to keep them going; clergy have received a bag of maize and so have been able to stay in their parishes to minister to people's needs.

John and Anne praise God for the great privilege of such a varied and fulfilling ministry, particularly in East Africa.

- **Gillian Blair** (Clarke), a physiotherapist, who thought her time at St Michael's (1959-61) was training for service with CIM (OMF). Instead, in her last term she became engaged to the Revd Patrick Blair (formerly curate at Harwell), chaplain at Oundle School, and they were married soon after Gill left Oxford. They were to serve God together overseas, and to bring up a family of four children. First there was a happy ministry at Oundle where Gill's physiotherapy skills were much appreciated for 'rugger' injuries. But their time there was short for in 1964, Patrick was appointed a lecturer and Archbishop's chaplain at St George's College, Jerusalem. Now it was learning Arabic and settling their two children into a new routine of ministry in the home, where they held fortnightly Bible Studies, and in the College.

But in 1966, perhaps to their surprise, they faced another move, this time to Khartoum, where Patrick was to be Provost of the Cathedral, in the Church of the Sudan. Of their life there, Gill wrote in 1967:

> Life in Khartoum is never straightforward or leisurely. Pray that enough time may be found for prayer, study and the needs of the family.

By this time they had three children; Mark, Ruth and James. Services, classes and other organisations all brought involvement with many Sudanese people. It was a happy time and lasting relationships were made.

In another prayer letter in 1968 they wrote about the work of the CMS Hospital in Omdurman:

> Cares for some ninety leprosy in-patients and hundreds of out-patients who come from all over the country. Many walk miles on ulcerated feet to receive treatment. A physiotherapist friend of Gill's stayed with us on her way back to her work with the Leprosy Mission in the Far East. She gave some very valuable advice and practical ideas for assisting and re-habilitating the patients.

At that time, this was the only hospital in the Sudan where leprosy could be treated.

The pillar of cloud moved and so, in 1970, the family returned to England, Patrick to an incumbency in Chester-le-Street, Co. Durham. This was an exciting ministry. They saw the church growing, and its story is told in the book 'Ten growing churches'.

The next move was to Barking where Patrick became Rector of St Margaret's Church and Gill honorary parish worker. Life was very busy. It was a parish renowned for weddings - a hundred and eighty a year! Gill wrote:

Pray for meetings for engaged couples: also work is slow in developing on a housing estate but we hold Sunday worship in a flat, and a Bible Study midweek in another. I continue to do part-time physiotherapy in Hospital and home visits in the community.

Here in 1986, Gill and Patrick celebrated their silver wedding. But there was no resting on their laurels. In 1988, they were off again, this time to Tunis, North Africa, where Patrick was to be chaplain at St George's. Their previous experience in Africa was of use to them in their ministry to another congregation. They were to stay for five fruitful years until, in 1993, Patrick was invited to become Provost of St Paul's Church, Nicosia, and Rural Dean of Cyprus. The Diocese of Cyprus and the Gulf was created in 1976; although St Paul's Church had been founded in 1893, it was only made a Cathedral in 1981. From Cyprus, Gill wrote:

> I am involved in prison visiting and other parish activities. Our four children are all in London. Greetings to all old St Michael's students who know me.

Now, after those further nine years abroad, Gill and Patrick have retired to the New Forest living in a parish which covers three villages, and where it is certain there is a ministry for them.

- **Rosemary Hyde**, Eire, moved from horticulture to missionary work with Bible Centred Ministries International. She wrote in 1996:

> There is much to praise the Lord for: the clubs and camps for children continue to be a blessing. The Church is growing both spiritually and numerically. I am moving to the Dublin area after sixteen years in Newbridge. My work will continue much the same - accounts, administration, special projects, camp preparation etc.

- **Nicky Hockey** (Walsh) Taiwan and Oxford, who was one of the early students, leaving St Michael's for further training with CIM in 1954. In the autumn of 1955 she sailed for Singapore, underwent language study and arrived in Taiwan (Formosa) in 1956. After passing her third language examination in Mandarin, Nicky moved to Neipu in the south of the island where she had to begin mastering Hakka, the language of a group of Chinese people originally from China. She wrote in 1959:

> As in so many places, there is the stumbling block of nominal Christianity. We need the fire of the Holy Spirit and some special manifestation of the Lord's power for Christians and non-Christians to be shaken from their lethargy.

Soon after that Nicky came home on furlough with the lovely news of her engagement to Wallace Hockey, a fellow CIM missionary, from South Africa. She had a white wedding in Taiwan, in a church filled with Chinese friends and missionaries and a Chinese feast which more than fulfilled their expectations. Soon they moved to Makung on the Pescadore Islands where their work chiefly amongst Service personnel was greatly blessed. After the birth of their son Christopher in 1962, Wallace and Nicky felt that the Lord was calling them to preach the Gospel among the million Hakka people in Taiwan, and they moved to Miaoli in the North of the island.

During their next furlough, spent partly in South Africa and partly in Oxford, Rachel their first daughter was born. The family returned later in 1965 to Kung Kuan, near Miaoli, in a Hakka area. They were linked with an evangelistic team of the Presbyterian Church, and wrote full of praise for the blessing seen in summer evangelism.

Nicky's health, during her next pregnancy gave cause for concern (she was bearing twins) and this, with other factors, led to them re-locating to Oxford for their children's growing years. But all their experience of working with Chinese and their mastery of the language was to be put to full use again. They were to see the founding of the Chinese Church in Oxford; to be supporters and advisers to the many Chinese men and women who came to Oxford; to make close personal friends, and to be active prayer partners to others called to serve the Chinese community. Wallace was very deeply involved when in March 1996, the Lord suddenly took him 'Home' - a very great shock to his family and the Chinese Church. His funeral service in St Andrews, Old Headington, can be described like that wedding in Taiwan. The Church was packed with Chinese friends, and the service was again followed by a feast prepared by their many friends.

Over the walls - to engage with the world

St Michael's did not only seek to train women for the three spheres of work, in education, in parishes, and the overseas mission field. The aim of the College was to deepen the spiritual life of everyone in the community, to equip them better to live for Christ, and to attract people to Him, wherever they would be in the world. So courses were adapted to individual needs, and individuals to courses. Women chose to come and to stay for varying lengths of time, a few weeks, a term or two, a year or two, or even longer. Most of them left, usually enriched and inspired to go out, sometimes to a secular job or to another training, in this country or often, as in the case of continental students, abroad.

This list, taken from newsletters, reveals what a great variety of work was taken up. It is representative but not exhaustive: speech therapy, physiotherapy, occupational therapy, radiotherapy, nursing of all kinds, social work, work with the elderly, with children with special needs, with the blind, work in offices - Christian and secular, personnel management, one, into horticulture, yet another a parliamentary secretary in the House of Commons. All were appreciative of the regular prayerful support of the College. They sent in their news and prayer requests, of which the following is a very small selection:

- she writes of a great need among the people with whom she works and would value prayer for her own personal witness.

(Zurich)

- how grateful she is for prayer - she now has a post as assistant in a children's home at Chesieres-s-ollare, Vaud.

- asks for prayer for young unmarried mothers who have been converted that they may be established in the Lord.

(Mission of Hope)

- has been doing the work of a personnel officer in cotton mills - many sad problems - asks us to pray for monthly evangelistic rallies.

(Manchester)

- attached to the Family Service Unit - please pray that my contact with these families may genuinely help to ease their distress.

(Bradford)

- at Atholl Crescent Domestic Science School - pray for her contact and witness among all her fellow students.

- on the Staff of the YWCA Hostel - please pray I may continue to witness for our Lord in everything I do, whether taking Bible Study or mending sheets or just being friendly with the residents.

(Plymouth)

- Health Visiting in Surrey - taken on a Gypsy Camp - pray for wisdom in dealing with them and talking about Jesus Christ.

- with Barnardo's caring for families affected by Cystic Fibrosis ... emotionally demanding, particularly when it involves the death of a child.

- my voluntary hospital work finds me working closely with Radiographers and other Nursing staff, often giving practical help in the X-ray department of this biggest hospital in Europe.

(Southampton)

- I am progressively more involved in the world of Speech Therapy (difficult in a multi-lingual society) advising, researching, and doing some treatment. We are both very involved in local Church work, visiting etc.

(Khartoum)

- the local authority has just erected thirty-two small flats for the elderly and I have been appointed Warden.

(Wootton-under-Edge)

- I am still busily involved in local activities in connection with the Farncombe Community - we hope to begin a prayer group.

(Flintshire)

- I am still working for Commonwealth and Continental Church Society and am in charge of the Sunday School by post.

(Lillingstone Lovell)

- Ward Sister - G.P. Hospital - in charge on a block of three wards, male and female, medical and surgical - please pray for me in the many opportunities both in the Hospital and the local Parish Church.

(Haywards Heath)

- I am working as a school secretary locally and love every minute.

(Glasgow)

- assistant, Diocesan Office of Social Responsibility (Moral Welfare) - I would appreciate prayer in regard to advice and help often necessary and/or expected to be given sponta-neously to the many who 'phone with varied personal, family, social and spiritual problems.

(Winchester)

To close this chapter we quote a news/prayer request sent in by Miss Snow after her retirement to Privett. It was in the form of a P.S. to her letter to former students. It shows how she applied the teaching at St Michael's to herself first:

- please pray, not only for our Sunday School but also for a weekly class I have for about ten adults in spinning, dyeing and weaving. I am getting to know these enthusiastic stu-dents, some old, some young. One has already talked to me about a marriage problem. Pray for her that she may come to know the Lord, and for the rest that they may all do the same, for not all are Christians.

CHAPTER 20

Sabbatical

When Miss Snow had been at St Michael's nearly twelve years, the College Council offered her a Sabbatical term. She was overjoyed, and began at once to plan a journey to visit her sisters in India, and as many former students as possible who were working in India, Nepal and Pakistan.

Her own account of her travels, including her prayerful preparation for it is recorded here from the 1959 and 1960 newsletters.

Breaking the news (1959)
My dear St Michael's Family,

We have just finished our academic year, and as I look back over the years since St Michael's opened in 1948 with five students, to the present time when our numbers are nearer forty, I feel that we have much to thank God for during these last eleven years.

This leads me to a piece of news which may come as a surprise to many of you, and for which I ask your prayers. As I have been so long at St Michael's, our College Council has decided to give me a Sabbatical term. This is made possible by the very excellent staff that the college has at present and I hope will long continue with us. Please pray for them as well as for me during my absence.

I am planning to take next Hilary Term off, as not only is it the shortest term, but by that time new students will have settled in, and there are no public examinations at the end of it. Incidentally it is a good term for me to go East, which is what I am hoping to do.

S.S. Carthage
I have for a long time very much wanted to see our students' work abroad, but up to the present time this has not been possible, and even now I cannot go round and visit you all, much as I should like to do so. I am, however, hoping to visit part of India, Pakistan and Nepal. I expect to leave England on S.S. Carthage on the 8th of

January 1960. This should give me about two months in the Indian sub-continent before returning near the end of March on S.S. Canton. It does not look as if a visit to South India will be possible, much as I should like to visit our students there and Jo Roberts' work in Ceylon, but Jo is in England at present and has been down to see us. Mr Dain and Mr Norrish of the B.M.M.F. are very kindly arranging an itinerary for me, in order that I may see as much of missionary work and as many of you as possible. Please don't all plan to come home just as I am about to get out to you!

A plea for prayer

I do want this trip to be not just for pleasure and refreshment, but also one which will give me first hand experience of missionary work, which will make the work of training our missionary students here more and more useful for them as they prepare to go abroad.

I could wish very much that I could fit in Africa and South America, and Israel and the Far East, but that joy, if it ever comes to me, will have to wait until I can take longer time off and have saved some more passage money!

Please pray about the trip and all it will entail, and pray too that if God has any work for me to do during it, that I may be ready in the day of the Holy Spirit's power.

The months passed, and, the journey accomplished, Miss Snow wrote in the 1960 newsletter:

The Michaelmas term was so full and busy and there were so many things to be done before I left England that I could hardly believe I was going to India until I was on board S.S. Carthage on January 8th. I seem to have been given the right kind of inside for travelling on board ship, and I found the journey out most relaxing and restful on the whole. There were a number of Christians, chiefly missionaries, on board and we soon got prayer meetings, Bible and missionary studies, and Sunday School and evening services going. The Sunday morning service is, of course, always taken by the Captain.

We were able to spend half a day at Aden on the way out, and saw the Headquarters of the Red Sea Mission at Sheikh Othman, which is north of Aden, where Marie Thorsen worked with the Scottish Mission in this almost all Moslem city.

After Aden, Bombay was our next port of call where I disembarked. Beryl Wilson was there with the others to welcome us. After having lunch there in the University College where one of my sisters is Vice-Principal, I travelled to Nasik with the B.M.M.F. missionaries. I stayed there long enough to see the leprosy work, the Canada Hospital, and the American School. We went on to Manmad by road where I saw the children and home where Dorothy Diggens had worked, and then I had a long journey across India, which took two nights and a day, to get to Patna. Ruth Neve met me at the junction at Mogul Serai in the middle of the second night, and landed me at the Teck hospital early the next morning, where not only she worked but also Bertha Parker. I stayed a few days in Patna and saw some of the sights. Rosemary Harris took me off to see something of her work amongst students, to one group of which I was asked to speak.

Nepal - a New Testament experience
From Patna I flew to Kathmandu, where I spent a weekend at the United Mission and was well looked after by Dr Anderson, Sister Fleming and Ursula Meisel. After waiting about two hours in the Secretariat I managed to get a visa to go up country to Pokhara and Tansen. The journey to Pokhara was an easy flight over fascinating mountain country - the foothills of the Himalayan range. In Pokhara I stayed at the Leprosarium with Barbara Best and Betty Bailey. These were new friends for me, but I found that Barbara Best had known my elder brother in England years ago. While at Pokhara I visited the little Church and the Shining Hospital. Pokhara is beautiful with wonderful views of the Annapurna range of mountains, sometimes fully visible with their great snow covered peaks 26,000 feet up; at other times hidden in the mist, so that all that is seen are the brown foothills and the river valleys. The work here is fascinating, almost like that of the New Testament, for Nepal has only been open to foreigners comparatively recently. Do pray for the work that it may be "kept by the power of God".

Pokhara was on my way to Tansen, whither I was to be escorted by a Norwegian nurse, Sister Ingeborg, who came to Pokhara to collect me and two Australian missionaries from Darjeeling.

A nerve racking drive
We flew out of Pokhara to Bhairawa, not a very pleasant frontier town where we had some difficulty in getting transport over the

twelve miles to Butwal, the starting point for our trek up into the mountains of Tansen. Eventually we boarded a lorry, already somewhat full. Of all the journeys I made abroad, this was the most nerve racking, for the road was never level and never without potholes, so it seemed that at any minute we might overturn. The lorry broke down sixteen times en route, and after five miles or so of stopping for repairs and breaking down again, it gave up its struggles at last and refused to go any further. After a long wait by the side of the road in the moonlight we got into another lorry already full, and were perched precariously on our luggage at the back. We had to hold each other to keep from slipping off as we lurched from side to side and plunged in and out of the potholes.

Sister Ingeborg managed to have some conversation with some of the travellers. She was a most faithful witness to the Faith, and also had a good knowledge of Nepali. We spent the night at Butwal, dossing down in a rest room, three of us on the floor and one on a string bed. I being the oldest was given the bed and warned about possible bugs, but my prayers were answered and none appeared!

The trek to Tansen - an endurance test
After tea and a little food we aimed to leave at six a.m. for the long sixteen-mile trek up the mountains to Tansen. This is an arduous journey travelling from 1,000 feet above sea level to about 6,000. The scenery is magnificent, beginning with about five miles through a river gorge along a path cut out of the rock. Tibetan caravans of laden donkeys or ponies passed us with a merry tinkle of bells. There was just room on the narrow trail for them.

By the time we had reached the first village we were glad to stop for some breakfast after five miles of walking. Here I met the milkman from Tansen, whom Mary Cundy had sent down with a pony for me. As the next part of the journey was steep climbing, I was glad to get into the saddle but rather sorry for the good little pony, which was only about thirteen hands and who must have found me very heavy. He was a wonderfully agile beast. The track was almost perpendicular in places and never before have I ridden an animal that seemed able to climb up what looked like a stone staircase! One of the Australians, who was not a good walker, took turns with me on the pony, so our progress was slow. We reached Tansen at ten p.m. after fifteen hours on the track, but we had got there, and how glad I was to see Mary Cundy and to drop into bed in the little bungalow she shares with an American nurse, Anne Avis, of the R.B.M.U.

I spent the best part of a week in Tansen. Then Mary and I rose early one morning, and went down to Butwal again. We had a pony for part of the way and managed the return journey in about ten hours. We were taken by lorry to Nautanwa where we spent the night in the dispensary, and where many years ago an old friend of mine, Dr Kitty Harbord, worked.

Gorakhpur - Lucknow - Delhi

Mary and I spent the night on the balcony of the house where Miss Steele and the Wards have their headquarters. We left between five and six a.m. the next day and travelled to Gorakhpur by train. Here we visited the nurseries founded by Miss Warburton Booth. Then Mary and I parted, and I went on by train to Lucknow, where I stayed at the Kinnaird Hospital. Here Edna Bourn has been Sister Tutor for some years, and Sheila Nixon, who left St Michael's recently was also staying in the hospital compound doing language study. She and Edna showed me some of the sights of Lucknow, including the Residency and the Botanical Gardens.

After a few days in Lucknow I went by night train to Delhi where I was the guest of Barbara (Farrell) and Ken Jolley. They have two small children, Philip and Esther, who go to school now each morning, while Ken goes on his scooter to the Christian Literature shop, where a very good work is being done with most attractive looking Christian books. Barbara is able to do some secretarial work for the E.F.I. (Evangelical Fellowship for India) and both she and Ken have contacts with students.

I was able to see something of Delhi, which is a fascinating and beautiful city, and I also paid a visit to Sikandra's tomb and the Taj Mahal and the Old Fort at Agra.

From Delhi I was also taken in a jeep by Beryl Wilson to see village work in the district around Bulandshahr.

Family reunion - Ludhiana

From Delhi I went on to Ludhiana, where my doctor sister met me and drove me to the Medical College and Hospital of which she has been principal for about twelve years, and which I have wanted to see for a much longer time. As most of you know, this piece of medical work was founded by Dame Edith Brown and carried on by Dr Aileen Pollock, to train Indian women as doctors, nurses and midwives, in order that they might be medical missionaries to their own people. On Dr Pollock's premature death my sister, who was her great friend, was asked to take her place. Of late years the college has grown and is now co-educational. We have had four old students there - Dr Mary Eldridge, now home on furlough, Sister Ruby Holmes, who was doing eye camp work when I arrived and whose camp I visited the next day, Sister Alice Masih, and Georgina Lauckner. Georgina has had to come home owing to her father's illness (and we have just now had news that he has been called Home to God), but she is missed in Ludhiana. I have met so many of the Ludhiana staff in England that I felt very much at home there.

Surprise meetings in Pakistan
From Ludhiana I went over the border to Lahore, where Anne Cooper and Betty Cox met me and took me off to the United Hospital. Here I met Taj Mall, now Taj Unwar, and also her husband who came to a meal one evening. Elvina Masih was away unfortunately. There is much to see in Lahore, the Kinnaird School, the Kinnaird College, as well as various places of historic interest. Anne and Betty were excellent guides. I stayed for a few days at the hospital, and a few days at the Kinnaird College, where I was the guest of Miss Mangat Rai, the Pakistani Christian Principal, whom I had already met twice in England. While I was staying at the College, Sir Henry and Lady Holland were also revisiting Pakistan. Sir Henry is over eighty but was determined to go up to the N.W. Frontier where he used to work. He is an indefatigable traveller. When last we met it was in London and I did not expect to find him in Lahore.

Dorothy Boswell lectures in the College and took me out one afternoon to see Janangir's tomb and mosque and the lovely gardens in which it stands. At the Kinnaird School I also met Margaret Wilson, who is now here doing a course with us as she had gone out on short service without missionary training. We hope to have Mary Cooper from the College with us next year.

Indisposition - a change of plan
I had hoped to get up to Peshawar to see Muriel Gideon and the N. W. Frontier, a part of the country with which so many of my family have had connections, but time was against me and also an element of human frailty. I had been slightly ill for a day in Delhi,

and a couple of days in Ludhiana, and felt unable to face too many more long journeys.

I had one more before me, but this was after I returned to Ludhiana, for after a few more days there I left for the long journey down to Bombay which takes two nights and a day by train. In Bombay I stayed for a few days with my sister and was able to visit the Queen Mary High School, but otherwise rested before going on board the S.S. Canton for the journey home.

Although I had a strenuous time I have been so glad that I had the opportunity of visiting so much about which I had only heard but not seen. I visited fifteen mission stations and saw fifteen old students and met three present ones - Margaret Wilson of Lahore, Dr Shanti Lal from Patna and Kalyani Shome from Calcutta.

The voyage back was wonderfully relaxing. It seemed curious to leave roses and sweet peas behind and come back to daffodils and primroses in England. After the long journeys in India, the one from London to Oxford seemed to flash by.

❖ ❖ ❖ ❖ ❖

Miss Snow returned to a great welcome. In prayer and through her letters during her absence, everyone had had a share in the tour she had made. Typical of her humility, and in keeping with the spirit of the New Testament missionaries, she made light of the difficulties and discomforts of the journey. But we know from Mary Cundy's account of her visit that there were many trials, among them a distressing attack of diarrhoea on their return journey to Butwal; the night on the balcony at Nautanwa a chattering monkey kept them awake and Mary had a disastrous experience with an oil lamp. Also, there was the disappointment she felt of being unable to get to Peshawar to see Muriel Gideon, Head Mistress of Elizabeth High School, which was made even more sad when, only a few months later, news reached Miss Snow of Muriel's sudden death.

Not only was this a memorable Sabbatical for Miss Snow, but all those she visited were greatly encouraged that such a faithful Principal who was not young, should make such a journey to encourage them and to enable her and the College to pray for them with greater understanding.

CHAPTER 21

Prayer Fellowship,
Newsletters and Reunions

How has the family of St Michael's retained its close fellowship for
half a century since re-opening in Oxford in 1948, and for thirty
years since the merger with Dalton House? The answer must surely be by prayer, by newsletters and reunions.

Prayer fellowship

From the beginning, St Michael's was a place of prayer.

It continued to be central as it had been in the Mildmay and St
Catherine's Deaconess Houses. Miss Snow believed whole-heart-
edly in the power of intercessory prayer. She wrote in an early
newsletter:

> We are giving news from all those who have written to us
> during the past year. We would like you all to know that you
> are remembered by name regularly in prayer in Chapel, and,
> if your name is not on the list, we would love to have your
> news so that we may pray intelligently for you.

Former students and staff will recall the lists of names so carefully prepared by Miss Long and others of those serving God all
around the world, in different kinds of work, as their prayer
requests came in. In this way the names of many former students
were learnt, although we had not met them. Dr Mary Eldridge,
who spent a short time at St Michael's writes:

> I truly appreciated the informed intercessory prayer for past
> students at the daily Chapel services, knowing that such sup-
> port would continue when the present church workers, teach-
> ers and missionaries were scattered world-wide.

Within the house there were many times of prayer; privately, in twos and threes, and as a family, especially when there was a grave emergency such as the serious illness of a student or member of staff. A quote from Miss Cooke's letter in 1967 describes how wonderfully God answered such corporate praying:

> During the year (1966-7) we have seen some remarkable answers to prayer in College. At Easter, a Parish Worker Student, Ann Stowe became seriously ill with an "ideopathic anaemia". At one point we thought she would never take up her training again. But we prayed constantly and sacrificially for her, and now I am able to tell you that Ann has resumed her training here this term, and will, D.V., complete it in 1968.

Ann went on to many years of service as a parish worker and deaconess, finally marrying and retiring in 1990. In the same letter reference is made to Dss Tatton who suffered much ill health:

> In the Summer Term, Dss Tatton became ill again, and our hearts sank as we learnt that she too must be hospitalised and face serious surgery. But once again our prayers were answered. She has made a good recovery and is back with us working too hard (as usual) but very much appreciated for all she does.

Small groups met to pray for different missionary societies with which they or former students might be serving. Students and staff could be found praying anywhere, in their own rooms, in the Chapel, in the garden - wherever 'quiet' could be assured. Such prayer fellowship greatly strengthened the participants. Felicity Bentley-Taylor recalls:

> Kneeling beside a chair in my room, with my Bible open before me at Isaiah 41:9 - and the words seemed to be directed to me, personally: "You are my servant and I have chosen you and not cast you off."

These words inspired a hope which sustained her in years to come.

Another remembers being petrified at the thought of speaking at a morning chapel service, and, having met the Senior Student,

Kathleen Lefroy (Clark) on the way, being whisked into her bedroom. Kneeling by the bed, Kathleen quoted "His banner over me is love" (Cant. 2:4) and confidence was restored. About forty years later, meeting each other at a funeral at Holy Trinity, Eastbourne, where Kathleen was non-stipendiary deacon, they spoke again of this incident.

No one could have passed through the house without being faced with the challenge of the old chorus:

> I believe God answers prayer
> I am sure God answers prayer
> I have proved God answers prayer
> Glory to His Name.

Newsletters fuelled prayer

The Annual Reports of St Michael's Deaconess House issued in 1938 and 1939, were precursors to the newsletters. In these there were accounts of College activities and a record of former students' placements. This was the pattern followed soon after Miss Snow became Principal. The first letter was circulated in June 1950 and is full of interesting news. Miss Snow wrote in it:

> As this first number of the St Michael's letter goes out, I feel that we should, first of all, express our praise and thanksgiving to God for all the way that He has led us from the enrolling of the first five students for the Michaelmas term of 1948 to the filling of the College with a full quota of students a year later.

In the same letter the Senior Student editor, Anne Morgan, wrote:

> The beginning of a new venture is always a great occasion, and if the St Michael's newsletter has a rather humble guise in its inaugural issue, it follows in a great succession. It was from small beginnings that the Christian Church sprang and that the first great missionary enterprise was undertaken, when two men, Paul and Barnabas, sailed from Seleucia, to 'turn the world upside down'.
>
> We have no ancient college tradition but we are creating precedents for those who, under God's hand, will follow us.

Already the fellowship of St Michael's has become something real and of value to us all. With our high percentage of over-seas students (about fifty percent) we are doubly conscious that we are 'all one in Christ Jesus'. There is a strong family spirit in our midst, and we are proving the truth of Ephesians 2:19 'We are no more strangers and foreigners, but fellow-citizens with the saints of the household of God.'

Every year after that, a newsletter was produced and circulated to former members of the College and some friends. As well as prayer news from those who wrote in, there would be a letter from Miss Snow and a report by the Senior Student. By 1962 it was being sent to the Middle East, Africa, India, Pakistan, Sri Lanka, Nepal, the Far East, Canada, USA and South America, as well as to Europe and many different areas of England.

When, in 1968, the amalgamation with Dalton House took place, Miss Snow and Miss Cooke felt that it would be very helpful to try to keep up the production of a letter which would maintain the fellowship of prayer and strengthen the many friendships that had been made over the years. Since then the collection of information, the production and distribution of the letter have involved many folk. The first secretary was Jill Thomas, the last Senior Student in Oxford. She was succeeded by Jill Palfrey (Hubl) in 1971 who has nobly organised this ever since. Others have kindly helped in the very arduous task, and the family of St Michael's is grateful beyond words to everyone for all the love, work and prayer that have gone into it. In any one year, up to one hundred and seventy former students have sent in news - and at the time of writing the letter goes out to about two hundred and fifty people.

In the 1955 newsletter Rika Takacs (mentioned in chapter 6) while at St Michael's wrote:

Another source of endless joy is the visit of old students and going to visit others. The former is also an opportunity for the new students to meet those for whom they are praying. So, please, come and see us, write to us, pray for us, as we are praying for you, that each of us may realise to the fullest extent what it means to be children of our heavenly Father.

Newsletters over the years have made exciting reading. Every year, items sent in spoke of new things attempted for God, difficulties overcome, fruitfulness in retirement ('re-tyre-ment'?), families expanding, health failing, continual rejoicing in what God is doing still, all over the world. Here are some excerpts from the 1998 letter to illustrate:

> Bible Study Home Groups - Sunday School Class - Services in O.A.P. homes - Open House for Sunday Tea.
>
> (Norfolk)

> Have angina and arthritis problems - learn to live with them - family and Church commitments - pray faithfulness to the pure Gospel in God's Church today.
>
> (Lancs)

> In May '98 I was licensed as a Reader and will work in my parish and local Deanery.
>
> (Lincs)

> During the last year I have been able to develop the training side of the Diocesan Counselling Service. We certainly don't feel retired and life is just as full.
>
> (Argentina)

> May God guide our moves in retirement so we don't all rush away to leafier and more 'comfortable' places. Let us wear out rather than rust out.
>
> (Yorks)

> Five years since my Clergyman husband died of cancer. My four children are now, mostly grown-up - I have gone forward to offer for ordination - 24 July, 1999. I am learning a lot and loving it.
>
> (Eire)

> Reader, Exeter Diocese - I enjoy being a Mothers' Union speaker - I hope to get my Diploma in Pastoral care and have set my sights on an M.A. Theology, and pastoral work in the psychiatric wards of our area hospital.
>
> (Devon)

Retired, but keep very busy with locums, preaching, hospital chaplaincy, committee work etc. Sponsored cycle run at end of May through Outer Hebrides in aid of work amongst ethnic minorities in Glasgow.

(Scotland)

God is good and we see Him at work in many corners of Europe. Our four married children are all missionaries, for which we thank the Lord.

(Europe)

Our first and second Alpha Courses have led to a regular evening for anyone who wants to move on in the Christian faith. What took me to St Michael's and where the Lord has taken me since has brought me much blessing.

(Hants)

Surely what Rika wrote in 1955, sums up for many, what it meant to belong to St Michael's, not just for one or two years or a couple of terms, but for all the years that have followed? Who can begin to understand what it meant to folk overseas in lonely outposts, teachers struggling with difficult classes, parish workers coping with interregnums, and others in unfamiliar situations to know that numbers receiving the newsletter would be standing with them in prayer?

Reunions

A popular event each year in Oxford was the Annual Garden Party held on a Saturday in the Summer term. The tradition began in 1939, for Head-Deaconess Crathorne had written in the 1938 Report:

We hope to have a Reunion Garden Party and Sale in the Summer term. This will afford an opportunity for our people from a distance to come over and see our charming House and grounds.

And so it was that year by year many friends and former students, including those on leave from overseas, made their way back to Oxford, to meet each other and to enjoy the ministry of a visiting speaker. The gardens of 117 and 119 Banbury Road were perfect for such gatherings, but, as recorded in newsletters, the weather was not always kind. Thus in 1954 Betty Osborne and Mary Eldridge wrote:

> The Whitsun Garden Party, the social event to date did not, this year, live up to its name. To the great grief of those students who had laboured furiously in 3 days to do the weeding which they should have been doing over many weeks, the weather was too unsettled to permit of more than the briefest visit to the garden. Because of this inclemency the opening was held in the library. This time it was impossible even with the utmost ingenuity to get everyone in, and a quite impressive overflow listened from the hall. This year Miss Snow introduced three students representative of the different branches of the work at St Michael's, the first, a teacher the second, a prospective parish worker, and the third, a missionary recruit. After they had spoken briefly the Revd M. Kenworthy, Vicar of St Clement's, Oxford, addressed the guests. The company then dispersed for tea. It was then, as students observed with alarm the crowd overflowing the common room and dining room, that the need for an extension became even more urgently apparent!

It seems there was always great interest shown in who the visiting speaker would be - Joan Botterill wrote in 1963:

> Of course there was the usual tension as we all wanted to hear who was going to speak at the Garden Party. The weather on that day was lovely and it was grand to welcome so many visitors.

Many will remember with a smile that all-out effort to make the gardens respectable for this event, even - it may be recalled - going on hands and knees with scissors on the lawns to remove stalks which had resisted the lawn-mowing. But it was all worth it as this description in the 1964-5 newsletter shows:

> Pauline Dolby (Sturges)
> The day itself was warm and sunny and the meeting held in the Dining Room with opened French doors was one at which we were very aware of God's presence. Mrs Allison

closed by speaking in a simple stirring way of His grace which is always enough. This was something each of us had proved again and again - it gave us real cause to exalt His name together, as we parted, for we knew that neither His grace nor He Himself would ever fail.

After the closure of the College in 1968, there was strong desire to plan opportunities like this for coming together from time to time. At first these were arranged twice a year, once in Oxford, once in London. It was a great joy to Miss Snow to come to some of these until illness prevented it. Always there have been 'new' faces - and an opportunity to link people with their already familiar names. More recently reunions have been held more or less annually, alternating between Oxford and London. Each one has been a time of inspiration, of renewing friendship and sharing in the fellowship of prayer.

Special occasions

Three particular reunions should be mentioned. On October 30th, 1993 there was a very special reunion at 117 Banbury Road (see chapter 8 'The house next door') when between ninety and a hundred people were present. It was special for two reasons: the first that it was the **twenty-fifth** occasion when ex-students had gathered for prayer and fellowship **since 1968**; the second that it was taking place in what had been Latimer House of St Michael's - now the North Oxford Overseas Centre, a Christian hostel for overseas students. This gathering surpassed everyone's expectations; and many met folk they had not seen for perhaps thirty or more years, and others who had until then been simply names in a newsletter.

The Communion service conducted by the Revd Canon Keith Weston and assisted by former students was a time of heartfelt praise and thanksgiving.

The second reunion was the occasion of the **twenty-fifth** anniversary of the founding of Trinity College, Bristol, held in November 1996. A good number of St Michael's ex-students were able to attend functions in Trinity College and the Celebration in Bristol Cathedral at which the Most Reverend Dr George Carey, Archbishop of Canterbury, former Principal, preached. They felt glad to be there and to be praying for the work of Trinity, of which St Michael's had become a part.

The third reunion and most recent was the **fiftieth** Anniversary of the re-opening of St Michael's, after the War, in October 1948, with Miss Snow as Principal. It was arranged at rather short notice, nevertheless more than fifty ex-students, some with husbands and friends, gathered for lunch and tea at St Andrew's, North Oxford, on Saturday, September 19th, 1998. It was a wonderful afternoon! Many years of students at St Michael's were represented. **Ruth Batchelor** (Anderson) one of the first five in Michaelmas Term 1948, was present with her husband Peter. Others were from the years between 1948 and 1968, when St Michael's left Oxford. They came from far and wide, England, Scotland, Wales and Ireland. Between them, they had served in Europe, Africa, Middle East, India, Nepal, Pakistan and South America in every kind of 'work' - as clergy, clergy wives, teachers, nurses, doctors and so on.

During the afternoon, we all united in a glorious time of praise, thanksgiving and prayer for the world-wide St Michael's family - the singing almost raised the roof! Canon Keith Weston brought a riveting message on 'St Michael and all angels' from the Bible which encouraged and challenged those present. This happy time of remembering came to an end all too soon, but everyone left with the words of the closing hymn in their minds:

> No more we doubt Thee, glorious Prince of life;
> Life is nought without Thee, aid us in our strife;
> Make us more than conquerors, through Thy deathless love;
> Bring us safe through Jordan, to Thy home above.
> Thine be the glory, risen, conquering Son
> Endless is the victory Thou o'er death hast won.

People - not buildings

Writing in the newsletter in 1968, **Miss Snow** had spoken of how one day she was feeling sad at the loss of St Michael's in Oxford, when a former student, **Pat Masterman**, called on her:

> As Pat talked to me about the work (Pat was a Chaplains' Assistant in the Royal Army Chaplains' Department, at Aldershot) and its problems, and the hunger of some of the Service women to know about God - of whom most of them know nothing - God was using Pat to change my sadness over the loss of the buildings, to joy over our witnessing old stu-

dents. I have now come to see that St Michael's is not 117-119 Banbury Road, but a company of four hundred or more Christians who have lived, worked, prayed and studied with us in Oxford and are now proclaiming the eternal Gospel from as far East as Japan right across the world as far west as Chile.

It was as students left St Michael's that they could look back and appreciate what that prayer fellowship would continue to mean to them:

Now as some more of us become "old students" how we value the knowledge that we, too, will be prayed for so faithfully at St Michael's. How we praise the Lord Who called us, and has been equipping us, and preparing the place where we shall serve Him. Again and again His way, His time, His plan, has proved to be perfect. As Miss Snow reminded us in her Chapel talk on our last day, this same Jesus Christ "will never, never let go your hand ... will never, never forsake you." With such assurance in our hearts as we face new work and new situations, we may boldly say, "The Lord is my Helper; I will not be afraid."

Doreen Begernie (1962)

Staff and Students, 1966.

Some 1968 students.

The Revd. Canon David and Mrs. Valerie Gillett – Principal 1988-1999.

Dr. Francis and Mrs Renee Bridger – Principal 1999-

Trinity College Bristol

Bishop Peter Dawes, the Principal, the Archbishop of Canterbury, and Bishop Michael Nazir Ali after the Jubilee Service in Bristol Cathedral.

Jean Cooke.

Joan Garwood.

CHAPTER 22

Farewell - To Miss Snow and to Oxford

Miss Snow made known the date of her retirement from St Michael's in the 1963-4 newsletter. She had decided it would be December 1965. It would mark the end of seventeen years during which the College was blessed in its dedicated Principal. She had been the lynch pin, the hub at the centre of all that took place. Much that had happened would have been deeply discouraging to another. She faced limitations in accommodation, equipment, financial resources, and sometimes even a lack of understanding by those to whom, at the human level, she was responsible. Her joy in the Lord had kept her strong in spirit throughout. In this way she wrote:

> When I came here I dared not attempt the work without the praying support of many friends. In the very beginning I knew this was to be God's work and that I was only to be God's servant doing what He wanted me to do, because he had called me to it. It would take too long to tell the whole story of how I came to St Michael's, but it cannot be too much stressed that what has been achieved here has been what God has wrought for His glory, and that I and our staff, both academic and domestic, have been 'workers together with Him'.

> So, the years have slipped by. They have had their problems and difficulties, their ups and downs, times when things have been difficult, times of much rejoicing and always times which have proved over and over again, the faithfulness of God.

In the Michaelmas (Autumn) Term of 1965, everyone was conscious that it was Miss Snow's last term. It was mentioned in chapter 8 that the whole College travelled to London on November 8th for her Farewell. Many paid tribute to her, including the Most Reverend Dr Donald Coggan, Archbishop of York, and the Revd

Basil Gough, Principal of Clifton Theological College and former Chaplain of St Michael's.

The Archbishop launched the Appeal for the new Extension which was planned for 117, Banbury Road, and the future of the College looked secure. However, unknown to any but the St Michael's Council, all was not well. But at the time a new Principal had been appointed. Miss Jean Cooke, a teacher of Religious Instruction in Cardiff, was to succeed Miss Snow on January 1st 1966. Some years before, Miss Snow had corresponded with her about joining the staff as a tutor. But because of family circumstances that was not possible. Now, it seemed, the time was right for her to come to Oxford. Interestingly, her qualifications and experience were similar to Miss Snow's. She had a Degree in Biology, a Diploma in Theology, and many years' teaching experience in both disciplines. She was also deeply involved in leadership of classes and camps in the Girl Crusaders' Union.

Leaving St Michael's was not easy for Miss Snow. She needed to find a home for herself and her two sisters, Olive and Eileen. Students and staff prayed much about her future. It was wonderful that, within a couple of months, the way opened for her to join the staff of the Anglican School in Jerusalem (managed by Church's Ministry among Jewish people) in a voluntary capacity. She was needed to teach both scripture and biology, to do maths coaching and be form mistress of a lively class of fourteen year old boys and girls. At the school she was delighted to be teaching alongside ex-students, **Marion Allen**, **Ann Altham** and **Muriel Nie**. She even found time to study modern Hebrew.

By the time Miss Snow returned from Israel in April 1967, her sisters had procured 'Forge House' in Privett, for their retirement, so she was able to return to a home (and to Andy) and to settle there.

A new era begins

Miss Cooke and her elderly father left Cardiff and came to St Michael's for the beginning of Hilary (Spring) Term 1966. They were given a suitable flat in 119, largely because of the care and concern of the Revd John Sertin (Secretary of St Michael's Council) and the vision of Mr Kenneth White (College Architect). The students and staff gave them a warm welcome. They thought Mr Cooke had great courage in joining an all-female community. In fact he was soon looked upon as a great friend, and his practical contribution to the College, particularly in the garden, was much appreciated.

A year of building

This is an apt description for 1967. New relationships were built within the community. In March that year, the builders 'Bill' and 'Ben' (nicknamed by Auntie J) began work on the Extension to 117. As a slow and steady stream of gifts was coming in, the St Michael's Council decided to proceed in spite of growing uncertainty about the future. For various reasons the work extended over a whole year, during which carpenters, painters and more and more workmen descended on 117. What a relief and joy, when, with the new study bedrooms furnished and curtained, the dedication of the building and the new Chapel took place on Gift Day, 6th May 1967 (this has been described in chapter 8).

The beginning of the end

In October 1967, the new Wing and the new Chapel were in full use. Staff and students rejoiced in the improved facilities, and it was hoped that these would help to attract more applicants to St Michael's. But this did not happen. Numbers applying to come continued to fall. From a peak of between thirty and forty students in the early sixties, numbers fell to the twenties. There were several reasons for this; one was that once the three-year training for teachers had been introduced, there was less demand for the one-year Supplementary Course for teaching religious knowledge, and the Ministry of Education withdrew finance for it; another was the amalgamation of a couple of Missionary Societies (the Church Mission Society and the Church of England Zenana Missionary Society) with the consequence that candidates would go to another training house. Then, there were fewer women opting for parish work training (perhaps owing to the uncertainty felt over Women's Ministry). Finally, at this time, the swing towards co-education in theological training was just beginning to take effect, and was being encouraged by 'the powers that be'. Even so, at this point, St Michael's had more students than the other two recognised training houses for women.

In February 1967, Miss Cooke wrote in the newsletter of the serious excess of expenditure over income, in spite of stringent economies. The St Michael's Council considered the situation at every meeting and began to look at options. Only two courses seemed to be open to them. One was to raise large sums annually for subsidising the work at St Michael's, so recognising that it was a piece of missionary Christian work; the other would be to amalgamate the College with another which was also evangelical and missionary-hearted. Church Society, the owners of St Michael's, chose the second alternative. The decision, though regrettable, was understandable. The Society had lost a considerable sum of money on St Michael's over the years, and did not consider it right to continue in debt at a time when the bank interest rate was high. Moreover it faced financial problems over its schools. It had only recently had to close Oakfield School, Kirkby Lonsdale, and amalgamate it with Luckley School, Wokingham.

Discussions took place with the Councils of other colleges, and visits were made to them. In the end, in the spring of 1968, the decision was taken to amalgamate St Michael's with Dalton House, Bristol, on the Bristol site, in time for the Michaelmas Term in that same year. Although the actual decision was not a surprise, the Principal, staff and students were deeply shocked by the directive to close in Oxford within a few months. That left almost every member of staff both homeless and jobless, and a number of students wondering where they could complete their course. When the news became public, former students and friends of the College were horrified and many wrote letters of sympathy and support. Some were very critical of the Church Society. But the Chairman of the St Michael's Council, the Revd John Bournon, was kind, sympathetic and supportive throughout the ensuing weeks.

When Miss Snow heard of this turn of events, she confessed to being 'quite bowled over' at the thought of there no longer being a St Michael's House in Oxford. However, after sober and prayerful reflection, she was able to write in the 1968 newsletter:

> I was comforted, for God showed me another way of looking at the whole situation, and this is what I want to pass on to you all. Nothing can happen to God's children that He does not know about and that He does not allow to happen.

She could even point out some advantages in the amalgamation:

> Before I left Oxford I suggested to our Council that it should consider the possibility of making St Michael's co-educational, which is becoming the present pattern of training. At that time

the Council did not feel able to do this, but Dalton has gone ahead in this direction, and shares lectures with the men's theological Colleges in Bristol,

and again:

I have known Dalton House, its Principal and staff for a number of years and you could not have a better team of teachers. You will also go to a delightful house in a lovely position on the Downs overlooking Bristol and you will be working in much more bracing air than in Oxford's very relaxing climate.

Like others, Miss Snow was deeply concerned about the staff and wrote feelingly about them:

I expect you know that none of these ever received a salary comparable to what they would have received in a secular post, but they all took the equivalent of a missionary's pay to serve you all. So do remember them and uphold them in your prayers at this time and onwards.

The next few months were difficult. A working party was set up, consisting of members of both College Councils and members of staff. So many practical things had to be considered. The buildings were to be sold, so everything had to be disposed of or re-located - the well-stocked library, furniture, equipment, and so on. Other matters were considered, the name of the new College, students fees, bursaries, courses and so on. It was truly the united desire that all should be done under the guidance of the Holy Spirit and with all possible human imagination, insight and foresight.

"It is certain," wrote Miss Cooke, "that the new group of students who begin the Autumn Term at Bristol will have the exciting task of creating a new community in which the best features of the training previously undertaken in both Houses will be combined for the benefit of all."

Many were concerned that there would now be no Women's Theological College in Oxford. It has already been mentioned that the founder, Bishop Chavasse of Rochester, had been absolutely sure that Oxford was the place where such a Training House should be. Some have asked "Why could not the merger have been in the other direction, and the Dalton House community, where there was a smaller staff and fewer students, brought to Oxford?" There were several answers. First, the building in Bristol had some kind of covenant on it so that it could not be sold. Secondly, since Dalton House was the Women's Training House of the Bible and Churchmen's Missionary Society, it made good sense to keep it alongside the Men's College, Tyndale Hall, of the same foundation in Bristol. Thirdly, Church Society felt that they needed the revenue of the sale of the two excellent Oxford properties to help solve their financial problems.

It was nothing short of a miracle that, by the Autumn of 1968, the untiring work of the staff and friends, meant that everything had been dealt with. Staff and students had made plans for their futures, and the College in Oxford had closed. An era had come to an end, but only the end of life in the Oxford buildings. The work and witness of the College would continue, beyond those walls, through the hundreds of former students, and, for future students in the new home, in Bristol.

In due course the two houses were sold. What happened to 117 has been described in chapter 8. The story of 'Ridley', 119, is very different. Many believed at the time, and they were proved right, that this lovely house and garden was worth a great deal more than the Church Society received, £60,000 or thereabouts. The buyer, University College, intended turning it into a student residence, for which it would have been suitable. But planning permission was not granted, so it remained empty for some two years, and was at times vandalised. It was then sold, for £100,000 to the Abacus firm of builders. They pulled it down (in spite of efforts made to save it for its historical value) and built thirty-three luxury flats in its place. Many of the beautiful trees had to be preserved. Two other bits of information are of interest. Firstly, when a name for this development was being considered, Miss Cooke was able to inform Abacus that the original name of the house was 'Thackley'. Accordingly they named it 'Thackley End' and it remains that today.

Secondly, there was in Ridley Library a large book of photographs of the house and its rooms as Professor Wright had built it. In 1995, this book was accepted by the Taylorian Institute in Oxford to be kept with memorabilia to do with Professor Wright who was such a distinguished figure in the University. Giles Barber, the Librarian, wrote this letter of thanks to Miss Cooke:

> This is just a formal little note to thank you for so kindly coming in and giving us the fascinating album on Professor Wright's house 'Thackley'. Several members of the staff were, like me, most interested and I am sure that we should keep the book here. It will bear a presentation book plate explaining that you gave it and why.
>
> Once again many thanks for this evocation of Joseph Wright's world.

For Miss Cooke, it was, naturally, a vast disappointment that her time at St Michael's covered only the brief span of two and a half years; also that much of that time had been spent in discussions about the future of the College. However, as with Miss Snow, the Lord enabled her to accept what was happening with faith and courage, believing that a Christian must never be offended by what He allows. Her feelings were expressed in the 1968 newsletter:

> Finally, some of you have expressed dismay on behalf of some of us - the Staff of St Michael's, who are not needed in Bristol. We - "Auntie", Miss Manners and I, thank you most sincerely for your concern, your love and your prayers. The Lord is increasing our faith during these weeks of uncertainty with regard to our future, and enabling us to rejoice with those whose futures are made more secure by the 'merger'. He is also giving us a better understanding of the difficulties of others who become redundant in these days, through no fault of their own. We all believe wholeheartedly in the truth of Romans 8:28 for all God's children. For the present, please continue to write to us at St Michael's. In due course we hope to have private addresses to which to invite you.
>
> I would like to end on a really personal note. I have greatly appreciated these two and a half years at St Michael's and would not have missed them for anything. I have gained so much more than I can do justice to in words. There has been a wealth of experience of every kind. I have made many new friends - and I am sure have learnt more than any student. At St Michael's in the worship and work of the community, my own knowledge of the Lord, of His Word, and of people, have all increased and for all this I am profoundly grateful. I can

only say thank you to the many students, both present and former, and staff who have helped me in so many ways, and been so patient with a "beginner". I am deeply sorry to leave a sphere of work which I so enjoyed but God does not make mistakes and I trust Him fully. A friend wrote something to me which greatly helped. "Remember Elijah - he must have been puzzled when he was guided to a brook which dried up soon! But the Lord had the next place ready for him." It may be that some of you have been facing some kind of "loss", a personal bereavement, a removal of opportunity or responsibility, some change of circumstances that you would not have chosen. May you be enabled to show your utter reliance on God and His faithfulness by the way you accept it.

During the summer of 1968, Miss Cooke was seeking to re-enter the teaching profession, as well as a new home in Oxford (where they had decided to stay) for herself and her father. In a wonderful way, God provided both. In that September she took up a post in Religious Education at Wycombe High School, and there she remained for ten happy years. In their new home in Headington, former students and staff were often welcomed. The closure of St Michael's was not the end of Miss Cooke's connection with the College. Through the prayer fellowship, and reunions, she has continued to pray for and keep in touch with many who passed through the College. It has led to enriching friendships in a worldwide family held together by bonds of prayer. For this she will always be grateful. Her time at St Michael's had been only slightly more than that of most students. Yet, as for them, those years had been small hinges on which a large door had opened. In February 1967 Miss Cooke had written a message of encouragement in the newsletter. It was to prove a strength to herself most of all:

I think we are increasingly conscious of the desperate need of the world in which we live. From all sides, at home and overseas, in the Newspapers we read, in the Missionary letters we receive, it is brought home to us. If we are to 'bless' (i.e. make truly happy) the people we seek to help, it can only be as we bring the Lord Jesus Christ to them in loving unselfish service, and them to Him in prevailing, interceding prayer. Perhaps some of you are feeling discouraged in your attempt to do this? If so, may I commend to you the words of a great Frenchman - Adolph Monod (1802-1856):

"Looking unto Jesus, and not to the apparent success of our efforts. Apparent success is not the measure of real success, and besides, God has not commanded us to succeed but to work. It is of our work that He will require an account and not of our success: why then take thought about it before the time? It is for us to sow the seed; it is for God to gather the fruit: if not today it will be tomorrow; if not by us it will be by others. Even when success is granted us, it is always dangerous to let our eyes rest upon it complacently; on the one hand we are tempted to attribute something of it to ourselves: on the other hand we thus accustom ourselves to give way to relaxing our zeal when we cease to perceive its effects, that is to say, at the very time we ought to redouble our energy. To look to success is to walk by sight; to look to Jesus, and to persevere in following and serving Him in spite of all discouragements, is to walk by faith."

CHAPTER 23

The Light Still Shines

We have been heartened and encouraged as we have reviewed the history of St Michael's to realise how ongoing is the work which began so many years ago. Because it was spiritual, the light of Christ continues to shine, not only in the lives of former members of the College, but in thousands of lives touched and transformed by their message, in both life and lip. Teachers, doctors, nurses, secretaries, parish workers, translators, writers, wives and mothers have proclaimed the gospel of Jesus Christ. Through them many have received salvation and the power of the Holy Spirit.

Many ex-students are now enjoying 'active' retirement. Not a few have been 'called Home' to Heaven, to hear the Lord's words, 'Well done, good and faithful servant'. However, many others remain on 'active service' in this country and abroad.

God has His own ways of ensuring that a work for His Kingdom, begun in His name, and under His guidance will remain to completion. So it has been with St Michael's. The work which grew and flourished in Oxford continues to do so in **Trinity College, Bristol**. There, in any one year, about two hundred full and part-time students study together in preparation for a life-time of Christian service. Much that the lecturers of St Michael's deemed important has continued in Trinity. Writing in a 1998 newsletter, the **Revd Canon David Gillett**, Principal, says:

> We have long accepted the vision to be a **College without walls**, a college that is committed to breaking down the barriers between cultures, between training for ordination and lay ministry, between men and women in the church, between college, the church, the city around us, etc.

Dalton St Michael's

In the summer term of 1968, just ten students were in the middle of their courses in Oxford. Of these, four chose to go to Bristol, three

to Cranmer Hall, Durham, and three to London Bible College. In
the new environment all completed their courses successfully, gaining their certificates and diplomas. The change to Dalton House
was relatively smooth, largely due to the care and consideration of
Miss Florence Weeks, the Principal and Miss Joyce Baldwin the
Vice-Principal. The Revd Basil Gough, who was Principal of
Clifton Theological College, and his wife Stella also welcomed the
students. They were generous with their hospitality. **Dss Ann
Butler** was one of those students and writes of that period:

> Yes, it was a long time ago when we all faced changes that
> year (1968). I don't know if I really took it all in at the time.
> For instance I did not know the background against which
> things were happening and tended to pick up whatever I
> could and begin to adapt accordingly.
>
> I felt quite sure that St Mike's was the right college for me at
> the time and wanted to move to Dalton/St Michael's because
> at least it would be similar instead of moving to a completely
> different set up.
>
> The one change I found difficult was the extra work we had to
> do because the course for parish workers had altered. I hardly
> did any practical work in order to give more time to study, con-
> sequently I was very tired at the end of that year and could not
> wait to leave. Four years (two at Ridgelands) was long enough.
>
> However, we four who moved to Bristol were made to feel at
> home by the Goughs who were at Clifton, often going to
> Sunday tea. Miss Weeks also understood our difficulties very
> well and often smoothed the path for me - I cannot speak for
> others!
>
> Looking back over a long period I see that my ministry was
> undergirded by the moves. I learnt to adapt and to trust the
> Lord. Since then I have gone through four interregnums. I
> therefore feel the whole exercise was preparation for some
> very bumpy rides later on. Also lots of joy too.

Another of those students, the **Revd Anne Wright**, now
Regional Assistant for the Midlands for the Church Pastoral Aid
Society, has written:

1967-68 I was a student at St Michael's House. It was during this year that we learnt that the college was going to amalgamate with Dalton House. I remember Joyce Baldwin and I think it was Anne Quilliam, coming to Oxford and meeting with us. We also had the choice of going to Cranmer Hall if we wished.

Moving from one college to another was quite an upheaval but a few of us moved together so that helped.

The move to Dalton House proved good for me. I was very happy at DH and made more friends with students and staff. Indeed I am still in touch with some of them. I also enjoyed sharing lectures with Tyndale Hall and Clifton Theological colleges. It gave us a much wider breadth of lectures and lecturers. We were privileged to have Bible expositions each Friday evening from Alec Motyer, Jim Packer, Stafford Wright and Colin Brown.

I never found studying easy. I have since learnt that I am more suited to the non-book culture, i.e. I prefer to receive information in a non-linear and more practical way. I think I would do better in today's multi-choice way of studying!

We had not been at Dalton House too long when we heard talk of the three colleges becoming one. At that time there were many problems in the men's colleges, especially Clifton, but I can't remember the details.

Shortly after I left Bristol, Trinity College was formed and seems to have gone from strength to strength. I believe it is now one of the best evangelical colleges for training ordinands.

The Birth of Trinity

In October 1968 no one could have forecast the events of the next few years which would lead, through much travail to the birth of Trinity College. A new **Dalton St Michael's** Council was set up under the Chairmanship of the Revd H.A. Birch. An Inaugural Service took place on October 4th in Bristol Cathedral. Many supportive people attended, though the number of women students in the College that Autumn term was only twenty. Talks about another possible amalgamation with Tyndale and/or Clifton were already taking place. Early in 1968, the Church of England published a report called 'Theological Colleges for tomorrow'. Sir Bernard de Bunsen was the author. It sent shock waves through the Theological Colleges recommending an optimum size of one hundred and twenty and a minimum of eighty students, in future, at any one College.

Such a goal could only be achieved by mergers and/or closures. This report prompted many consultations between Councils and Staffs of different colleges, the details of which need not be recorded here. But it seemed obvious that Clifton and Tyndale, both being evangelical, and in close proximity, should come together. However, it was not all plain sailing! Tyndale was the Bible Churchmen's Missionary Society's men's training College, founded in 1925. (It was soon followed by the opening of Dalton House for women in 1927). Clifton had come into being through a breakaway of Staff and Principal from Tyndale (although it was not called that, then) in 1931. Both Colleges had since developed in their own way and neither really wanted to give up their independent status. But with the threat of an enforced amalgamation, or worse still, closure, 1969 heralded an urgent need to talk seriously again about coming together, and possibly to include Dalton St Michael's. But there were too many obstacles in the way and this first attempt proved abortive.

However, in 1970 the Church Assembly debated the future of theological education. It decided to reduce the twenty-one theological Colleges to fourteen - this to be done by 'consultative planning'. A Commission, chaired by the Revd Robert Runcie (later Archbishop) would suggest how this should happen.

In October that year, the Runcie Commission recommended that theological education should cease at Bristol. Clifton College would amalgamate with Wycliffe Hall, Oxford, and Tyndale Hall with the London College of Divinity, which had recently relocated and become known as St John's, Nottingham. This edict shocked everyone in Bristol and stimulated the staff and Councils to an even more serious attempt at local amalgamation. But was it too late? The future of Dalton St Michael's was also at stake. For if both men's colleges had to leave Bristol, it was not likely to survive on its own. One wonders even with this threat whether those most concerned realised what a parlous position they were in.

As late as November 1970 no merger had been agreed and the future of the colleges was uncertain. It looked as if Clifton would be forced to amalgamate with Wycliffe Hall, and Tyndale to close on October 1st, 1972. It was a very difficult - not to say traumatic - period for college councils, staffs and students.

Then - it seems at the eleventh hour - a miracle took place. Many would say it was Divine intervention. In a General Synod debate on February 18th, 1971 Archbishop Ramsey allowed the Revd Colin Craston to intervene on behalf of the Bristol colleges. "If" - he pleaded - "even at this late stage, Clifton, Tyndale and Dalton St Michael's agreed to merge, could theological education remain in Bristol?"

The same evening the House of Bishops met and considered the matter; amazingly Archbishop Ramsey agreed a conditional reprieve for Tyndale. This was their recommendation:

> In the opinion of the House of Bishops, the continuation of training for ordinands at Bristol is only possible if Tyndale Hall, Clifton and Dalton St Michael's agree to amalgamate on the Clifton site. The House therefore asks that the Governing Bodies of the Colleges concerned should immediately explore this possibility and submit their decision to the House of Bishops not later than May 1971.

So the Colleges were given another chance to 'save themselves'. A joint body consisting of representatives of the three colleges was set up, chaired by the Right Revd Oliver Tomkins, Bishop of Bristol (he did not want to lose theological education in his diocese). They considered the name, staffing, finance, doctrinal basis and administration of the combined college. Even so, difficulties emerged. At one point during those months it looked as if the merger would founder. Again, it was in the goodness of God that it survived, and on January 7th 1972 Trinity College was born. Dr Jim Packer who had been deeply involved, and was appointed Associate Principal, regarded its founding as being like the Exodus - "something remarkably long and protracted - but with a wonderful goal - a promised land - in prospect, which when finally reached, brought much joy and relief."

A letter was sent to all former students and friends of the Colleges, signed by the Revd Alec Motyer (Principal), the Revd Gervais Angel (Dean of Studies) and Miss Joyce Baldwin (Dean of Women). It included this paragraph:

The final realisation of Trinity College may properly be described as a story of death and resurrection. When it is so described the glory is given where it alone is due. To the God of all grace Who has stretched out His hand to establish what otherwise would have perished. We cannot but share with you our testimony to the wonder-working, gentle and sovereign hand of God, and call you to worshipping, praising and loving Him.

And in the St Michael's Newsletter of that year, Miss Baldwin wrote:

Praise God with us that Trinity College has been a going concern since January. We are looking forward to beginning our first full academic year (1972-3) with a new intake of about forty students. Of these ten are women making a total of twenty-five - the same number as last year. Please pray that, right from the start, there will be an atmosphere of dedication and earnestness as well as of joy and fellowship.

God is faithful - twenty-five years on

In Trinity College News, Summer 1996, the Principal, Canon David Gillett, looked back to the founding of the College, and forward to the celebrations and beyond:

For many of you reading this, it will come as a shock to realise that some of today's ordinands were tiny babies when you were among that first group of students who took part in the move from Tyndale, Clifton, or Dalton House with St Michael's - to Trinity.

Trinity began as a united enterprise in two stages. In the autumn of 1971 the three colleges embarked on a joint programme; in January 1972 they all moved onto the same site.

We rejoice in the name **Trinity**. It reminds us of the Sovereignty of God, the Lordship of Christ and the work of the Spirit in our midst. Throughout these twenty-five years, our commitment to the fullness of God's truth and the reality of His working among us has been our central focus.

At Trinity today we are particularly concerned to retain a wholehearted commitment to a clear Biblical faith together with and enthusiasm for **Mission**.

We continue to praise God for the way He has blessed Trinity with success. The College has had notable Principals and many dedicated, highly qualified members of staff. The Revd Alec Motyer brought the new College through many teething problems. He was followed (as mentioned in the Introduction) by Dr George Carey, who came from St Nicholas, Durham. Since his appointment was for the Autumn of 1983, and Alec returned to parish ministry in 1982, Miss Joyce Baldwin nobly delayed her retirement and led the College ably for twelve months.

Dr Carey's Principalship was all too short, for in 1987 he was appointed Bishop of Bath and Wells. There was rejoicing and congratulations for him, but sadness within Trinity. However, there was even more rejoicing at his promotion to Canterbury in 1990. Jill Palfrey wrote to him and Eileen to give our (St Michael's) congratulations and to assure them of our prayers.

In 1999 there was another surprising change. Canon David Gillett who had followed Dr Carey, was to be inducted as Bishop of Bolton. Again there was rejoicing but more sadness. For more than a decade David and Val his wife had given outstanding pastoral leadership to the College. On June 12th a moving Valedictory Service was held in St Mary's Church, Stoke Bishop, at which they, and leaving students were commended to God. The appreciation of their service was evidenced by a standing ovation. They took up their new responsibilities upheld by many prayers.

The new Principal, the Revd Dr Francis Bridger, met and married his wife Renee, who is also ordained, at Trinity in the 1970s. Francis was Vicar of St Mark's, Woodthorpe from 1990, having previously served on the staff of St John's College, Nottingham. He has written several books. His most recent publication was 'The Diana Phenomenon' which looked at responses to the death of Princess Diana. Francis has recently been appointed Adjunct Professor of Pastoral Care and Counselling at Fuller Theological Seminary in California where he will have a visiting teaching role, and he hopes to develop a strong relationship between Trinity and Fuller.

Students at Trinity today have a very wide age-range and come from a great variety of denominations and countries. There are single men and women and families. Younger children are cared for in an excellent day nursery. A language school is run for non-English speakers. In the curriculum there is an important course for a Certificate or Diploma in Evangelism. Postgraduate and research degrees in Theology are offered, and are validated by Bristol University. Students who leave Trinity go all over the world, just as St Michael's students so often did; some return to the countries from which they came; they go to witness for Christ, perhaps in secular employment, or to an ordained or lay ministry. They go better equipped to serve God with wider usefulness in a fast changing, multicultural, ever more needy world.

Mission into the new Millennium
As Christians we are watching and waiting for the promised return, in Glory, of our Lord Jesus Christ. We need to be ready, but, while we wait we also need to be faithful in His Service. Many millions of people still have no knowledge of Jesus Christ and the salvation which God offers to all, through Him. We believe the Lord is still speaking those words, heard by the young Isaiah more than two thousand years ago:

> Whom shall I send?
> And who will go for us?

It is our prayer that God would use the story of St Michael's House, of those hundreds of women who said:

> Here am I. Send me!
> (Isaiah 6:8)

to call someone today who will also respond to His call, and go, where He leads, to bring His light to those who live in darkness.

APPENDIX 1

Members of St Michael and All Angels Trust, Ltd. (1938)

The Right Rev. The Lord Bishop of Manchester.
The Right Rev. The Lord Bishop of Southwell.
The Right Rev. The Lord Bishop of Worcester.
The Right Rev. The Lord Bishop of Leicester.
The Right Rev. The Lord Bishop of Sodor and Man.

The Rev. G.P. Bassett-Kerry, M.A.
Miss Baring Gould
The Hon. Mrs. M.H. Corfield
Dr. H.M. Churchill
The Rev. C.L. Cresswell, M.A.
*Mrs. W.L.B. Caley
*The Rev. C.M. Chavasse, M.A. (Vice-Chairman)
*Deaconess E.E.D. Crathorne
The Rev. E.A. Dunn
The Rev. E.G.A. Dunn
*The Rev. C.N. de Vine, M.A.
R.H. Everett, Esq.
*The Rev. G. Foster-Carter, M.A. (Warden)
The Rev. J. Glass
The Rev. T.W. Gilbert, D.D.
*Deaconess C.L. Hankin
*Mrs. E.M. Hellicar
*The Rev. J.M. Hewitt, M.A.
*The Rev. C.W.J. Harbridge, M.A.
The Rt. Hon. Sir Thomas Inskip, M.P
Mrs. C.M.G. Merrin
The Rev. S. Nowell-Rostron, M.A.,B.D.
*S.D. Pears, Esq.
The Rev. A.W. Parsons
*The Rev. H.S. Phillips, M.A.
Mrs. H.S. Phillips
W.A.F. Platts, Esq., M.A. (Hon. Sec. and Treas.)
The Hon. Mrs. W. Talbot Rice
Mrs. E. Rigg
The Rev. Canon Guy Rogers, M.A.,B.D.
The Rev. O.R.M. Roxby, M.A.
Deaconess Mary Stanton
Deaconess Catherine Sandeman
*The Ven. E.N. Sharpe, M.A. (Chairman)
The Ven. F.G. Sandford, M.A.
Mrs. Tottenham.

* Members of Board of Directors.

Memorandum of Association of
The Deaconess House of
St Michael & All Angels Trust, Limited. (1944)

1. The name of the company (hereinafter called "the Association") is "The Deaconess House of St Michael & All Angels Trust, Limited."

2. The registered office of the Association will be situate in England.

3. The objects for which the Association is established are:

    (A)   To train on an evangelical basis women to be deaconesses or other diocesan recognised workers of the Church of England.

    (B)   To appoint with or without remuneration chaplains or other suitable persons as tutors or instructors in connection with the objects of the Trust.

    (C)   To promote and propagate the principles of evangelical Churchmanship and to provide means of intercourse between persons professing evangelical Church principles.

    (D)   To spread education; to promote morality and peace.

    (E)   To provide for the delivery and holding of lectures, public meetings and conferences on religion and allied subjects.

    (F)   Subject to the provisions of Section 14 of the Companies Act 1929, to purchase, take on lease or in exchange, hire or otherwise acquire any real or personal property and any rights or privileges which the Association may think necessary or convenient for the promotion of its objects, and to construct, maintain and alter any buildings or erections necessary or convenient for the work of the Association.

    (G)   To sell, let, mortgage, dispose of or turn to account all or any of the property or assets of the Association as may be thought expedient with a view to the promotion of its objects.

    (H)   To undertake and execute any trusts which may lawfully be undertaken by the Association and may be conducive to its objects.

APPENDIX 2

"Such a Candle"

By Dorothy M Barter Snow, B.Sc., B.D.

(Principal of St Michael's House, Oxford)

It was over at last - the close confinement in London, the nine months in the Tower. Over, too, was the time in prison together of the four Cambridge men, men whose names would one day help to make history. The conditions in the Tower prison had been miserable, but yet one of the four could say of the time: "We were thrust into one chamber, as men not to be accounted of, but God be thanked, to our great joy and comfort! There did we read over the New Testament with great deliberation and careful study".

Then on an April day came the breaking up of this prison fellowship. Three of the four said farewell to John Bradford, their fellow prisoner, and left the Tower to make the journey to Oxford. At that time this took two days and was broken by a night at Windsor, but at last they reached their destination where they were no longer to share a common prison, but were lodged separately. Yet, although they were no longer to have the intimate companionship which had helped their prison days in London, they were not in truth divided, for these men were "one in Christ Jesus".

Men of Learning

Who were these three who in London had been imprisoned "as men not to be accounted of"? Why were they treated as criminals, yet with a difference, for it was recognised that they were men of learning and had held high offices in the Church?

One was Thomas Cranmer, Archbishop of Canterbury, a scholar, a Doctor of Divinity, and at one time a Fellow of Jesus College, Cambridge. He had once been offered a Canonry in Wolsey's Cardinal College in Oxford, the great foundation which afterwards became Christ Church. Cranmer had refused the honour and in Cambridge continued to insist that the candidates whom he examined in Divinity should have a real knowledge of Holy Scripture. To him the English Church was one day to acknowledge its debt, for the Book of Common Prayer, steeped in Holy Writ, was largely his work.

On his arrival in Oxford this honourable old man was thrust into the Bocardo 'a filthy and stinking prison' over the north gate of the city, hard by St Michael's Church and overlooking the Cornmarket; while his two companions were lodged, one with the mayor and the other with the bailiff.

Cranmer's two friends were also men of note. Nicholas Ridley, Bishop of London, had had a distinguished career at Cambridge where he had been both a scholar and a fellow, and had held the Mastership of Pembroke Hall.

The third man, old Hugh Latimer, Bishop of Worcester, had at one time been Fellow of Clare College, Cambridge. He had also been in his early university days a doughty opponent of the Reformed Faith and had preached vehemently against the reformers. Then had come a day when he had heard the confession of a man, little in stature, but great in faith, who had found, through reading the New Testament, that indeed "Christ Jesus came into the world to save sinners".

Little Doctor Thomas Bilney of Trinity Hall, Cambridge, who had led Hugh Latimer to his Saviour, had already sealed his faith in the fires of martyrdom outside the city wall in Norwich, even as these three other Cambridge men were to "glorify God in the fires" outside the city of Oxford.

The Trial at Oxford

The trial of Cranmer, Latimer and Ridley was preceded on Saturday, April 14th, 1554, with a Mass of the Holy Ghost sung by the choir of Christ Church. From thence a procession proceeded to the University Church where thirty-three commissioners and a crowd of students and townsfolk gathered to hear three Cambridge men defend their faith in Oxford.

The three accused were told to prepare for separate days of trial. Cranmer was ordered to appear on the Monday, Ridley on Tuesday, and Latimer on Wednesday. On Friday, April 20th, all three were condemned after a trial or disputation which had developed into a farce, for the three men were baited and ridiculed, interrupted, and taunted with gibes while they sought to defend the

New Testament teaching concerning the Lord's Supper as against the Roman doctrine of transubstantiation.

Yet although the men were condemned as heretics, execution of their sentence of death was postponed. It was more than a year later when Ridley and Latimer were brought to the University Divinity School at 8 a.m. on the 30th September, 1555. Archbishop Cranmer was ordered to appear later still before his judges.

For Bishops Latimer and Ridley the end was in sight. At long last were finished the questionings and disputations, the arguments and the ridicule. Although Cranmer's execution was to be postponed to the following year, Latimer and Ridley were to die and to die shortly.

A strong stake was driven into Balliol ditch outside the city wall and on October 16th, 1555, the two bishops, both of them the greatest preachers of their time, were led out of Oxford city to be burnt alive in defence of "the faith once delivered to the saints".

"Be of good comfort, Master Ridley, and play the man. We shall this day light such a candle by God's grace in England as I trust shall never be put out." Thus did old Hugh Latimer encourage his fellow martyr, Nicholas Ridley, as they were led out to die on an autumn day four centuries ago in Oxford.

Did they die in vain?
Did they and the martyrs before and after them, who gave their lives for the Faith, die in vain? Was the lighted candle of truth put out in England? Surely not.

After Queen Mary's disastrous reign the Church of England broke from Rome and was reformed, and her Prayer Book is a lasting memorial to Cranmer and his work. In spite of difficulties, setbacks, and even disloyalties, the Church of England is, according to her articles, a reformed church, accepting no doctrine which is not based on, or in accordance with, the teaching of Holy Scripture.

Was the candle put out at Oxford?
Certainly not. Oxford has had its struggles to maintain the Evangelical witness, but the candle of truth has been kept burning ever since the Reformation. In the Broad, the wide street, which was once a ditch, there lies embedded in the middle of the roadway, a cross which marks the place where Latimer and Ridley died that there might in England be lit "such a candle by God's grace". Just

round the corner in St Giles, the graceful and beautiful Martyrs' Memorial stands as a witness that Cranmer, Latimer and Ridley did not die in vain and that they are remembered still.

These are material memorials, but there is more than these in Oxford. To-day there are at least half a dozen or more Evangelical churches in the city, and several of these, in addition to a large regular congregation, are crammed with undergraduates and other University members during term. The Reformer Wycliffe's name is perpetuated in an Evangelical College for ordinands named after him. The Bishop Jewel Society and the Oxford-Inter-Collegiate-Christian Union are flourishing Evangelical Societies in the University. The Reformed Faith defended to the death in Oxford by Bishops Latimer and Ridley in 1555 and Archbishop Cranmer in 1556 is still faithfully preached and taught in Oxford in this fourth centenary year of 1955, when, on Whit Monday, loyal church people from all over England will come to Oxford to give thanks for the Reformers who died there for the Faith.

St Michael's House
There is in Oxford a more recent centre of Reformed teaching than any of these just mentioned. Seven years ago an Evangelical theological college for women was opened. St Michael's House began its present work in 1948 with five students. It has now sent nearly a hundred trained women to work for God in Evangelical parishes in England, to schools where old St Michael's students teach as Scripture specialists, and to the far places of the earth where other old students are doing missionary work, evangelising, teaching, healing. St Michael's has old students in Israel, Arabia, Uganda, Nigeria, Ethiopia, India, Pakistan, Ceylon, and most European countries, as well as in England. Shortly the college will be represented in Malaya and the Far East.

St Michael's outgrew its original house just over three years ago when it moved to Banbury Road. The work has continued to grow and for some time we have had to sleep students out with very kind hostesses in the vicinity of the college. We have prayed much about some kind of extension to our present premises, but to build what would be adequate for our number would be a most expensive undertaking with the present costs of labour and materials.

Any plans we have made for building have been frustrated because we feel God has all along had something better for us. We have been told that this autumn the next door house will be available and this would give us far more than would have been possible had we tried to build at the same cost. After much prayer our Council has felt that they should agree to purchase this house, especially as we have some money in hand sent by friends for this extension in answer to prayer.

To complete the purchase, make certain necessary alterations, and buy extra furniture, the sum of just over £8,500 is needed. This is for us a very large sum, but we are praying that as the need is made known, God will lay this work on the hearts of those whom He would have support it.

What would God have you do?
In this year 1955 when we celebrate after four centuries the martyrdom of Latimer and Ridley, who lit the candle of the Reformed Faith in Oxford, there may be some whom God is leading to celebrate the year by helping to extend a work which stands for the Evangelical Reformed Faith for which the martyrs died. Perhaps this year some are being called to keep burning in Oxford "such a candle by God's grace ... as ... shall never be put out".

St Michael's House is, and always has been, a venture of faith, and we believe that in answer to prayer God **will** supply all our need so that we can go forward, unhindered by lack of means and accommodation, to work for the extension of His Kingdom to the glory of our Lord Jesus Christ. For this we ask the prayers of all Christian people.

APPENDIX 3

Poetry and Prose

Most of the following have been extracted from annual newsletters.

And was the Son of God born in a manger?

1. And was the Son of God born in a manger?
   That cannot be!
   To man, the promised One was but a stranger
   Of low degree.

2. Yet did He toil and sweat? Did He too sample
   A busy day?
   Christ Jesus lived on earth as our example,
   Showed us the way.

3. Surely He was not tempted by the devil,
   Yet without sin?
   Empowered by Him, we too may conquer evil,
   His peace may win.

4. Did He, heart-burdened, kneel to God His Father,
   Each detail share?
   If Jesus watched long hours, then how much rather
   Do we need prayer?

5. But was it possible that Christ could languish
   Upon the tree?
   For us Our Lord endured that bitter anguish
   At Calvary.

6. He bore our sins - surely you are mistaken -
   How could this be?
   Upon the cross, made sin, He was forsaken
   For you and me.

7. Tell me again how Jesus rose victorious,
   Quitting the tomb!
   Buried with him, we too may claim a glorious
   Eternal Home.

8. Compelling Love! How can we still disown Thee,
   Saviour adored?
   We bow in awe, and in our hearts enthrone Thee,
   Redeemer, Lord.

Wyn Cornish

Buffaloes in the Bathroom

Actually there was only one buffalo, and she was only half in, but even one half of a buffalo is a rather disconcerting fellow-inmate of a bathroom.

Perhaps, being a water-buffalo, she wanted my bath water. Perhaps she was merely curious. Whatever the reason, as I entered the bathroom from my bedroom, there she was, half in, and half out of the outer door by which pails of water are generally brought in. Her owner was pulling her tail, but there wasn't room for him to push past her and drive her out. Fortunately she found my entrance as disconcerting as I found hers, and backed clumsily out.

When I had been in India only a very few weeks there was a great shouting and jumping around in the dormitory I had just locked up. The children should have been going to sleep, so I raced across to see what was the cause. It was not a buffalo in the bathroom this time, but a snake in the shoe-cupboard!

The children's method of dealing with this situation was to leap from bed to bed with squeals of excitement. I did not know the proper method, but this seemed to me to lack efficiency, though they seemed to enjoy it. I took a shoe brush and swept the snake into a shoe box, carried it out, and emptied it over a wall into a field below. I have since been told this was not the conventional method!

A more common and dangerous enemy is the mosquito who can ruin your sleep, waste hours of your time just evading the blow you aim, or perhaps give you malaria. Malaria feels like gastric 'flu alternating with a tense shivering, such as you would feel under the dentist's drill in a refrigerator. A mosquito inside a mosquito net is the worst kind of mosquito, and though it will find its way in if there is a single thread broken, it will never find its way out.

There are lovely animals too. Tiny deer, about as big as a fox-terrier, called mouse deer, can often be glimpsed in the jungle. Grey squirrels with three dark stripes on their backs leap everywhere in the trees. The story is told, that when one of the gods was wandering about on the earth one day he lay down and slept under a tree. He slept so long that the shadow of the tree moved round and his head was in the sun. A squirrel living in the tree saw the danger, and sat near the god, shading his forehead and eyes with his tail. The grateful god, on waking said "You dear little thing", and stroked the squirrel. The marks of his fingers can be seen to this day.

Peacocks and parrots, often startle eye and ear by their bright colours and harsh call, and bul-buls which have robin-like characters sing as sweetly as nightingales.

The main difficulties of Indian life are not the discomforts of bats in the rafters or rats on one's pillow, or even a panther in the garden - though all these may be there. They are the spiritual difficulties of maintaining one's faith against a steady pull down. Everyone else accepts lower standards, and when these are matters merely of feeding, clothing and pay, the Christian foreigner should, I think, welcome them: but in matters of conscientiousness, efficiency and consideration for others, and above all spiritual standards, no compromise is possible. She is often unable for weeks or months at a time to meet other keen Christians and this steady pull against downward forces of inefficiency, slackness and even deliberate purposeful evil, demands an hourly dependence upon God. One must have learnt beforehand to get one's spiritual food direct from God, not only for oneself, but for those thousands upon whom Our Lord has compassion - about whom He says to us "Give ye them to eat".

Beryl Wilson

Some Netball !

Miss Snow, St Michael's Warden, has a brilliant
    netball side,
They've never had a beating, tho' the Wickers men
    have tried.
Two afternoons of last term, when they ventured out
    to play
The Mickeys donned their fighting spurs and won
    the well fought day.
The Wickers men, who quite ashamed crept back
    into their Hall
Were greeted by their student pals, "chaps, this
    won't do at all".

So now St Michael's tremble when they think of
    their next game,
They've lost two stalwart players - now will they
    lose their fame?
For Wickers will come armoured, with shield and
    banner bright
To beat up poor St Michael's and win the glorious
    fight.
The battle will be furious as they tear from post to
    post
The shooters working overtime, to try and score the
    most.

A final word should just be said, but I will keep it
    curt,
Discreet young maids leave games alone, if you
    would not get hurt.
True love and netball are alike, in these I'm sure
    you'll find
The rough and smooth go side by side, and leave
    their scars behind!

Anon

A Day in the Life of a Student

What an awful noise! Oh, the rising bell as usual - and the alarm clock - enough to waken the heaviest sleepers. And so the day begins.

It is wonderful how different we all are at six thirty a.m. Some annoyingly cheerful, others just sleepy, and longing to creep back into a warm and comfortable bed which is always most inviting at that hour. However, we revive after a cup of tea, brewed by a thoughtful student - who has had to do it because it's her turn!

Another bell is rung at seven a.m. and the day begins, as it should, with the Lord Himself. The precious half hour slips by all too quickly - especially if wandering thoughts have their way - but we rise to tackle the day's work with the sure and certain knowledge that the Lord is there to strengthen and uphold. Now the attack on dust and dirt is launched, and figures scurry round waving dusters and mops - noble banners! Alas! sometimes the said dust and dirt are conquerors, aided by their old friend "procrastination".

While we are busy this way, Miss Carpenter and her helpers are also busy, seeing to the needs of the inner man (or woman!). Appetites are keen in this corner of Oxford, and many an Oliver Twist cries "More please" and gets it! If a visitor should happen to visit us some morning and finds that conversation is non-existent, the said visitor would find the explanation - kippers!

Prayers follow breakfast when we unitedly seek God's blessing on the day that lies ahead.

The morning passes all too quickly. Lectures and study soon fill the time as we read in, and around, God's Word in order that we may ourselves learn, and then endeavour with His help, to teach others.

Just as mental and physical exhaustion reach their peak, a bell rings in the distance. Dinner! At this meal all the stops are pulled out, and everybody seems to talk at once - it is very reminiscent of a zoo in some respects!

Most days follow the same pattern, so we'll choose Saturday - which is sometimes unique in that we are livened up by a netball match against Wycliffe. This game can be very exciting in many ways! For one thing it is highly unorthodox in that the ball has a fatal fascination for a few members of both teams, and if it should fall to the ground they hurl themselves at it and hold on for dear life! Mercifully our umpire is adept at breaking up such cliques. So far, which is really not very far, we have managed to win. But tables may be turned some day, and the not so gentle maidens may suffer defeat.

Saturday night can be spent in a variety of ways. "Getting ready for Sunday" ranks high in the list, as we complete our talks for Sunday School or Bible Class. Many attend the OICCU Bible Readings, where together with many like-minded people, we join in praising God, and listen to one of His servants expounding the Word. How good it is to be here and have these opportunities of learning of Him on weekdays and on Sundays. Learning, that we may eventually teach to others the precious truths He imparts to us.

Lack of time prevents further mention of many other activities, which are packed into the students' day. Lectures which are sometimes light-hearted and lively - but not always; visiting in homes and hospitals, seeking by God's help to bring a message of hope and comfort from Him; Sundays when we attend our various churches to worship the Lord, and seek and find strength to go on. Again, those gay and sociable gatherings after supper when a few of us meet in one room or another and congregate over the inevitable "cuppatea", and bedtime when hot drinks are brewed - cocoa and ovaltine for some, tea for others.

And so to bed, having sought the Lord's forgiveness for the failures of the day and found rest and peace in His forgiveness and the promise of strength for tomorrow.

Anon.

My Impressions of England

It might be safer to write something like this when one has left the country, but I will try not to write anything that could hurt anybody's feelings. Anyway, I believe that I shall not get into any trouble, because the English people are too polite to come and blame me. Politeness was the first impression I had about the Englishmen. Everybody was ever so polite to me (and they are still!): sometimes I felt quite uncomfortable because I did not know what they really thought. Now after eight months I have still sometimes that feeling but I know now that some people are frank.

I did not expect that people here would know much of my country Finland, but I was a bit surprised to find that many of them only knew the Olympic Games, and some perhaps Sibelius. England is a beautiful country, but my country is more in its natural state. The English love their gardens and parks and keep them really beautiful and always in good condition. The English Spring with various kinds of flowers and fruit trees is a simply lovely experience for one from the North.

One can see nearly anywhere beautiful buildings, old castles, fascinating colleges and magnificent churches, but I am always a little shocked to see how dirty and black the outside of these wonderful buildings is. England is a clean and tidy country, but it is strange to see that in cafes the cakes are kept on the window-sill for many hours and then brought to the table. When one buys biscuits at the grocer's the girl puts them in a bag with her dirty hands - we generally use tongs.

The English gardens are beautiful, but the graveyards look very sad and untended. I can say that ours are beautiful with their trees and flowers. But then - our highways are often in a poor state, and in England they are smooth and marvellous. Here we come to the difference in the wealth of the countries again.

I knew before I came to England that those English people who go to church attend very regularly. I thought at first that it was a tradition, too, but now I know that they go there for their heart's desire. The English Christians have a marvellous discipline, for example, in regular quiet times. They have a very living, personal interest in missionary work, and every Christian feels the responsibility for those who do not believe.

258

Now when the Coronation is so near it is moving to see how dear the Queen is to everybody, and how people pray for her.

The English tradition - you dash against it every now and then. When things have been like this for hundreds of years, they say, why should they be changed? I first thought it very funny that students wore their robes even on bikes, looking quite serious - we have only a cap - but one gets used to them, too. Is it because of the tradition that the English houses are so cold? They are not built for the winter, I have heard. In the bathroom there is no shower and in the kitchen only one sink for washing up. There are lots of little and big things like these if you start to think.

I do admire English people in their letter-writing. They write to a great many people and very often, too. The secret is probably that these letters are very short and to the point. The Continental letters have been called "novels" by the English people. The English have a good sense of humour.

My impressions of England are both good and bad, but I think that the good things outweigh the bad. I like "merry old England" very much. I shall be glad to go back to my own country, but probably I shall sometimes be homesick for England, for its gardens and parks, in spring bloom, wonderful old colleges in Oxford and Cambridge, for St Michael's House and all the dear friends. When I am rich I shall come back to see what I think about England then, being an old lady!

Elli Mollari (1953)

Grass Green Novices

Grass green novices in College evangelical
Treading through their paces in matters strictly Biblical
Putting all the prophets in an order chronological,
Studying sound doctrine in matters theological,
Making sure that answers are absolutely scriptural,
Clothing not their ignorance in metaphors elliptical,
Stepping very carefully in matters metaphysical,
Grass green novices in College evangelical.

Felicity Foster-Carter

The Voice

Insistently I heard a voice,
My arms were folded round myself,
I stretched them out to touch the world
And found His hands in mine.

Felicity Foster-Carter

The Wind

Lord, I don't like the wind
It unsettles me.
I shiver in its path
It means things are changing.
But, Lord You made the wind
It can scatter the seeds
As well as destroy.

Things are always changing, Lord.
Without the wind how dull life is.
We need it blowing us from lethargy to life.
It can scatter new ideas
And sweep away misconceptions.
Lord, thank you for the wind.

Anne Sankey (Gathercole) from *"Towards Tomorrow"*

Prospect and Retrospect
(With apologies to Browning)

Oh to be in Oxford,
Away from parish strife,
Where the woes of green-frocked workers
Make a travesty of life!
For the youth club riots and the children wrangle,
Visitors crowd and the meetings tangle!
'Though we sound depressed, we're quite content
Where we've been sent.'

Oh to be in Oxford,
Now that summer's there,
For whoever wakes in India
Sees each morning - weather fair,
And the sun will scorch and the missionaries drip,
The brain will clog and the creatures nip!
But the Word goes forth in St Michael's way
In India - today!

(by Students)

All Angels?
(To be sung to the tune of "Cargoes")

Students from St Michael's trying hard to be as good as gold,
    And learning the Kings of Israel!
With their Bibles and note-books, pens and pencils,
    Wondering about the date of Daniel.

Busying themselves with weeding or with making paths of brick,
    (Oh what is the theme of Habbakuk?)
With their trowels and pitch-forks, mops and dusters,
    (Who cares if philosophers would love a duck?)

Pedalling down the road to get to Timm's in time to punt,
    Wondering which college "eight" the bumps will win,
(With their doctrine text-books far behind them!)
    Knowing that Man's grace to see is not a Sin!

Mary Cawthorne (Bogg)

Parish Workers in Training

If you ever go to Oxford
Then call at 119;
It's there they train the ladies
In a very special line.

You'll always tell they're coming,
For they're dressed in neatest green;
They're really most efficient
The smartest ever seen.

They are given special training
In how they are to cope
When they're landed in a parish
(They'll be every vicar's hope)

They are taught to ride a cycle,
The oldest one you find,
They can cook upon a candle
And never seem to mind.

They are used to making do
On the smallest kind of fee;
They'll turn their hand to anything
No matter what it be.

They are taught to speak to ladies,
To keep the children good,
To type the vicar's letters
And do everything they should.

They'll do the baby sitting
They'll visit you in bed,
They'll go on all the outings
And work until they're dead.

But still they're only humans
Not come down from the sky;
They may appear like angels
But you'll never see them fly.

So, vicars, are you listening?
Then take a tip from me,
If you want a Lady Worker,
St Mike's is where she'll be!

Anon

Happy Memories of my Oxford Year
1959-60

Oasis - in a city? Yes,
St Michael's House - a training place
For those who sought most earnestly
To serve the Lord in various ways those years ago.
The Parish Workers with their uniforms of green.
And Teachers, Missionaries, Clergy Wives and 'Others'.
Communal living and its discipline
Was necessary for our learning.
Sharing rooms and experiences.
Confessions written in the late book.
Our housework so the 'ship' remained afloat.
Lectures and weekly Bible knowledge tests.
Our own research (by books it all was then).
And daily worship in our lovely chapel.
The panic for some to discover that
Hats were obligatory on Sundays.
Also no use of public transport then.
For me the memories are precious
Of that unique experience: a year in Oxford
(Quite beyond my wildest dreams at school!)
Seeing famous places and meeting famous people.
Even attending the Keswick Convention
As part of 'the Course'.
I gained some documents of academia
To certify my studies were successful;
I have them yet (along with scarf and blazer -
still donned occasionally!)
And Andy, butter tubs, the Judas tree.
The pillared portico of one one nine,
Playing for chants and wearing a 'skid lid'
As a pillion passenger (both new to me)
Are all part of my history
And contributed to the learning process
Because - οικονομιαν πεπιδτευμαι.
My pilgrimage continues!
Thank you SMH.

Nancy H Dear (died 1998)

The Beech Hedge
St Michael's House 119, Banbury Road, Oxford.

Oh beech hedge, so firm and so enduring,
I praise the Lord who made thee so.

The dejection of Autumn
Was dispelled by your glory -
The net brown crisp of your leaves,
Michaelmas daisies and red hot pokers
Piercing the purple with daring ease.
Could one look and still be wrapped in pity?
Enjoying dejection with selfish thought?
Not for this was salvation wrought.

In front of the hedge
The daffodils came,
The tulips too, with wonderful colour.
The leaves were renewed
And grew tender and green
Filled with new life rich and free
Given by Him who giveth to all
New life as they wait for His dew to fall.

Today the hedge is bathed in sunlight
The lupins lift their heads in praise.
The splash of scarlet reminds me of One
Who gave His life for a world undone.
The pale yellow irises, delicate, lovely
Speak of the peace that pervades the whole scene.
The ramblers that wave and nod in the breeze
Joyous and right as they add to the view.

O Father, how gracious Thy bounty
To give me this sight
And through it to teach me
That Thine is the Hand
Which gives so much richness
And warmth to delight.

O beech hedge you helped me and pointed to God
And just by existing have shown me so much.
In days that may come you will be used again
To reveal to some seeker that sunlight in rain

And enable another to join in the praise
To speak of the wonder of His Holy ways

Kathleen Lefroy (Clark) June 1958

O God Accept the Worship

O God, accept the worship of a creature
Stirred by Thyself in autumn,
Warmed by the sun on dew-damp grass,
On burning height of trees
And in the glow of glad chrysanthemums.
Receive thanksgiving for the fleeting scent
Of bonfire smoke among gold leaves,
And for the purging light of day
Which paints the postbox up the road.
O God, accept the worship of a creature
Whom Thou dost visit with Thy beauty.

O God, receive thanksgiving from Thy creature
For transcience of autumn,
For funeral days of loveliness
And all the grief of death,
For all that leaves our soul unsatisfied.
Perfect in me the praise of Jesus Christ
Who in His glory never dies,
And in compassion ever lives
To bind myself to Thee in love.
Father, fulfil Thy purpose in a sinner
To whom in autumn Thou art Spring of life.

Felicity Bentley-Taylor (Houghton)

Psalm 91:1

"Under the shadow of the Almighty", what a
    wondrous place to be,
For it's there I find refreshment, I'm assured of
    victory.
For the shadow of the Almighty means that God is
    very near;
And that myself is hidden, that His Glory may
    appear.

If I know I'm in His shadow then in anguish I'll
    not fear
For I know my Saviour loves me, and tho' hidden,
    He is there.
I have proved His promise often, in the place of
    darkest night,
And I know He will not fail me - that at eventide
    there's light.

In the shadows of the morning, when the
    dangerous tests I meet,
The Lord will be my Counsellor and guide my
    wandering feet.
But no shadow lasts for ever; tho' defeated once or
    more,
When the morning comes, I'll see Him standing on
    the new day's shore.

Joanna Crick (Goodwin)

The Hope of the World

"Not by might, nor by power, but by
My Spirit, saith the Lord of hosts."

Zechariah 4:6

Not with the tramping of armies and not by the
    might of sword,
Came the supreme Revelation, the begotten Son of
    the Lord.

A Baby born in a manger, Messiah Who suffered
    and died,
Thus to the world came redemption -
    God incarnate, God crucified.

In the deep calm of His Spirit is strength for war,
    peril and loss,
Peace through the Babe of the manger, victorious
    life through the cross.

Dorothy M Barter Snow

They Left One Oak Tree

They left one oak tree
when they rebuilt the Church.
I thought it was dead.
Now I can see leaves
of celebration.
You left one spark
when you rebuilt me.
I thought it was dead.
Today I heard a cuckoo
with joy in my heart.

Anne Sankey (Gathercole)

Bandage my Heart

Bandage my heart
With absorbing love
Which will staunch
The gentle flow of grief.

It is like bleeding
Seeping through the stuff
Of daily living,
Staining, colouring
All of my days.

Yet comfort is coming
In the reality of aloneness
After the tearing apart ...
The division of oneness.
The exposure that is negative
Must gradually become positive.

The bandaging is being done
By the gentleness of friends
Who open their hearts and homes,
Who love and accept
Who care and act.
Through letters and cards.

Words chosen with thought and prayer,
Words poured out
In spontaneity of love and shock ..
Practical kindness
Expressed with love
Binding wounds
Bandaging with the touch
Of the Master Physician.
Firm, loving, true, gentle -

Then the convalescence
To a different life -
With the ongoing healing
Wholeness and holiness
From the Holy One.

Kathleen Lefroy (Clark)
September 10th, 1998.
After the death of her husband, John.

King of the Universe

"He emptied Himself of His glory ...
Wherefore God also hath highly exalted Him."
Phil 2,7,9 (Lit translation)

Bend, lowly bend as you enter the stable
And worship the Babe in a manger Who lies;
Heaven was His throne and the earth was his footstool,
Winds were His chariots sweeping the skies;
Angels bowed low had hastened to serve Him,
King of the Universe - lowly He lies,
Outcast and poor in a mean humble manger
God looks at men through a Baby's soft eyes.

Lift up your hearts, for the Christ of the Manger
Living with men through the long starless years,
Died for their sin, but the grave could not hold Him,
Triumphed o'er death, over sin and earth's tears,
King of the Universe - stooping to enter
Your heart and mine if implored as a guest
Soon will return in His glory and power
To set up His kingdom of peace and of rest.

Dorothy M Barter Snow

Pilgrimage

As a child
At my mother's side
I learned to pray
In a simple way.
To understand
How a Father's hand
Could protect and guide
Or gently chide.
Then, later, to grow
And begin to know
The truths of His Word
In reverence heard
Or quietly read,
Its power to spread
From head to heart
And faith to impart;
Faith in His Son
Whose victory won
Salvation for man,
Fulfilling God's plan.

I sought to find,
Engaging my mind
The paths of His will,
His way to fulfil.
He granted a Guide
In my heart to abide
So tender yet strong,
Reproving the wrong,
Affirming the right;
Revealing His might
As I learn to obey,
To fathom His way,
The journey goes on,
Many seasons now gone;
New challenges wait -
Opportunities great -
More lessons to learn,
Some simple, some stern;
Much yet to attain
Through experience and pain
Till, the pilgrimage past,
I reach Home at Last!

Jean Reader
from *'Upward and Onward'*

I Thank You Lord

I thank You, Lord that I can talk,
That I have legs, and I can walk,
That I have eyes to see around,
And ears to hear the slightest sound;
That I have hands with which to serve -
Great blessings I do not deserve.
I dedicate my all to Thee,
Whilst I have strength, Lord, please use me.

Dss Annette Tatton (died 1982)

APPENDIX 4

Some books written by, or about, St Michael's ex-students or staff

Author	Book Title
Cynthia Bunch	Developing an Approach to Primary RE The World's Best Seller (Project pack for children) Ludhiana Hospital Blood Bank Christ Lives Here - Adult discussion material for a video (S Korea and Japan)
Anne Cooper	Ishmael My Brother Heart to Heart
Joan Crewdson	Christian Doctrine in the Light of Michael Polanyi's Theory of Personal Knowledge
Margaret Cundiff (Smith)	Called to be Me and Following On I'd like you to Meet Living by the Book My Kind of Day Good Morning it's Margaret Travelling Light The Cost of Living One More Step Northern Lights Miracle in the Dales The Church around the Corner Something for the Journey
Mary Cundy	So great a God Better than the Witch Doctor Muriel's Children (story of Muriel Ainger, Gorakhpur Nurseries)

Margaret Habermann (Morris)	Persistent Whisper
Gillian Hunt	All the Pieces Fit
Edith Mullins (Gooding)	Equal but different
Margaret Price (Neve)	Social Studies for Pakistan Books 1-5 A primary social studies series for English Medium Schools in Pakistan, with accompanying Teachers' Guides. At Work with Words Books 1-4 English as a second language, for use in Pakistan.
Anne Punton (Dexter)	View the Land (by Anne Dexter) The World Jesus Knew (by Anne Punton)
Jean Reader	Stepping Stones (Poems) Upward and Onward (Poems)
Helena Rogers	Reaching for the Crescent Moon (Mike and Mary Cawthorne [Bogg])
Anne Sankey (Gathercole)	Stoughton, Guildford, People and Places Towards Tomorrow (Poems) From Yesterday (Sarah Cadle's Notebook 1887 - 1906)
Ruth Stranex	Amudat Sister (Ruth's story)
Margaret Wardell	Entering another's World Sharing Good News Chapatis for Tea Lions, Princesses, Gurus When Love Prevails

APPENDIX 5

Languages, Societies and Educational Establishments in other Countries

During the course of their ministries former St Michael's students mastered **many languages**, some of them are listed below;

Amharic	Marathi
Arabic	Mataco
Burmese	Nepali
Guarani	Pakistani
Hakka	Pokot
Hausa	Singhalese
Hebrew	Spanish
Hindi	Suk
Hokkien Chinese	Swahili
Japanese	Tagalog
Lengua	Urdu
Lugbara	Xavante
Mandarin	

They also served in **many different Societies**, including:

Africa Inland Mission
Bethel Mission
Bible Centred Ministries International
Bible Churchmen's Missionary Society - Crosslinks
Bible Medical and Missionary Fellowship - Interserve
Canadian Caravan Mission
China Inland Mission - OMF International
Church's Mission among Jewish People (CMJ)
Commonwealth and Continental Church Society - Intercon
Edinburgh Medical Missionary Society
European Missionary Fellowship
Jane Furse Hospital, Transvaal

Ludhiana Fellowship
Methodist Missionary Society
Mission to Mediterranean Garrisons - Mission to Military Garrisons
Nurses Christian Fellowship International
Qua Iboe Mission
Regions Beyond Missionary Union
Rwanda Mission
South American Mission Society
Students Christian Association
Sudan Interior Mission
Sudan United Mission
Sunday School by post, British Columbia
Swedish Evangelical Mission
The Christian and Missionary Alliance - Netherlands Branch
The Evangelical Alliance Relief Fund (Tear Fund)
Thonon Evangelistic Mission - France
United Mission to Nepal
World Evangelisation Crusade
Wycliffe Bible Translators
Zenana Bible and Medical Mission - Interserve

Some of the educational establishments in other countries in which St Michael's students worked:
Bishop Azariah High School, Viyayamada, India
Wynberg-Allen School, Mussoorie, India
Woodstock School, Mussoorie, India
Kimmins High School, Panchgani, India
The Christian Writing Institute, Nasik, India
St Hilda's School, Ootacamund, India
Paton Memorial School, Bombay State, India
Orphan Homes and Schools, Sholapur, India
The Women's Christian College, Calcutta, India
St Faith's School, Gajra, Lyallpur, India
Elizabeth High School, Peshawar, Pakistan
Boys Public School, Peshawar, Pakistan
Kinnaird College, Lahore, Pakistan
Kinnaird High School, Lahore, Pakistan
The Sharp Memorial Blind School, Rajput, Pakistan
St Denys School, Murree, W Pakistan

Sudan Mission Schools and College, Gindiri, Nigeria
St Anne's School, Ibadan, Nigeria
St Peter's College, Kaduna, Nigeria
Elelenwa Girls' School, Nigeria
Goli Schools, Uganda
Kinyamasia Teacher Training College, Uganda
Hunters Trees Teacher Training College, Kenya
Njase Girls School, Zambia
Orthodox Church School, Makalle, Ethiopia
The English School, Addis Ababa, Ethiopia
Primary School, Dabat, Ethiopia
Kamunting School, Malaysia
CMS School, Hong Kong
The Noor School, Teheran, Iran
Lebanon Evangelical School, Beirut
Lebanon Evangelical School, Tyre
The Evangelical School, Ramallah, Israel
Tabeetha School, Tel-Aviv, Israel
The CMJ Anglican International School, Jerusalem, Israel
Ahliyyah Girls School, Amman, Jordan
Mission School at Makthlawaiya, Paraguay, South America
St Andrew's College, Asuncion, Paraguay
St Paul's School, Vina del Mar, Chile
The University of Chile
The Mackay School, Chile
Union Theological Seminary, New York, U.S.A.
West Nottingham Academy, U.S.A.
Kilkenny College, Eire.